A SEASON IN HELL

A SEASON IN HELL

The soccerati's state-of-the-nation
fin-de-siècle guide to
Scottish football league grounds

David Bennie

MAINSTREAM
PUBLISHING

EDINBURGH AND LONDON

For Lynn — with love and thanks

First published in 1997 by
MAINSTREAM PUBLISHING COMPANY (EDINBURGH) LTD
7 Albany Street
Edinburgh EH1 3UG

ISBN 1 85158 904 X

A CIP record for this book is available from the British Library

Typeset in 11 on 13pt Van Dijck MT
Printed and bound in Great Britain by Butler & Tanner Ltd

CONTENTS

'Une Saison en enfer'
— Albert Camus (attributed)[1]

'East Fife five, Forfar four.'
— James Alexander Gordon[2]

'When ideas fail, words can come in very handy.'
— Johann Wolfgang von Goethe[3]

'I promise results, not promises.'
— John Bond[4]

'There's no fun in soccer anymore . . . We'll end up playing in cemeteries.'
— Terry Venables[5]

'Free love is like playing football without goalkeepers.'
'Aye, well, Musselburgh Athletic would still be goal-scoring virgins even after extra time in the Scottish Junior Cup.'
— Two men conversing in a Portobello pub[6]

'We are all the author of our own fiction, but none of us knows the plot.'
— Douglas Kennedy[7]

'Everything I know of life, I owe to football.'
— Albert Camus[8]

FOOTNOTES

1. This is the title of a long-lost novel by the Nobel Prize-winning writer and French Algerian ex-goalkeeper. The plot revolves around the recruitment by Third Lanark FC of a midfield maestro and murderer called Meursault, whose death sentence in 1942 has been commuted to five years' hard labour and who, after starring for Mondovi Tangier, transfers to the (now-defunct) Glasgow club. After almost a year of hell in the old Scottish First Division, Meursault's existential angst resurfaces, and, despite helping Third Lanark to win the Scottish Cup against an 'Old Firm XI', the hat-trick hero garrottes a linesman with his 'lucky piece of piano wire' after being incorrectly given offside for 'racialist reasons', before stringing up the bloodied official by the feet to swing from a crossbar. The SFA supervisor in the stand criticises the referee in his report for his 'moral and physical cowardice' in not sending Meursault off, but although the hapless official later pleads that to have done so would have 'caused a definite riot', he is nevertheless dropped from the Grade One list of referees.

The typewritten pages of this 'revisionist future footballing fantasy and extrapolation of a favourite character's life' were mysteriously removed in 1960 from the car-crash wreckage in which Camus died, only for the original extant MS to reappear in Scotland in the early 1990s, where it was rejected by Canongate, Polygon and John Donald, all of whom cited 'dubious provenance' as their lily-livered reasons. After the MS was authenticated by Lord Trevor-Roper, however, Magnus Linklater (who was slipped an E-tab after asking for an aspirin), Wallace Mercer and a French trialist for Falkirk who claimed to have read all of Proust's *À la Recherche du temps perdu* 'without skipping', Mainstream secured the rights and decided to exploit the increasing market for football literature with an initial 40,000 hardback print run of an English translation (by the aforementioned bilingual trialist, but whose claim to have studied at the Sorbonne later proved to be as disingenuous as Jeffrey Archer's oft-boasted Oxbridge credentials).

At the last possible moment, though, review copies had to be hurriedly recalled, when Bob Crampsey's meticulous textual analysis threw a *soupçon* of doubt on the book's authenticity. 'Definitely not the work of a humanist genius like Camus,' the Glasgow *Evening Times* 'Now You Know' columnist declared. 'Far too funny for the black, bleak muse which inspired *The Outsider* – or *L'Etranger* as we refer to it here on the sports desk.'

Shaken by this bombshell from the erudite writer, entertaining broadcaster and Brain of Britain 1965, who scored maximum points on *Mastermind* with his specialist subject knowledge of 'The Scottish Football League Management Committee's Agendas, Motions, Minutes and Points of Order 1890–1990' – and who only lost the final by a point because he didn't know who the lead singer of Simple Minds was (rather than 'pass' he incorrectly guessed 'Pat Kane') – the Mainstream directors felt compelled to postpone publication, in order to consolidate their well-nigh incontrovertible evidence from at least one more unimpeachable source. While attempting to track down the touring Jim Kerr – who the publicity department felt would be a major PR *coup de théâtre* – an unsolicited endorsement by a self-styled 'sexy savant of stentorian slapheids' who wrote a column called 'The Man the PC Police Couldn't Gag' in a sport-and-sex comic disastrously undermined book-trade confidence in the project. The fatal on-air phrase delivered using a portable phone during a live radio phone-in, verified the veracity of the work as 'categorically one-hundred-if-not-more per cent pure dead brilliant *Ka-muss*'.

As a result, the mountainous pile of valueless volumes were seized and pulped under the Obscene Publications Act of 1959, since the shocking extracts of anal penetration and *odour d'excrement* in the after-match shower scenes were difficult to defend on the usual basis of 'artistic value' because the author was not accepted to be a genius like Camus but an opportunistic literary fraudster. Not only were all printed copies destroyed but the original MS and all editorial and translation proofs were too. A carbon copy of the text remains, however, which I have in my possession, kept safely but separately from my first handwritten draft in O-Grade failed-F French, and which

I transcribed using a 1948 Olivetti Olympique typewriter (with inflected and umlauted keys) filled with reams of yellow copy paper (surplus stock from the offices of the left-wing newspaper *Combat*, which Camus and Simone de Beauvoir's 'dear little being' Jean-Paul Sartre co-edited for three years after the Liberation).

Camus and Sartre actually 'broke' with each other over 'irreconcilable ideological differences', which first began to manifest themselves on the sports pages of *Combat* (the former always reading it from back to front, to the intense irritation of the latter). Sartre hated football but was a keen political devotee of Moscow Dynamo, funded and controlled by the KGB, but Camus genuinely supported Moscow Spartak because it was the only club in the Russian capital not in thrall to vested interests and which up to five million people freely followed. In contrast, CSKA were the Red Army in shorts, Lokomotive a subsidised symbol of the Soviet railway system, and Torpedo the sponsored sports club of the Zil limousine factory. Squabbles between the two writers invariably ensued over the political slant to be given to Dynamo v Spartak derby match reports, but the arguments became volcano-heated when Sartre began demanding 'positive propaganda' for all the Dynamo clubs set up by the secret police in conquered Eastern Europe, such as those in Berlin, Bucharest and Dresden, even when playing against French opposition. The pair finally came to blows when Sartre wrote and Camus spiked an editorial demanding that Beria, head of the KGB and honourary president of Dynamo, have the star player of Spartak, Nicolai Starostin, shot in the back or ice-picked in the eye rather than allow him to serve out the rest of his ten-year sentence for sedition in a 'holiday camp' gulag. Camus knocked the merde out of Sartre when the editorial appeared in a late edition and henceforth declared himself to be an official 'Spartakian' – a normally dismissive term used to describe the club's uneducated support, with their inclination towards counter-revolutionary hooliganism and 'intellectual-bashing' of anyone caught carrying copies of *Pravda* rather than *Sovietski Sport* into their section of the Lenin Stadium (which they shared with a distinct lack of collective solidarity with Torpedo – whose fans they taunted with chants of 'Zil Zombetskis' and the universal gesture for dickheads). Simon Kuper gives greater, and more reliable, details of the Marxist realpolitik which underpinned the rigged Soviet soccer system in his classic book *Football Against the Enemy* (Orion, 1994).

A Season in Hell is also the translated title of a book by Eric Cantona's favourite poet, Arthur Rimbaud (and which, like Eric's IQ, is probably overrated).
2. Apparently the voice of the classified results on Radio 5 Live has never actually had to read out this legendary result. The nearest he came was when the 'five' and 'four' were transposed one Saturday afternoon, which, although requiring serious reading concentration, is not nearly such a Spooneristic mouthful as the above – apocryphal? – result. Nevertheless, Alexander Gordon does have a wooden leg, which must be stress-relieving to take off and bite on when faced with terrible typos sent up by the typing pool just prior to 4.45 p.m.
3. As a newspaper man in Frankfurt in the 1770s, Goethe was spared the torture of

having to interview football managers during post-match press conferences, but this quote has been an inspiration to coaches of all nationalities and at all levels ever since it was coined. In contemporary parlance, it's an excuse for talking absolute nonsense in monosyllabic clichés. But whereas Berti Vogts can get away with mumbling '*Sturm und Drang*' to assembled *Bild* reporters – meaning 'storm and struggle' and/or 'emotional turmoil' – Terry Venables always sounded less intellectually well equipped with equivalent English phrases like 'A game of two halves, Gary, first sick as parrots then over the moon' (or 'over the world' as fumbling ex-goalkeeper and now bumbling ITV presenter Bob Wilson attempted to sum up the atmosphere and spectacle of Euro 96's opening ceremony).

4. The ex-Manchester City 'Boss' and unpaid male model for Burton's Medallion Man range in the 1970s must have promised to play his son in defence in every game, no matter how many embarrassing OGs Bond Junior – Kevin – flashed into his own net as a result.

5. Presumably this quote was a reference to the half-empty Wembley terraces during the run-up of uninspiring friendlies to the European Championships, but after the Euro 96 semi-final penalty shoot-out defeat to Germany, the memorial headstone inscriptions for the England careers of Tony Adams, David Platt, Stuart Pearce and Gareth Southgate (*Why didn't you blast it?* – 'Mum') must be close to lapidarian completion.

6. This overheard snatch of dialogue sounds like a variation of the Robert Graves quote about free love being like playing tennis without a net.

7. This is a phrase which Kennedy used when reviewing Paul Theroux's *My Other Life* in *The Independent*, and hopefully it won't turn out to be percipiently portentous with regard to the travelling itineraries and literary endeavours that this author has committed himself to undertake for this book.

8. Even great writers like Camus can occasionally be caught out talking soundbite silliness.

INTRODUCTION

'The Scottish Football League — A Seventh Circle of Soccer Hell?'

If the Earth is a polluted *pissoir* of a planet — orbiting and illuminated by a skittishly sallow 20-watt sun — part of a senescent solar system on the nicotine-stained fingertip of a spindly spiral arm, 30,000 light-years from the clustered galactic core of the miasmically mediocre Milky Way (there being as many galaxies in the universe as there are grains of sand on Seamill beach), cannot the Scottish Football League be regarded as being just as unimportant and peripheral as the wee globe on which we eke out our short-lived but increasingly deadened existence? Especially in relation to the ever-expanding number of exciting league structures elsewhere in the more glamorous galaxies of world soccer?

Human life may have originated in Africa, but the Dark Continent is not exactly noted for its civilised democracies today. Similarly, Scotland (and/or England) may have invented association football, but North Britain is no longer sending out football missionaries in the form of sailors, soldiers and engineers to teach the rest of the world how to play the game. Indeed, the Scottish Football Association's current commission on the future of Scottish football has co-opted at least one foreign expert — Rinus Michels — to help review the tartan game and the Independent Review Commission is estimated to cost almost a million pounds over its three years of deliberation. Its interim and final recommendations are intended to push the soccer infrastructure of Scotland into the 21st century, but at best seem more likely to drag the country kicking and screaming into the 20th — with not a year to spare.

As humankind approaches the millennium we have had to learn to accept that Homo Sapiens Ununited — restricted to home games only against nobody but ourselves at Terra Firma Park — are far from the centre of cosmic creation and nowhere near the pinnacle of universal understanding. And just as modern man has had to adapt to the realisation that his positional role in the grand scheme of things is one of time-spatial quarantine in a celestial corner of boondockian remoteness, so too most Scottish football clubs are having to reassess their historically inflated sense of self-importance. The vast majority of the 40 League members are being steadily shuffled out of the centre-circle of attention, brusquely escorted away along the halfway line towards banishment on the sidelines, leaving them to look forlornly on from the precipitous edge of the soccer dramarama.

In the beginning, though, the Scottish Football League and the Football League in England were the cynosured centre of the soccer solar system, Big-Bang binary stars in an otherwise football-free universe (notwithstanding the cup and international matches organised by their respective, and even older, Football Associations). However, the Anglo-Scots people's game soon spread to 'all four corners of the globe' (as ex-Coventry manager and ITV co-commentator Ron Atkinson¹ wouldn't hesitate to describe the geographical phenomenon), and even before 1953 and 1954 – when, respectively, the Magyar Marvels of Hungary became the first team to beat England at Wembley (6–3), and Scotland were booed off the pitch by a Basle crowd after losing in the World Cup to Uruguay (7–0) – the foreign students were beginning to eclipse the original masters of the most popular team sport ever devised.

Like the bone-tossing ape at the beginning of Stanley Kubrick's *2001: A Space Odyssey*, the west-of-Scotland Cro-Magnon centre-half (circa 1893) has seen his leather-and-laced football spiralling upwards into the stratosphere to be transformed into a fantastic space-age structure (to a Deacon Blue soundtrack rather than the *Blue Danube*) – only instead of transmogrifying into a geosynchronous satellite station it has metamorphosed into a state-of-the-art soccer stadium back at ground level. In this case the technology has come to rest in Amsterdam, with Ajax opening their retractable-roof, 50,000-seater super-stadium in time for the 1996–97 season.

As Simon Inglis has pointed out in his awe-inspiring tome *Football Grounds of Britain* (Collins Willow, 1996, third paperback edition), this kind of architectural design flexibility could soon lead to not only individual football clubs coming together to share expensive super-stadiums, but soccer and other sports combining in single showcase stadiums. Such super-stadiums could cater for the additional requirements of, say, rugby union and grid-iron football (as in the case of the Scottish Claymores paying rent to the SRU for Murrayfield, a stadium that both Hibs and Hearts have lobbied to have used as a neutral football venue and which Raith Rovers considered using for their home tie in 1995 against Bayern Munich in the UEFA Cup).

At the time of writing, Newcastle United's chairman Sir John Hall has just applied for outline planning permission to build a multi-million-pound super-stadium a quarter of a mile away from the current ground at St James's Park, designed to incorporate football, rugby, ice-hockey and Alan Shearer 'We're not worthy, pet' rallies/revival meetings. Since they now have the architectural technology, Newcastle could also incorporate the additional six-million-dollar facilities necessary for athletics, grid-iron, basketball, baseball, beach-volleyball or even cricket.

In Scotland, for example, the only way that cricket could 'take off' in commercial terms would be if it formed part of a portfolio of sports operated under the umbrella auspices of the Old Firm, although the rules of this most English of games would definitely need tampering with to make the sport less soporific as a spectacle for a Scottish audience of sectarian sadists. The sound of leather on willow would require aural amplification from the more satisfying smack of lead on wavellite (compressurised phosphate of aluminium) or that of uranium on titanium. Additionally, batsmen would require Rollerball-type protective equipment to cope with compulsory bouncers and beamers aimed at batsmen's heads and permitted once per over. Sightscreens could be massive JumboTron videos displaying psychedelic patterns, subliminal messages and hard-core pornography. Wide balls instead of being given as one-run byes could be detonated in the field anywhere before the boundary barbed wire, activated by a button at the top of the batsman's handle. With a few more innovative adjustments Glaswegian cricket could be successfully marketed as a completely new sport using the strapline slogan 'Braveheart Bodyline Bodybag Baseball'. Or maybe not . . .

On the park the Scottish game has continued to evolve, albeit at a snail's pace held back by unnatural selection and survival of the fattest, but our closest genetic cousins in England have now hunted down their most lumbering on-pitch dinosaurs to the point where, if not exactly extinct, they are certainly in danger of becoming endangered species – thereby leaping ahead in Christmas-tree-type formations of outfield players with forward-directed eyes and using goalkeepers with opposable thumbs.

Even more impressively, our Continental and South American relations appear to have succeeded in hitching their wagons to the chariots of the footballing gods; as if during the UFO-sightseeing boom of the 1950s they benefited from direct alien intervention in their fast-track development, with flying saucers hovering above forest and jungle clearings laser-sculpted into the shape of rectangular football pitches, before beaming down gift sets from the 'Golden Goal Gods of Golconda' which contained high-tech Predator boots, lightweight vinyl balls and collapsible five-a-side goalposts (as well as coded coaching manuals which, when deciphered, revealed the arcane mysteries of Sirius C's existence, the *libero*, *catenaccio*, 3-5-2, Total Football, weekend training camps, high-protein diets and pre-match warm-ups – but which if intercepted by the extensive network of multilingual Scottish spy-cum-scouts operating on mainland Europe and in South America would either self-destruct or were programmed to mistranslate into nuggets of wisdom like 'pre-match warm-ups knacker players' or 'hanging about on the verge of offside is a sign of effeminate homosexuality').

And even though the Bonnybridge Triangle in east central Scotland appears to be a favourite attraction in the 1990s for saucer parties of retired extra-terrestrials on guided flying tours over the tackiest tourist traps on Earth – along with every small town in America such as Roswell, Beameup, Ufofield, Knuttville, Suicide Bluff, Apocalypse (Pop. 666) and Velikovski-ville – their predecessors seem to have taken a grey-gilled pleasure in dumping football-kit hampers onto post-WWII bomb sites in the industrial belt, where the demob-depressed and shell-shocked survivors engaged in chest-beating squabbles over the joke's-on-you-mate contents of: hobnail-and-toe-reinforced boots, 'magic sponges', fixed-odds coupons, starched jockstraps, midgie-attracting liniments, flat caps and bobble hats, ricketies, methylated spirit mixers, unfiltered fags and medicine-balls which, when headed in wet-weather match-play conditions, could compress-fracture skulls or snap spinal columns.

Then, while huddled around smoky fireplaces in single-ends, mid-century professionals worshipped at the alter of mantelpieces draped with damp woollen socks. Not knowing any better, they coughed themselves hoarse extolling the obvious virtues of the long punt up the park, the undoubted aesthetic beauty of a well-timed, knee-dislocating tackle from behind, and the well-proven benefits of a rigid 4-4-2 formation (whether deployed by a tactical genius like Alexander Haig on Flanders Field or by an away manager whose team were sinking into the even more muddy and blood-soaked surface of Dumbarton's Boghead quagmire).

But no matter how many times the Morlockian Scots might lose 7–0 to effete Eloi XIs, they would continue to regard the sun-kissed interlopers from abroad with projectile-diced-carrot-vomiting contempt. After all, real football men didn't eat pasta.

Nevertheless, interstellar (or interconference) mating has produced dribbling demi-gods such as Pelé, Maradona, Platini and Cruyff. Contemporary examples from Euro 96 who are almost in the same superstar league would be Davor Suker, Hristo Stoichkov, Matthias Sammer and Paolo Maldini. Neanderthal 'Ingerland' have at least produced the idiot-savants of Paul Gascoigne, Peter Beardsley, Darren Anderton and Paul Ince. Cro-Magnon Celticland are currently uncovering missing links like Andy 'the Golem' Goram, John 'Gorbals Goblin' Spencer, Duncan 'Bar L' Ferguson and Gordon 'Juke Box' Durie.

Needless to say, Scotland in Euro 96 managed to find a new nailbiting way of not getting past the first round of a major tournament. Instead of being balked by inferior goal difference, we went out having scored one goal less than Holland (whose goal difference was equally negative). But even if we had managed statistical inseparability from the Dutch – by beating the

Swiss 3–2 – we would still have been eliminated because of an inferior 'rating co-efficient factor', as calculated before the competition by UEFA actuaries and which had been fiddled about with to favour any tied team with the largest and most lucrative television audiences.

Deconstructing the reasons for the boom in British football during the 1990s, when the 'beautiful game' became culturally ubiquitous and the predominant icon of late-20th-century capitalism, would require a book in itself (*Das Futbol: The New Opium of the Masses*, for example, in which a Jewish East German Marxist academic who fled to Liverpool or Leicester before the Fall of the Wall – *and who has never been to a football match in his life* – could expound at unreadable length on his theories about the surplus value of superstars, divisive fan conflict, the exploitation of the season-ticket-holder, and the alienation of man after play-off relegation).

Football has never been an exclusively working-class concern, anyway, but the stampede of the suburban soccerati[2] towards soft seating, Sports-pages soccer shelves and Sky subscription sports since the start of the decade has helped propel football to the respectable end of the cultural spectrum, from red-shifted regressiveness to blue-shifted becomingness, scattering the sense-of-irony-failure skinheads to the Four Winds saloon bar in section-eight discharges from the Hooligan Hussars of Hotspur, Huddersfield and Hibernian *et al*. The Charge of the Petite Bourgeoisie has not only turned the tide in the tactical battles of Wounded Knee, Fractured Skull and Scarred Face, but looks set to win the strategic *zeitgeist* war (even if the Genghis Khan Casuals continue to wage intermittent guerrilla warfare on the approach roads to the newly captured and consecrated grounds).

The main catalysts of football's rehabilitation and renaissance are well known and although oft-stated probably deserve very condensed reiteration: Hillsborough in 1989, the resulting Taylor Report in 1990 legally requiring moves towards all-seater stadiums, more middle-class fans of all ages and both genders, Sky's 1992 deal to deliver live footie to the satellite-and-sofa supporters, the success of USA 94, rule changes to make the game more exciting, foreign imports like Laudrup and Cantona, increased media coverage, and finally three points for a win and the introduction of play-offs which lead to fewer meaningless games.

These developments have nearly become self-sustaining and self-perpetuating phenomena, recent past investment in a club *almost* guaranteeing future expansion and helping to feed – and/or create? – a new public's ferocious appetite for yet more fantasy football, a feeding frenzy that has led to the phenomenal growth of the football souvenir business.

The new five-year-plan way forward for an ambitious club, north or south of the border, became pretty straightforward. It would start with temporary bench-seating being installed in an Archibald Leitch-designed ground, the recruitment of an ageing but charismatic player-manager, the selling of the ground to a supermarket and a move to a greenfield site where a new 'decorated shed' stadium could be built, the signing of a geriatric or psychotic foreign superstar (whose weekly wages could well exceed an average fan's *yearly* salary), new shirt sponsor and kit manufacturer capable of producing away strips in puce pink, slime green or bowel brown (or any combination of the three), hiked admission charges, expanded retail floor space in the club shop (by knocking down the adjacent Premature Baby Unit if necessary) in order to stock all kinds of club-crested kitsch, diversification into financial services, catering, etc, a minority share issue to supporters, and finally even the possibility of a successful flotation on the stockmarket – since wealthy individuals and financial institutions are beginning to invest in *big* football clubs *simply to make money and get a good return on invested capital.*

Following this formula the rich get richer, the poor get poorer, and those in between can go either way, depending on the one unquantifiable factor in the equation: namely, performances on the pitch by gobsmackingly greedy but frustratingly fallible players (whose standard of living no longer depends on generous win bonuses that would have had their predecessors of just a decade ago bursting blood vessels in the brain or playing through the excruciating pain of haemorrhoids the size of golf balls). Super-rich clubs can, of course, guarantee some kind of success by buying matching sets of superstars if need be, but if one superstar – or foreign free agent with a skilfully edited video of fantastic goals (against Alpine-village amateurs) – is carrying the hopes and aspirations of a whole town, or one half of a city, he can always break his leg while making a cash-dispenser withdrawal or refuse to bust his contractual gut if he doesn't like the shade of red on the club-supplied Lexus or the lack of EU Blue-Flag bathing beaches within a ten-minute drive of downtown Motherwell or Wolverhampton.

In the summer of 1996 BSkyB agreed to pay £670 million to show English Premiership matches live until the year 2000. In Scotland, however, a figure of £11 million was agreed for the same period of time. No satellite spokesman was quoted as saying, 'If we're only getting monkeys, they're going to have to accept peanuts.' That is the subtext of the separate Scottish contract, though, which would have been even cheaper if not for the fact that all eight games selected for live coverage in season 1996–97 involved at least one of the Old Firm.

Although satellite and terrestrial television rights are still an important source of income north of the border, it is interesting to note that in the forthcoming season – excluding European rights – Manchester United expect to rake in almost £20 million but Glasgow Rangers less than £2 million, partly because the Ibrox side are not part of an autonomous Scottish Super League and have to watch revenue that they generate 'trickle down' a pyramid of lower leagues, as do the champions of Serie A. But ever since the top 20 English clubs broke away in 1992 with all the satellite shekels, they have had a much larger cake to split.

South of the border the football bubble continues to expand, the successful staging of the European Championships encouraging England to follow up Euro 96 with a planned bid for the World Cup finals in 2006 (which they are not willing to consider co-hosting with Scotland apparently, even though South Korea and Japan combined successfully in their joint bid for the finals in 2002). They won't get them, though, not even by bragging about having 'a Notre-Dame or two' amongst their present stadiums – even Old Trafford is hardly comparable to the Gothic splendour of the cathedral that was featured in the opening shot of Kenneth Clark's 1966 TV series *Civilisation* (as Michael Henderson of *The Times* pointed out when debunking the BBC's hyperbolic Rob Bonnet).

The intellectualisation of soccer supporting has also resulted in a book-publishing free-for-all, with the traditional duopoly of Mainstream and Stanley Paul having to cope with fierce 'de-regulated' competition – but benefiting from a vastly expanded market of 'chattering class' book-buyers keen to get their twice-a-year-checked teeth into literate sportswriting with a bit of intellectual meat on funny-bone prose. The resulting let's-jump-on-the-bandwagon-blindfolded-egg-and-spoon-three-legged-sack race to get books into the Sportspages/*Independent* Top Ten[3] – and thereafter into the Bookwatch/*Sunday Times* equivalent – is like the London Marathon run during the capital's Monday morning rush-hour traffic (i.e. not a pretty sight with casualties being carted off to remaindered oblivion by the score).

Excellent football authors abound, but the backlash against impressive-vocabulary, unique-angle or individual-tone-of-voice publications has already begun, with one fanzine editor asking his lip-moving readership 'Should Nick Hornby be taken out and shot?' (How dare he criticise St Nick, the patron saint of the soccerati, prematurely bald men and extremely ill-at-ease guests on BBC2's *Fantasy Football League*?)

England's upstairs neighbour has mostly watched in jealous awe the mega-buck partying, on-and-off the park, and we are running out of other countries that we can make fun of and feel superior to.

Just as the Third World has taken its football forward in leaps and bounds, especially in Africa and Asia, the good old US of A can no longer be regarded as the Jurassic Park of world soccer either, after the success of USA 94 and the setting up of the Major Soccer League in 1996 (even with such bizarrely named franchises as New England Revolution, LA Galaxy and Kansas City Wiz). The average MSL attendance of nearly 30,000 is more than any Scottish club outside of Glasgow – even if they do insist on stopping a clock running backwards from 45 minutes when injured players receive treatment.

If the SFL cannot really be compared with Spielberg's movie – an analogy probably better saved for the Australian lager-lout leagues which get Littlewoods and Vernons through the summer months – a better comparison might be one of the *Lost* films – e.g. *Continent, Horizon, World* or even *Weekend*. In other words, a self-contained but isolated colony that time forgot, whether you think of it as a Sargasso Sea of soccer run by a Scottish Inquisition (from West Regent Street and Park Gardens), a South African plateau full of prehistoric life, or a Tibetan valley where the weather is always crap and men die early because of coronary heart disease.[4] Whatever – definitely an inverted sort of Shangri-La. (The importation of a world superstar like Gazza to Rangers from Lazio in 1995 for £4.3 million was as incredible to this author as was the presence of a grand piano to critic James Agate in Frank Capra's 1937 version of *Lost Horizon* – since it had to be transported along a narrow one-person *ledge* with a two-thousand-foot drop on one side.)

Even the 'élite' Bell's Premier League is regarded as a backwater by those used to attending the Rothmans-Berger-Servowarm-Isthmian League in the 1980s (or even the Kentucky Fried Chicken Irish League). The reaction of pub patrons in London when BSkyB broadcast Scottish matches not featuring either of the Old Firm is painful for ex-patriate Scots to behold: 'Oi, landlord, ain't there 38DD topless darts from Romford on Eurosport?' Scottish fans, who attend more football matches in person than anywhere else except Albania, get the chance to see what they are missing from ever-expanding television coverage – Channel 4's *Football Italia* with live Serie A games every Sunday, BSkyB Premiership broadcasts, Eurosport's eclectic coverage, direct foreign stations' games (complete with 'Goooaaaal' commentators), as well as terrestrial Premiership highlights on *Match of the Day* and live coverage of the main European cup competitions. Purely Scottish games do not bear too critical a comparison.

Whether attending in person, or watching through a forest of fingers on the box, when top European clubs come to Scotland the cringe factor can be excruciating (even when it's not your team that's being played off the park). Last season when Rangers lost 4–1 away to Juventus in the Champions'

League, their supporters must have thought things couldn't get much worse – until they lost 4–0 to Juve at Ibrox. In the Cup Winners' Cup Paris St Germain came to Parkhead and positively strolled to a 3–0 away victory. In the UEFA Cup Motherwell lost 3–1 at home to MyPa-47 of Finland.

Yet every time a Scottish club gets drawn against Continental opposition, they invariably fall for the same old risible rhetoric from foreign coaches. 'Ve very negative at draw. Scot teams ve alvays struggle against. Ve don't like it up uz, as you in great humour say. Scot teams never say die, no?' Then with a straight face: 'Even vhen 6–0 down!' If you ever need to shut an Aberdeen fan up, two words will do it: 'Skonta Riga'.

The fact that attendances continue to grow in Scotland is largely due to Old Firm home gates and travelling supporters, because Celtic and Rangers account for over 70 per cent of fan loyalty, turnover, investment, etc – and sponsors like Bell's, Coca-Cola and Tennents aren't spending millions to reach supporters of Albion Rovers and Forfar Athletic.

Media Cassandras have been predicting bankruptcy for some of Scotland's smaller clubs at the start of every season for decades, as well as moaning about the century-old Old Firm hegemony, but all the other Scottish clubs manage to reach each season's end somehow. And today significant resources are being directed into revamped stadiums all across the country, up and down the Leagues, and although largely financed by the Football Trust and Pools money each club is having to fund stadium improvements from within as well. Hence, the current flat state of the transfer market.

Personally, the constantly rehashed debate about streamlining the structure of Scottish football (i.e. wiping out the wee clubs) versus the benefits of following tradition (i.e. giving the wee clubs subsidised gee-ups) leaves me passionately ambivalent. On the one hand, small teams that can keep going have the right to exist for their die-hard core, however small, and should be permitted promotion on performing merit so long as they can meet specified stadium criteria; on the other, historical anomalies and anachronisms are crying out for radical change.

As far back as 1952, when there were 38 League clubs, Stirling Albion argued for a 42-club total – a motion which, if accepted, would have introduced senior football teams to the new towns of East Kilbride, Cumbernauld, Livingston and Glenrothes (which were all in the process of being built or at an advanced blueprint stage). The move was, of course, rejected. It took until 1995 for Livingston to gain a League club, albeit at the cost of Meadowbank Thistle's enforced suicide/murder, when the Edinburgh club moved lock, stock and name (not even adding 'Thistle' to their new moniker of Livingston FC). A more sensitive way forward was adopted by Clyde in 1994 when they relocated to Cumbernauld, but retained their Rutherglen-based support by not becoming Cumbernauld New Town FC.

The Old Firm too dominant? Too many clubs? Too many games? Too many leagues? Not enough skill, entertainment or excitement? Not enough clubs investing in their infrastructure? Not enough fans for 40 clubs? Yes and no to each of these questions, I suppose, but this book is not intended to provide any definitive answers, merely to give a subjective snapshot of the Scottish game in season 1996–97, as it experiences a state of flux not matched since the game turned its back on amateurism in 1893.

While increasing (?) Old Firm allegiances are resulting in a new generation of supporters who can rarely, if ever, get tickets to see their teams in the flesh – the demand for expensive season-tickets and limited seating space meaning almost permanent lock-outs for pay-at-the-gaters – those playing for local minnows are almost on first-name terms with the staggeringly small crowds.

At present there are 37 grounds hosting senior football fixtures, with groundsharing in operation at Boghead (Dumbarton/Clydebank), Broadwood (Clyde/Airdrie) and Cliftonhill (Albion Rovers/Hamilton Accies) for all or some of season 1996–97, as all three guest clubs wait on their new stadiums to be built (although building work has not yet started anywhere).

Joining the Scottish '40 Club' (or '37 Club' as it is at the moment) has not been a long-cherished dream, I must admit, but for some reason Mainstream were not at all keen on 'a non-fiction book about trying to write an existential novel set in Venetian café society and written *in situ*'. But at least I'm doing it for a commissioned book with a travel-expense-covering advance – unlike the genuinely heroic Michael Pye, who has travelled over 22,000 miles to watch games at every ground in Scotland for the sheer hell of it (an example of truly obsessional behaviour, since he is a 38-year-old manager with Cadbury Schweppes in Birmingham and a Preston North End supporter, and whose self-imposed quest began when he was in his 20s).

Although featured in the *Independent*, Pye was a true 'ground-hopper' in that his pilgrimage was not undertaken for financial gain or public recognition. He just visited the grounds because they were there. Ken Ferris, however, visited all 92 English League grounds – plus Berwick! – between 10 September 1994 and 3 May 1995 in order to get into the *Guinness Book of Records* and publish the paperback *Football Fanatic* (which I have not, perhaps unfortunately, read).

In between these two ground-hopping extremes are the so-called Numpties, who have moved on from trainspotting in the '70s and plane-spotting in the '80s to ground-hop their way through the '90s. Sad individuals in anoraks, corduroy trousers and Jesus sandals, they tend to be bearded, balding and bespectacled – and have some amazingly arbitrary criteria that need to be fulfilled before they can tick off visited grounds on their checklists. Being there from kick-off to the final whistle is reasonable – I'm intending to meet it myself – but touching the ball, all four corner flags or both of the referee's buttocks is just ridiculous (if not symptomatic of manic-compulsive mental illness). Some Numpties even refuse to enter a stadium if no match programme is available or if they arrive even a minute late. Hopefully, these middle-aged maniacs restrict themselves to English League grounds, because they are definitely not the kind of people I want to share a crush-barrier with.

One basic tenet of feminist literary theory is that no criticism is neutral or value-free, and that any critic therefore has a responsibility to make clear any autobiographical similarities between their lived experience and the text. In a similar vein, I have to confess that Celtic are my first love, with mild romantic attachments to Hibernian and Raith Rovers.

1996 may have provided a great summer of televised sporting torture – with the White Shark's six-stroke lead in the US Masters being reeled back in by Nick Faldo in Captain Ahab mode, Gareth Southgate's penalty miss against Germany in Euro 96 almost making up for Gary McAllister's equally inept effort against England, Tod Martin visibly choking to defeat after being 5–1 up in the fifth set of his Wimbledon semi-final, and Lynford Christie looking like a Greek-Abyssinian God prior to the Olympic 100m final but fucking it up like a true Brit by being disqualified after two false starts – but Saturday afternoons just aren't the same without football (whether spectating at, match reporting on, or listening to the radio for).

By the end of this forthcoming League season – 10 May 1997 – I hope to have drawn a few tentative conclusions about the 'state of Scottish football' – assuming I survive a Scottish winter with every Saturday being an away game. Edinburgh would be a terrific place to live if not for the North Sea weather, which contributes to the worst climate in the world (baking summers and freezing winters being preferable by far to year-round wind, perpetually overcast skies and semi-permanent drizzle of a supposedly 'temperate' nature). Indeed, the influence of Scottish weather on the national psyche (negative) and the way we play football (at 100mph) cannot be underestimated.

The Scottish character as reflected in sporting *under*-achievement is an interesting question too, as is the public reaction to our relatively few successful sportsmen (and women in the case of Liz McColgan). Apparently, we like nothing better than a working-class nobody who comes out of nowhere, achieves a modicum of success, and then gets clobbered by hitting a brick wall of ignominious failure.

In this respect two small paragraphs in *The Times* (6.2.96) caught my eye. They gave the basic details about one Michael Volino, a New York police sergeant who won a competition in the USA to take a single place kick at the Pro-Bowl in Hawaii. The prize for succeeding was $1 million. He missed by inches. The capacity crowd then booed him off the pitch, whereas if he had scored they would have gone wild with delight. Everyone loves a winner, right? No. In Scotland he would have been booed and cat-called for kicking it through the posts, and possibly pelted with coins as well (which if he was cheeky enough to start picking up would definitely have started a riot). However, if the ball had rebounded from an upright, Murrayfield would have erupted in malicious 'Ah-kent-his-faither-the-bastard' glee.

As far as a methodology of writing approach is concerned, the *modus operandi* I intend following includes paying my way in as a spectator, seeing a bit of the town or city concerned, then getting home in time for the late-night Saturday movie on Channel 4 (programmed to send suicidal solitaries with no social life rummaging through their bathroom cabinets for a lethal cocktail of sell-by-date-expired medicines). I'll travel light with a backpack containing the minimum equipment necessary: a notebook, camera, *The Wee Red Book*, last year's *Tartan Special Scottish Football League Review*, *Fodor's Scotland* (1991), each Saturday's *Sun* for team news, something to read for pleasure, a packed lunch, and a three-pack of black-ribbed condoms (just in case I get stuck overnight in a fleshpot like Arbroath). I'm not expecting any life-changing dramas, but you never know. I could meet my future wife at a football ground or end up in custody in a police holding-cell beneath a main stand. Or at a *very* hard push, both at the same time (in the form of a WPC?)

This Introduction, rewritten *four* times before being word-processed, has been as tough as pre-season training for gutbucket footballers who've let themselves go during the close-season by pigging out on a daily diet of beer, pizza and Death-by-Chocolate. But I'm ready now. Depressed, anxious, bored and cash-strapped, but keenly anticipating the start of another football season.

Will it be *une saison en enfer*, a slow descent into the seventh circle of soccer-spectating hell? Hard to say with none down and at least 37 games to go. Not every game can be a seven-goal thriller but hopefully I'll see a few – along with exciting score draws, shock away wins and home cricket-score hammerings. But not too many boring 1–0 home wins and utterly tedious scoreless draws, please.

Roll on 10 May 1997, however, when I'll have done it. Although I suspect I may be totally done in too, if not completely done for . . .

David Bennie,
Edinburgh,
30 July 1996

FOOTNOTES

1. Ron Atkinson, or Big Fat Ron, or Atko, is a truly bizarre co-commentator and at times it's hard to believe English is his first – but undoubtedly only – language. During Euro 96 he had my sister and me holding our sides and weeping hysterically. We never could figure out what 'a real pumper' was supposed to be. Ian St John is justifiably famous for his 'couldnae score in a barrelload of fannies' description of Scotland foreplaying impotently around in an opposition penalty box. I have been unable to trace the coiner of the immortal line about a simple goal being 'as easy as raping your grandmother', but I think we can be sure it wasn't Arthur Montford.

2. Soccerati – a pluralised noun inspired by the generally accepted use of the term 'cognoscenti' (meaning connoisseurs or experts in any area). Difficult to define exactly, but while a well-read member of the soccerati will pride himself on his wide-ranging and critical football knowledge he (or she) will also read eclectically outside his main area of interest. For example a true soccerate will not only have read Nick Hornby's seminal *Fever Pitch* twice, he will also have read the same author's non-football novel *High Fidelity* (but only once, because although it is very good it's not *that* good, unlike say *Crime and Punishment*, *The Great Gatsby* or *Money*).

3. *Not Playing For Celtic: Another Paradise Lost* (Mainstream, 1995) crashed into the Sportspages/*Independent* Top 10 at No. 9 on 8.1.96, stalled there on 15.1.96, then disappeared for good on 22.1.96. Working in a press-clippings agency at the time my first words after 4.30 a.m. rises on these three successive Mondays were: *Te-ess!* . . . *Hmmmm* . . . and *Shit!* . . .

4. According to a recent medical survey, published in *Scotland on Sunday* (28.7.96), Scotland is top of the world league for coronary heart disease deaths in males over 40, ahead of both Russia and the Czech Republic. Where else can you buy deep-fried Mars Bars from fast-food outlets? They're an acquired but addictive taste – apparently.

HAMPDEN PARK
Queen's Park v Ross County
Coca-Cola Cup, First Round, 3.8.96

The Scottish people's parliament for 'ninety-minute patriots' holds a handful of world attendance records, but the amateur Spiders fail to feature in the roll-call of 100,000-plus crowds. Even without the alternative attractions of Sporting Lisbon at Parkhead, Arsenal at Ibrox and Oasis at Balloch, this fixture wouldn't have tempted more than a thousand paying customers into the eerily empty confines of the national stadium. In the circumstances, it did well to get 638 punters through the turnstiles of the new North Stand (even if a third of this total had travelled down from the Highlands) – and at six quid it was hardly bargain-basement pricing.

The sight of the old South Stand still standing was a major surprise to both sets of supporters, but since all the original oak seats from 1903 had been ripped out – for individual re-sale at £20 for an uncomfortable piece of football history – the demolition cranes and bulldozers must have been poised to move in, unless the logjam of early home fixtures for Queen's Park was already putting the construction of the two-tier replacement stand *further* behind schedule. Such organisational ineptitude may seem incredible on the part of the SFA/SFL schedulers, but not after the realisation that 16 teams outwith the Premier League and First Division were forced to run the 25 per cent risk of having to start their League campaigns having been knocked out of *two* competitions – namely the Coca-Cola and League Challenge Cups.[1]

As well as housing the Queen's Park boardroom (and *en suite* 'Code Blue' resuscitation area for the geriatric Committee members), the new stand will also accommodate the relocated offices of the SFA and SFL (who will doubtless install their respective but equally anonymous presidents, Bill Dickie and Yule Craig, at opposite ends of a long corridor, where they will only stop internal squabbling amongst their autonomous organisations' functionaries about sliding-scale-status shag carpeting and desk dimensions in order to present a united front when anyone questions the need for Scotland's two separate footballing bureaucracies, with their largely overlapping administrative functions). It will also incorporate the new Scottish National Museum of Football.

The Football Museum is temporarily housed in the Kelvin Hall's Transport Museum, and before this game I had an enjoyable stroll round the nostalgia-tripping and imaginatively displayed exhibits (of the Transport Museum, that is, not the single gallery of pathetically mishmashed football jerseys, cups and videos that made up the special Euro 96 exhibition; although when the real thing opens at Hampden in 1997, SFA chief Jim Farry's revisionist historians will have the opportunity to rewrite history with their doctored black-and-white photos and bureaucrat-censored text – with exhibitions entitled 'How We Qualified For Five World Cups in a Row' rather than 'How We Failed to Get Past the First Round of Five World Cups in a Row').

Outside Hampden I swithered about whether to join the home or away support (did they really need to be segregated?), since in the 'gentlemen versus players' dichotomy I've always tended to favour professional competence over amateur bumbling. However, Ross County's decision to sack manager Sandy Wilson because of finishing fourth in Division Three – behind arch-rivals but similarly unpromoted Caley Thistle – prejudiced me against them, especially since his replacement as manager was ex-Aberdeen and Rangers hatchet man Neale Cooper. As for Queen's Park, at least coach Hugh McCann had persuaded the octogenarian radicals on the Committee to steamroller through his proposal that they should start the new season with *ex*-professionals now eligible to play for the black-and-white hoops, a long-overdue decision that permitted former Spider and Celtic winger Mark Smith to return to the amateur fold.

By retaining their amateur status in the face of professional and semi-professional competition, Queen's Park have had to endure a truly appalling if unsurprising record of dismal failure, their last 'success' capable of being puffed on souvenir pennants being the 1980–81 Second Division Championship. Buyers of *The Men With the Educated Feet: A Statistical and Pictorial History of Queen's Park* – of whom there were none in the club kiosk despite a discount of nearly 50 per cent – soon run out of exciting plot developments, because the oldest and most reactionary club in Scotland have not added to their silverware since the turn of the century.

Waiting for the game to start I sipped my Fan Fayre Snax Bovril and attempted to answer the questionnaire about catering services. Would I buy any of the following items if they were added to the menu – jumbo sausage, chicken burger or popcorn? *Absolutely not.* Other (please state): *Pigeon-chest pastry, furred tongue fingers and recycled urine juice.* (A spray-painted 'Eat the Rich' example of graffiti on the filigreed entrance gates to the local park had got me thinking in unwelcome directions, as had an irritating advertising hoarding on Victoria Road which ambiguously stated 'We don't do blow football' – which must have been the start of a teasing seven-veils advertising campaign for a sportswear company, surely?)

For the first time during a football match I didn't hear the F-word, either as an exasperated exclamation or as scatter-gun punctuation in sentence construction. Despite finishing in a commendable mid-table position in

May, Queen's Park supporters obviously don't *expect* to win anything, not even home games. But even their considerable reserves of good humour were beginning to run out after the worst first half of senior football I have ever seen, with the Spidermen literally falling over their unco-ordinated feet, not miskicking so much as missing their kicks completely, and putting their goalkeeper Gordon Bruce into a flaffing panic with every pass-back – even gentle headed ones which looked easier to hold than palm away for unnecessary corners.

Amongst the fans there was no lack of passion and verbal irritation, but most of it was directed at the referee – even if expressed in bizarrely polite but apoplectic bellowing from the more unstable supporters, as in: 'For goodness sake, Mr Tait, are you not familiar with the current rules of association football? If he's in line he's *on-side*, you know . . . Honestly, that man is a disgrace to all Grade-One referees.'

When Ross County took the lead early in the second half through Derek Adams it wasn't unexpected, although the lead-up to the goal certainly was. Bruce redeemed himself with a stunning one-handed save, but from a diving header bulleted towards him by his own centre-half, Graeme Elder. As Adams over-celebrated his simple tap-in, Elder lay face-down on the grass for at least 30 seconds.

Queen's Park deservedly equalised with five minutes left, Ian Maxwell heading in a fine Martin McLauchlan cross. At the end of 90 minutes, with 30 minutes of extra-time imminent, the home supporters were leafing through their programmes in the forlorn hope of finding information about a 'golden goal' deciding things as quickly as possible. Half a dozen left rather than endure a further half-hour.

Although Marc Falconer and Kevin McGoldrick got the goals for a final 3–1 home win, the highlight of extra-time was the substitution of a County player who had dived earlier in the proceedings and got a sporting Spider unfairly booked. A few rows in front of me, an elderly father and middle-aged son had been getting very excited about the prospect of seeing Queen's win a Cup match, and as the substituted villain plodded towards the touchline they both stood up, pointed at the player and started chanting 'Cheat, cheat, cheat!'. 'Sit down and grow up,' someone advised them ill-temperedly – which they finally did after muttering madly to each other and looking over their shoulders in synchronised stares.

Man-of-the-match McLauchlan won a Coca-Cola mountain bike; and if the Committee had no moral objections to him accepting it, why don't Queen's Park just go the whole hog and embrace 'shamateurism'? They could still play amateurs but if they paid for a few battle-hardened Ayrshire Juniors and offered some money to the best young players constantly tempted away by the offer of filthy lucre, they could actually start competing on a level playing-field.

A successful Queen's Park, moving up the divisions and playing good football, could surely begin attracting crowds of 6,380 rather than 638. They'll soon have a refurbished stadium capable of holding over 50,000 people in seated comfort, and the surrounding districts of Mount Florida, Govanhill, Langside and Queen's Park are full of high-density housing, the tenements in particular subdivided into a profusion of lonely bedsits. (I know – I used to live in one, and if Celtic were away from home I could go for a whole weekend without speaking to anyone, before overdosing on too many Sunday newspapers.) If Queen's Park marketed themselves aggressively, priced themselves competitively and employed professional entertainers, they could become a real focus for the various communities which currently surround them but rarely interact (e.g. students, the unemployed, OAPs, schoolchildren, young couples, and the South Side Asians). The lack of brown faces amongst the Ross County supporters merely reflects the demographics of Dingwall, but although Hampden is situated in the centre of a large Scottish-Asian population, I didn't see one non-white supporter in the North Stand.

Without any attempts to broaden the fan base at Queen's Park, the new Hampden really will be a white elephant of a stadium. Ibrox and Parkhead are much more impressive grounds, and while Hampden may be useful for hosting Cup finals involving either of the Old Firm, its utilitarian value as a venue for the Scottish national team is increasingly open to question. The World Cup qualifiers required home games against Sweden, Austria, Estonia, Latvia and Belarus. Only the first two were 'glamorous' enough to attract 50,000-plus crowds, Ibrox and Parkhead play host to the Swedes and Austrians, which meant provincial Premier grounds catering for the rest – with Murrayfield another possibility for big games. (If Italy and Spain don't need a national stadium, why do we?)

Hampden may soon satisfy all the conditions of the Taylor Report and UEFA legislation for hosting European club finals, but it will never again be one of the world's *great* stadiums. Even when finished, it will betray all the signs of having been a political football in the past, with *ad hoc* cash injections resulting in an adequate but hardly inspiring design. Basically, it will always be a covered bowl whose gently sloping inclines lose even more atmosphere than necessary because of the pointless decision to retain the flat space between pitch and stands. Although not quite wide enough for a full-width athletics track, Celtic chairman Fergus McCann would solve this problem by removing the football pitch altogether and turning Hampden into an athletics stadium.[2] As a home for a Premier Division club, Hampden would be wonderful. As a national stadium, it looks like the result of too many compromises by a series of cost-cutting committees.

Walking back to Bridge Street tube station, the architecture of Govanhill/Queen's Park sparked off a multitude of memories from the time I lived in this strange district, a mix of Rachmanesque bedsits and expensive Victorian mansions. In Allison Street a police Peugeot 309 slide-skidded to a halt in front of Ladbrokes, where yet another punter was presumably running amok after losing the family-allowance Giro on a five-horse accumulator – or maybe, given its popularity today, a failed example of spread betting. *Plus ça change.*

Passing the refurbished Citizens' Theatre in the Gorbals, I found it hard to accept that more people watch plays than go to football in Scotland – and I for one don't believe it.

Back home in Edinburgh (after failing to find one of those blue heritage plaques dedicated to local-lad-made-good Jimmy Boyle), I was surprised how much I had enjoyed the Spiders' victory, but it was the supporters rather than the team that had charmed me. And the day ended perfectly as Roger Black failed to catch his American front-runner in the final leg of the 4x400 relay race in Atlanta – which was well worth staying up until nearly 2 a.m. to see.

FOOTNOTES

1. Ross County managed this depressing feat, kicking off their League season away to Arbroath after going out of the Coca-Cola and League Challenge Cups to Queen's Park and Ayr United, losing seven goals and scoring only one in this confidence-sapping prelude to their promotion push.

2. If the joint Glasgow–Edinburgh bid for the 2008 Olympics goes ahead Hampden could eventually be the venue for the track-and-field events. But it'll never happen – not even the proposed bid, because the man behind it is Glasgow's Lord Provost Pat Lally (who looks like the hideous young-old man on the steamboat in *Death in Venice* or like a ventriloquist's dummy jujued into voodoo life). In the unlikely event of the little megalomaniac pulling it off, Glasgow really ought to be renamed 'Lallygrad' in his honour.

EASTER ROAD
Hibernian v Kilmarnock
Premier League, 10.8.96

'Joint top of the division. Then the season kicks off.' So stated the Bell's
billboard on a prime-site Easter Road location – not that it dampened the
optimistic enthusiasm of the hundreds of Hibees pouring along Albion
Place and dreaming of their first League title since 1951–52. The start of
every League campaign is a glorious renewal of possibilities, with hope
triumphing over experience on a yearly basis. Leith Walk bookmakers may
have been offering shorter odds on a flying saucer piloted by Elvis Presley
crash-landing on the Loch Ness Monster than for Hibs winning the Premier
League (100-1), but on Day One every team started level with two-horse-
race favourites Rangers and Celtic – and a good win could have taken any
of the eight other clubs right to the top of the pile.

Two years previously I sat in the Easter Road press-box watching in
stunned disbelief as an opening-day 5–0 drubbing of Dundee United played
havoc with a miserly word-count and dyspeptic stomach. The old-fashioned
press-box may still have been driving journalists crazy with its finger-in-
the-dialling-hole Bakelite telephones, situated at the back of the Main
Stand, but since August of 1994 impressive new stands have been erected
at both ends of the famous sloping pitch.

These impressive structures cost between seven and eight million
pounds to put up and had seriously constrained manager Alex Miller's ability to invest in the transfer market. And although Kwik-Fit boss Tom
Farmer is the current owner, he is no football fanatic and is therefore understandably unwilling to sign personal cheques with six zeros to secure star
players. Farmer's refusal to divert all of his personal fortune into the club
frustrates a few season-ticket-holders, but his prudent business acumen
means that Hibs are highly unlikely ever to go bust. Especially not over
unpaid fuel bills for the club coach which, in the case of St Mirren a few
days prior to this game, started wildfire rumours about the entire first-
team squad being up for sale (rumours possibly started by the club's
bankers who, unlike the local petrol station, were owed £1.4 million). The
day after the story was rebutted – when the garage got its few hundred
quid – St Mirren crashed out of the League Challenge Cup 2–1 away to
Hamilton, two goals from one José Quitongo putting paid to a possibly
lucrative Cup run for the Paisley Buddies. (A week after this rebuttal, the
Saints' star striker Barry Lavety had been sold to Hibs for £250,000, assistant manager Kenny McDowell had been made redundant and boss Jimmy
Bone had resigned in protest!) If a club does disappear this season under the

Plimsoll line of unsupportable debt, it will be a major surprise but not seismically shocking – thereby joining the last football bankrupts of Third Lanark.[1]

Hibs, too, almost ceased to exist as recently as 1990, when a disastrous stockmarket flotation as a public limited company plunged them into financial crisis. In June of that year Radio Forth broke into their normal daytime programming with an 'important news flash'. My first thought, as my heart *ka-boomed* in my chest, was that the nuclear core of the Torness power station was heading for China. As I slammed the window shutters closed, the newsreader reported the imminent demise of Hibernian Football Club – first Club Champions of the World, European Cup semi-finalists, 7–6 conquerors of Barcelona – as Hearts chairman Wallace Mercer prepared to take control in a forced merger/unwelcome takeover designed to create an 'Edinburgh United' – *eventually*, after Hibs' best players had been incorporated into the maroon colours of Hearts for a few seasons and Easter Road had been flattened for a housing development.

A nuclear meltdown at Torness would have caused less civil unrest on the east side of Edinburgh than this announcement. The music format was immediately dropped for a special phone-in, during which a succession of hysterical Hibees displayed all the symptoms of disbelief, grief, and anger – but not acceptance. Not even when a quickly cobbled-together 'Death of Hibernian' feature was broadcast, which just prompted even more calls from distraught OAPs, tearful teenagers, furious middle-aged men and almost-speechless housewives. Even Hearts fans were phoning up to offer their condolences. Within a few hours, a 'Hands Off Hibs' campaign was up and running, and I attended a rally at the threatened ground which drew more people than an average League game.

Mercer eventually failed in his bid to gain 75 per cent of the stock for outright control – and one moral to be drawn from this sorry affair is never to trust a man who *always* wears short-sleeved shirts.

Paying £12 rather than a tenner was a premium well worth absorbing in order to avoid the bucket seats of the shabby East Stand, and my extra two quid got me a comfortably padded tip-down seat in the top tier of the new North Stand, with stunning views of the Firth of Forth, my old tenement block, Arthur's Seat and Calton Hill. The Killie fans in the bottom tier of the South Stand enjoyed an equally unrestricted view of the lush green pitch (with no irritating supporting pillars to block sight-lines).

A disappointing crowd of just under 10,000 made cash-entry into the North Stand easy – the overall capacity being about 15,000 – but the cheap seats in the East Stand were almost fully occupied, especially the mephitic jungle nearest to the away supporters (a sort of 'F-Side' section like that favoured by Ajax's most violent hoodlums) – where I have vowed never to sit again.

In December 1995 I saw Celtic demolish Hibs 4–0, after having bought a home brief for this all-ticket fixture from the Hibs shop. I found myself surrounded by 'tooled-up' Hibee Casuals, like Irvine Welsh's Begbie character but with B&Q home-improvement weaponry stuffed up their jukes. (I would willingly have exchanged places with an armless junkie using his tongue and teeth to retrieve a used opium suppository from the bottom of a blocked toilet-pan in Pilton.) As the goal tally mounted, less self-controlled Celtic infiltrators were being identified, 'swedged' and then roughly escorted from the stand by amused stewards and policemen. I was ever so slightly scared – more slightly scared than I've ever been in my life – especially when Leith's answer to Piltdown Man sitting next to me said he could 'smell Weegie fear from 30 yards'. Smiling wanly, I closed my eyes and concentrated on tightening my sphincter muscles. In order to avoid having to carry a colostomy bag as a permanent fashion accessory – after having my intestines ruptured by steel-capped DMs and tyre irons – I adopted a pantomime East Coast accent and cheered on Hibernian.

When Joe Tortolano was unable to control a short corner, and Celtic broke to score their fourth, I chanted, 'There's only one Joe Tortolano.' Thankfully the Hibee hoolies all assumed I was being sarcastic, since Tortolano was the most vilified player in the history of the club. He would even be booed during pre-match warm-ups. (Prior to the Kilmarnock game, the 'loyal servant' with 11 years' service was given a free transfer at the age of 30.)

During the pre-match stretching exercises, a line of Hibs players ran and jumped, heading imaginary balls – except for the lagging-behind Darren Jackson, who looked like he was nutting opponents in a visualisation exercise.

Within 26 minutes Killie were two up thanks to Ally Mitchell and John Henry, who went straight through the middle of Hibs' 3-5-2 system (an innovative idea that Miller had obviously picked up from his part-time post as Scotland assistant coach but which doesn't really work if your central midfielders all think of themselves as 'goalscorers' and your three centre-backs play as if tethered together like a chain-gang). Chants of 'Miller must go' were only choked off when Mickey Weir, a diminutive winger capable of tucking his flapping shorts into his socks, scored from 20 yards out two minutes later.

Thereafter, A.T. Mays-sponsored Kilmarnock were largely grounded in their own half, but their foreign rep – keeper Dragoje Lekovic – adroitly handled the few dangerous pelters that the Carlsberg-shirted Hibees managed to get on target. (Although the pretty passing of Hibs deserved a draw, by the end their attacking formations resembled the dance-floor of a Benidorm discotheque at two in the morning, with Jackson so desperate to score that he was trying his luck from the halfway line.) Having defended resolutely against the balance of play, their 2–1 win put Kilmarnock at the top of the table come 4.45 p.m.

Anticlimactic anger swelled in the departing ranks: 'Ah wish Ah hudnae bought a season ticket fir this shite, ye ken'; 'Fightin' fuckin' relegation already – unbelievable, like'; 'Man, Miller's just a mince merchant who talks BSE-infected bollocks'.

Miller had been in charge at Easter Road for ten years – winning the Skol League Cup in 1991–92 – and although a respected coach, he desperately needed quality players (and a sense-of-humour transplant). He worries, however, that a foreign import costing £3,000 a week would 'get a slap in the face' in the Premier League (a typical example of Millerspeak). Worryingly for him, Graeme Souness at Southampton was rumoured to be after 'pocket rocket' Kevin 'Harpo' Harper, Hibernian's best young prospect in years. Maybe George Best could be lured out of retirement once more, because in 1979–80 Hibs paid the bearded alcoholic £2,000 a week and saw their gates almost double. (They did get relegated as well, however.)

The two new stands can easily wait – like 'Edinburgh's Disgrace' of the uncompleted parthenon atop Calton Hill, Easter Road would probably retain more character by remaining 'unfinished' – but the supporters won't wait much longer for the arrival of some players who can be compared to the Famous Five of the '50s (even if they are only a Fantastic Four, Tremendous Three, Divine Duo or merely a Wonderful One).

So, out the flat after two o'clock and home again by half five, a pleasant walk enlivened by listening on my Walkman to Hibees on various phone-ins turning the airwaves green with enmity. I wrote up my notes in leisurely fashion, got one number in the National Lottery, had a pint of bitter and then tried to read the glossy £1.50 match programme as four beautiful Spanish señoritas cavorted in sexual abandonment at the foot of my single bed – where the black-and-white portable TV was tuned to Channel 4's *Belle Epoque*.

As I wrote out my entry to the programme competition for tickets to a Festival fringe show called *Albert Camus, What's the Score?* – about an unemployed goalkeeper who reads *The Outsider* and becomes a changed man[2] – sexy Luz was climbing into bed (with the hero Jorge Sanz). As old DHL might have put it, his man-root was a bronze Etruscan phallus of super-solidity. Flicking to the programme centre-fold, I almost spilled my cup of

Earl Gray when confronted by a puff-cheeked action shot of Keith Wright with a stapled midriff. And so to bed not needing bromide in my tea but more booze in my system . . .

FOOTNOTES

1. The demise of Third Lanark in 1967 is well known, but like most people I assumed they had gone out of existence because they had become a loss-making anachronism (like Accrington Stanley in England in 1961). In reality they were arguably the third force in Glasgow, having come third in the old First Division as recently as the early '60s. In its final season Cathkin Park was still attracting healthy crowds, but Third Lanark chairman William Hiddleston was literally trying to push it towards financial oblivion, so that the ground could be sold to property developers. Hiddleston personally turned off water pipes supplying the showers, gave free transfers to star players, insisted the team pay their own fares on public transport to away games, and kept the lottery jackpot for himself every week. After some extremely shady share-dealings the ground was sold and Hiddleston would have ended up behind bars if not for a timely visit by the Grim Reaper. It would be nice to think that Hiddleston and Robert Maxwell (simultaneous and therefore illegal owner of both Derby County and Oxford United) have eternity-ticket seats together over on the other side, surrounded by deceased Third Lanark supporters and departed *Daily Mirror* pensioners.

2. Quoting Camus and his famous remark about football having taught him all he needed to know about life is impressively erudite in the appropriate company, but when tattooed and scar-faced 50-something strangers in pubs start to do so, one's alarm bells should start ringing. If such persons proceed to expound on the insights into the human condition offered by writers such as Schopenhauer, Kierkegaard or – God forbid – Foucault, you can be pretty certain that the hauf-and-hauf autodidact who's bending your ear first hit the library books while serving his time 'in the jiles' of Barlinnie, Peterhead or Saughton. Foucault is the real red-light warning, and if you're invited back to a rented bedsit to discuss 'the history of madness, medicine and punishment' make your excuses and leave pronto – because your prospective host is probably an alumna of Carstairs, State Mental University of Southern Scotland. All offers of a bath should certainly be refused, unless you've always wanted to live out the shower scene in *Psycho* from Janet Leigh's point-of-view.

BROCKVILLE PARK
Falkirk v Albion Rovers
Coca-Cola Cup, Second Round, 13.8.96

'You'll find it in Falkirk' is the town's marketing motto, and despite only having reached the third milestone of my crisscrossing Scottish journey, I did indeed 'find it'. In a match of gloriously capricious Cup controversy, last season's 'worst team in Scotland' and wooden-spoon recipients for four of the past five seasons humped the Bairns of Brockville 3–2 – without the need for extra-time or penalty kicks and after losing a sloppy opening goal in just 20 seconds to Albert Craig. This was a wonderful advert for summer football, played on a sunny midweek evening.

When I arrived by the Dunblane train in downtown Falkirk, however, I wasn't expecting a lot from either the town or the team. The pedestrianised High Street was surprisingly affluent, supporting two shopping malls and two supermarkets (one of which would have paid up to £7 million for the football ground site in the early 1990s, but with a new retail park being developed close by, the Brockville acreage will do well today to generate over a million if sold to Beazer, Barratt or Wimpey for housing development).

Strolling amongst the new orthodoxy of high-street retailing – building societies, franchised opticians, video stores, fast-food outlets and the usual department store chains – I couldn't help but wonder how Falkirk's populace earned enough money to support such a capitalist cornucopia of consumer choice (especially since almost nothing on sale was made locally). Like everywhere else, I suppose, half the people must work *for* the council and *in* the retail outlets, while in Falkirk's specific case the rest of the community must commute to the petrochemical plants of Grangemouth. (The nearby Carron Ironworks may have been at the heart of the Industrial Revolution, but all the traditional mines, foundries and brickworks in its environs have long ago disappeared.)

Falkirk may no longer be the main market for Highland sheep and cattle, but maybe the UFO triangle of Bonnybridge, Callander and Falkirk is the secret of the area's wealth and plethora of luxury-car showrooms. Various 'black triangle' UFOs had been buzzing the area the night before my visit, in some kind of air display or dogfight.

If the town is prosperous and expanding, the stadium is impoverished and cramped. The optimism of a few short years ago – when a greenfield site and even European football seemed, respectively, probable and possible – has evaporated and the Bairns are now attempting to get back into the Premier League after having propped it up for most of 1995–96 (when they won six games out of 36).

Agents Mulder and Scully should have been called in as early as August of '95, when an X-file on the bewildered Brockville boardroom would have started to bulge. When Hearts offered a managerial job to Jim 'Jambo' Jeffries, Falkirk chairman George Fulston called in telepathic trouble-shooters headed by Paul Daniels and G. Gordon Liddy to try and persuade his talented young boss to stay put (as well as offering him a lucrative *seven*-year contract). The ensuing yes-no-maybe-possibly-aye-naw series of responses from Jeffries had psychiatric and philosophical observers fearing for the ontological well-being of the big man, as his heart and head pulled in opposite directions.

Having finally decided on his old playing club, Fulston locked Jeffries in a sensory-deprivation tank for seven hours, the chairman only emerging from the locked home dressing-room to recharge his electric cattle-prod and stock up on syringes full of sodium pentathol. Dishevelled and looking at the ground, Jeffries told the waiting news crews and reporters that 'I am not a numbered Jambo, I am a free Bairn'. Later that night, with the skies full of UFO activity, Jeffries made a dash for the Edinburgh train at Grahamston station, but big transparent bubbles bounced him back to Brockville.

Somehow Hearts got their man out, using abseiling lawyers, and Fulston reacted by appointing his close friend John Lambie as 'Number Two' (to the chairman's 'Number One'). As manager of Partick Thistle, Lambie had kept the struggling Glasgow club in the top flight but by turning them into a sort of Maryhill Crazy Gang (but without the practical jokes and wimpy cissiness of the Wimbledon originals). In Lambie's macho world, hetero-sexual male hairdressers were about as believable as goals created from inside your own half with 12 one-touch passes.

As relegation beckoned, the boo-boys of Brockville's terraces were pilloried by the media for being the most carping supporters in the country, as they demonstrated outside the ground after games, dominated radio phone-ins and, reportedly, attempted to liquidate Lambie. They certainly were 'guilty' of the first two charges, but the incident where a souped-up Skoda full of 'bad lot' Bairns overtook Lambie's Jaguar and waved clenched fists and made V-signs at him and his wife was dizzyingly spin-doctored in the press, radio and TV reports to the extent that one would have thought that they had tried to run him off the Kilsyth–Falkirk road and then shot out his tyres with sawn-off shotguns. Whatever the last straw was – possibly a powercut to the floodlights during a Scottish Cup game against Aberdeen which led to the game being abandoned – Lambie felt forced to resign. (Conspiracy theories abound over the fusing/short-circuiting of the power supply and the unusual suspects include – depending on which pub you're getting gutted in – Fulston himself, the 'Touch ane, touch aw' terrorist fan club, and of course the triangular black UFOs and the magnetic interference caused by their faster-than-light aluminium engines.)

After more than five years of rejected applications, planning permission for New Brockville at Westfield (towards Grangemouth) was finally granted in June 1996. But even if the finance to build it is eventually put in place, Falkirk will have to play out all of season 1996–97 at broken-down Brockville, with its rickety wooden stand and three sides of weed-strewn terracing (which, even if promotion is not gained, *must* be replaced by seats by August of 1997.)

Sitting right at the back of the Main Stand, as the Hawaiian-shirted-and-Bermuda-shorted fans in the Hope Street end basked in the setting sunshine, I smiled at the owner of the house whose gable end has a small window overlooking the pitch – which he stopped leaning out of and slammed shut the *moment* the actual game started. The parochial and obsolete advertising hoardings were amusing, too, especially the one which promised: 'Everyone enjoys Rosie's Niteclub' (which didn't sound like a raver's paradise of techno, laser lighting and line-dancing to the beat of Bolivian Marching Powder).

New manager Eamonn Bannon must have been pleased when he heard that he was to be presented with a complimentary car from a local dealer, but instead of a 3-Series BMW (even one with the bottom-of-the-range giveaway sign of a single exhaust pipe), the back page of the *Falkirk Herald* pictured him taking delivery of a nondescript white saloon with 'Square Deal Motors, Sponsors of Falkirk FC' emblazoned on the door panels. Not a vehicle to be seen in if crawling along the kerbs of Falkirk's red-light district (if it has one, but Bannon isn't a slow city-centre driver and Gladstonian saver of fallen women like some scandal-haunted managers down south).

With his capital connections, Bannon had brought in an Embra United of released crocks, which included Craig Nelson, Neil Berry and David Hagen (all ex-Hearts) and one-time Hibs full-back, Graeme Mitchell.

After scoring, the Bairns adopted a style of play reminiscent of the town's Scottish festival slogan 'The Big Heuch and Birl' (which could equally well be a description of centre-half Berry and keeper Nelson as a hapless comedy double act). Colin McFarlane equalised with an unchallenged header after Nelson stopped even punching innocuous crosses because of incessant booing. Back with my half-time pie before the half-time whistle, I was perfectly positioned to see David McKenzie's wonder-goal wallop, which actually gathered pace as the ball headed for Nelson's top-right corner. Albion's two-dozen fans in a crowd of 1,894 went wild in their row of the stand. So did the remaining 1,870 Falkirk fans in the stadium. A polyester-clad OAP near me turned round and started mock-hitting his head against the rear stand wall, but in real anger.

In the second half Falkirk's relentless pressure led to an equaliser, a looping header from Craig, but the Wee Rovers were hitting on the break like sophisticated Continentals (which would have been impressive enough from the basement proppers-up of Italy's Serie C2, but which from the team that habitually finished 40th out of 40 in Scotland was frankly incredible). Then Tony McNally scored direct from their first corner – not a banana bender curled into the far corner deliberately (as practised by the *Azzurri* in training), but sclaffed across goal and somehow in without anyone even deflecting it. Albion coach Vinnie Moore was out of his dug-out doing a St Vitus's dance of delirium. (Before beating Arbroath 4–0 in the previous round, the Rovers hadn't progressed beyond the first round of any cup competition for *five* years.)

Although Hagen hit the post in the dying minutes, Albion Rovers deserved their shock win. Falkirk merit praise, too, for making it the kind of game where even a neutral like myself was totally gripped by the non-stop action and pulsating atmosphere. So much so that by joining in the clapping, booing, shouting, whistling, jumping up and down, and feet-stamping all my personal worries – about approaching deadlines, mounting debts, decreasing sex drive, a receding future, etc – disappeared from my consciousness for 90 wonderful minutes. Such *total* immersion in sporting events outwith your control, although relatively rare, is extraordinarily cathartic and is one of the great attractions of closely contested and competitive football matches.

Almost getting crushed on leaving a ground is not – and is supposed to be a thing of the past. Nevertheless, those of us in the stand were forced to file through a small gap in a wall leading to the Hope Street terrace (an ambulance was supposedly blocking the Main Stand's concourse). There was no real danger as the queuers jostled to keep their feet traversing the bench seating, but if the little girl in front of me had tripped . . . And those jumping the front wall on to the pitch were shouted at to get off! New Brockville or no New Brockville, the sooner Falkirk meet the safety requirements of the Taylor Report, the better.

The general consensus amongst the fans I talked to about their attitude to chairman Fulston was 'Sod 'im'. Phil (aged 26) of Linlithgow thought Falkirk were heading back to the 'dark ages', would only believe in the new stadium 'when the *final* substandard brick has been laid' and wasn't at all happy about the absence of match programmes (because the game had been played on a Tuesday, he suggested that the club would probably have them delivered from the printers first thing on Wednesday morning). Although likely to be out of work by the end of the week, Phil wasn't nearly as depressed as the Bairns fan on the opposite platform of Grahamston station – who sat hunched forward with his head in his hands. He kept on mumbling one word over and over: 'Shocking'.

Although I was back home by 11 p.m., the Albion Rovers squad hit the Coatbridge night-spot Boozy Rouge to celebrate. If they get Celtic or Rangers away in the next round, their bank manager will probably party until dawn, whatever the result. And if they don't, the dream of qualifying for Europe by winning the Coca-Cola Cup can continue. Entertaining the likes of Chelsea, Cologne or CSKA at Cliftonhill would be a sight worth seeing. Falkirk may be good enough to gain promotion, but Brockville should be bulldozed as soon as possible.

SOMERSET PARK
Ayr United v Hamilton Academical
Second Division, 17.8.96

The handful of Accies fans alighting from the train at the terminus were welcomed to the capital of Burns Country and the Golf Coast in English, Gaelic (*Fàilte don Ayr*), French (*Bienvenue à Ayr*) and German (*Willkommen in Ayr*). A temporary sign in Yiddish would have been a nice gesture for the Israeli director Daniel Cohen, who had passed through the seaside town with his World Television News crew earlier in the week, on the way to cover an Ayrshire Juniors Cup-tie between Auchinleck and Cumnock further inland. (In their previous meeting supporters of the two village teams had engaged in hand-to-hand combat and lobbed chunks of masonry at each other's wives and weans – and if either of these bloodthirsty rivals ever decide to sign a trio of Serbian strikers the other will immediately up the ante further by recruiting half-a-dozen Croatian centre-halfs, thereby necessitating a tank corps of blue-helmeted UN peacekeepers to set up roadblocks at the crossroads of the A70 and A76 to prevent outbreaks of ethnic cleansing all over Southern Ayrshire.)

'Auld Ayr, wham ne'er a town surpasses, for honest men and bonnie lassies,' wrote Rabbie Burns after witnessing mixed-sex teams from Auchinleck and Cumnock demonstrating the new sport of 'contact gowf' (played over 18 grave-sized holes, but without balls, and whose only rule was 'You swing at your unconscious opponent where he or she lies').

Since 1996 was the bicentenary of the Scottish Bard's death, Burnsmania was in full swing during my visit, with local shopkeepers selling Made-in-China Burns baseball caps, Burns backpacks and Burns baby-bibs, etc. Just as Jesus Christ two thousand years ago never imagined that his crucified image would one day be incorporated in designs for religious memorabilia like battery-powered night-lights, so Burns himself two hundred years ago could never have envisaged his screen-printed profile adorning 'Ae Fond Kiss' T-shirts worn by obese Americans waddling down Ayr High Street.

Although Burnsians may outnumber Christians by the 40th century, like the King James Bible I find his *Collected Works* well-nigh incomprehensible (for every hour spent reading him, another 60 minutes is required to translate his words into English – which may in fact explain his popularity abroad where he is in print in almost every language except for Lallans Scots).

Arguably, Burns is a minor poet but major sex maniac, whose passionate personality and cultish charisma overshadow his sentimental and simplistic prose poems. In Scotland, however, the consensus in the cultural consciousness is one of 'Humanist Genius at Fuck' – a combination of Shakespeare, Sinatra and Solzhenitsyn (or even Jesus, JFK and Georges Simenon all rolled into one). Even my moral-majority mantra-ing father made an exception in the case of the fornicating farmer who fathered 15 children, six of whom were illegitimate. 'Rabbie loved them all passionately and exclusively,' my dad used to say of the women Burns brought to multiple orgasm, 'at the specific time and place of their lovemaking – and none of his lassies ever regretted their lustful couplings.'

In the 1790s Ayr may have been a sexual theme-park, but according to a Durex survey published just prior to my arrival, it was the least favoured holiday resort in Britain for torrid romantic encounters. (There's probably no connection but the newest sculpted statue in the town centre depicted in Soviet-symbolist style a fisherman holding a dead fish in outstretched arms – but even the fishing fleet has recently decamped to Troon's harbour.)

For the second game in a row I got stuck beside an angry old codger, while a few feet in front another middle-aged father and attractive 20-something daughter were watching their local team in filial togetherness. A Brockville brunette, in white jeans dangling a brown loafer at the end of a piquantly-bared ankle, had prompted a bizarrely erotic 'wet dream' . . .

Ever since seeing the bathroom seduction scene in *The Shining*, where a naked temptress in Jack Nicholson's arms transforms herself into a hideous old crone oozing patches of green gunge in between Nicholson's roving fingers, my relatively few erotic dreams have nearly always taken similarly terrifying turns into nightmarish surrealism – bladder-emptying bed-wetting only being forestalled by my sitting bolt upright in sweat-drenched shock. Even while daydreaming, my sexual fantasies tend to 'deflate' at my superego's insistence on introducing a bloody *condom* into Sharon Stone seduction scenarios.

I got a good viewing spot on the open north terrace of Somerset Park, enjoying the almost-forgotten 'luxury' of standing behind a crush-barrier – as well as having appreciated the directional presence of floodlight pylons when trying to find this neat little ground. Leaning against the next crush-barrier down, the silvery-haired papa stood proprietorially beside his very pretty daughter, dressed 'secretarial smart' in white blouse, blue-print skirt and slingback heels. Turning round slightly I saw the interesting inlet of her clavicle. Such heartbreaking beauty on the terrace of a football match . . .

Then I noticed the advertising hoarding right next to the home dug-out: 'Sexually Transmitted Diseases Clinics in Ayrshire', with separate tele-phone numbers for Irvine, Ayr and Kilmarnock (in Auchinleck and Cumnock the signs of tertiary syphilis are worn as sexual battle scars to be proud of). A similar half-page ad in the match programme shared advertising space with a Harry Fairbairn BMW dealership and Ayr racecourse. So a modern-day Tam O' Shanter could win a small fortune by betting his dole cheque on a five-horse accumulator, spend some of it on a *two-exhaust-pipe* 3-Series BMW, use its status-symbol pulling power to seduce the bonnie lass of his choice, and then make an appointment at one of the above clinics to investigate the cause of painful micturition and suppurating foreskin lesions – all because of the power of advertising as represented on page 29 of a £1 match programme.

Having dumped Premier League arch-Ayrshire-rivals Kilmarnock out of the Coca-Cola Cup, the Honest Men of Ayr were favourites to get their promotion push off to a winning start. The home team turned out in an all-white Real Madrid-type kit, except for black facings on the shorts (and although the Spanish giants refuse to sully their kit with shirt sponsorship, even they may have succumbed to the financial temptation that led to the *Ayrshire Post* replacing What Everyone Wants); Hamilton appeared in their 'Internazionale' away strip, although the famous blue and black stripes were somewhat disfigured by the name of Wilson Homebuilders (a somewhat ironic sponsor since the homeless Accies are currently tenants of Albion Rovers at Cliftonhill).

Over two thousand Ayr fans watched in mounting frustration as Hamilton continually hit on the break. In the 22nd minute the visitors went meritoriously ahead when 37-year-old Crawford Baptie – one of many ageing players on the Somerset pitch with a Premier past – headed across goal for Gary Clark to beat 40-year-old ex-Hearts keeper Henry Smith with an equally powderpuff header. The 50 or so Accies fans under the covered Railway End went impressively mental, the more excitable running up and down the terracing with their arms extended like wings. 'You're so shite, it's unbelievable,' they chanted, as a second goal looked increasingly inevitable.

While Ayr manager Gordon 'Dazza' Dalziel let rip at his charges during the interval, the half-time entertainment consisted of three people in Panda outfits taking penalties in front of the packed Somerset Road end. I got a good action-shot with my borrowed Panasonic Zoom camera, including the back of the aforementioned bonnie lassie's immaculately groomed head. Did I dare ask her to look away and yawn? (If posed pictures are good enough for Robert Doisneau, they're good enough for *moi*.) Nah . . . Having gone overboard on alcoholic beverages on Friday night – each section of this book having been written so far under the gravitational conditions experienced within Sylvia Plath's 'bell jar' – I felt as bad as I looked:

unshowered, unshaven, dressed in baggy Levi cut-offs and a Ribena-stained white T-shirt, and I was having a very bad hair day.

Then when I'd put my camera away in its case, she turned sideways and yawned naturally – just as one of the bloody Pandas blootered the ball over the bar. Great chance missed there, eh, Gerry?

I think I would have plucked up the courage to ask her to 'pose', if not for a truly embarrassing cow-lick standing to crooked attention on the side of my head (which no amount of water, gel or mousse had succeeded in battering into flat submission). Naturally thick hair and expensive rug-rethinks are vastly underestimated factors in the equation that determines masculine self-image and perceived physical attractiveness. (Personally, I can lurch from crippling shyness to garrulous gregariousness depending on the result of my Number Two-clippered haircuts.) Dazza, for example, would not have been described as 'drop dead gorgeous' by two pre-teen female fans if not for his Vidal-Sasoonish good locks. Similarly, Hamilton's new recruit from Livingston, ex-Hibee Joe McBride, wouldn't have been attracting wolf-whistles of admiration without his beautiful barnet (though it didn't stop him being substituted in the second half for fannying around ineffectively on the touchline). Would Melvyn Bragg be so televisually and flyleafishly attractive without his bouffant hair? Even Burns was lucky with his natural side-parting and sexy sideburns.

In the second half Angolan winger José Quitongo (one of 41 foreigners this season from 18 countries playing senior football in Scotland) continued to torment the Ayr defence. Great credit is due to the home fans, as not one racist remark emanated from the terracing, although Quitongo's two pig-tails drew some derisive comments. Both Quitongo and Paul Ritchie missed absolute sitters, but at one-up the Hamilton supporters felt confident enough to start serenading Smith with choruses of 'Henry, Henry, drop the ball'.

Ayr eventually managed to pin Hamilton back, but the Accies were hardly up against the ropes. Last-minute-call-up trialist keeper Colin Scott only had one outstanding-diving-save to make, from Paul Smith. With three penalty claims that only a 'homer' referee would have considered giving, Ayr were becoming increasingly desperate, but their fans continued to give them thunderous, high-decibel support, merely for earning corners and free-kicks.

With three minutes to go, three sides of Somerset Park erupted when Ronnie Coyle's sliced daisy-cutter was redirected into the net by Isaac English. A 1–1 draw was a disappointing result for Iain Munro's men, but in Quitongo they had the most exciting – if erratic – player on display. Although only 21, José speaks Bantu, Portuguese, Swedish, Gaelic, English

43

and Cliftonhillese – having played for Luanda Lions, Benfica, Malmo, Waterford, Darlington and now Hamilton Academical. Hanging about outside the Main Stand I got the following quote: 'Ich bin psittacosis as un perroquet . . . braw bonhomie with Accie boys but.'

Ayr chairman Bill Barr may be servicing weekly losses of approximately £6,000, but even without redevelopment Somerset Park will remain a great little ground – the old-fashioned but homely snack booths serving three sides of terracing, with both ends covered. The open North Terrace is obviously popular when it's not raining – even in the 1990s people like to stand behind crush-barriers – and the five executive boxes which overlook it are anonymous enough not to inspire envy amongst the seven-quid standers. The Main Stand's small extension gives it a capacity of almost 1,500, which is certainly adequate while Ayr remain in the Second Division. Still, having drawn Rangers at Ibrox in the live TV draw after this game for the Coca-Cola Cup, Barr should have a sizeable financial windfall to help reduce debts and get the team back in the Scottish Top 20, which they should never have been allowed to fall out of in the first place.[1]

On the way back to the station, I failed to find the 'Paki' newsagent shop that has been converted into a temporary mosque, despite vociferous protests from the Tory-voting bungalow dwellers in what sounds like an archetypal Ayr street. If the town can support a mosque, albeit small, surely Ayr FC could recruit either local or imported Asian footballers (who unlike their Afro-Caribbean counterparts have not yet broken through into the professional game in any significant way). 'Ooh, aah . . . Mohammeda' echoing round a Premier Division fixture at Somerset Park before the century's end would be something to aim for. After all, as the Bard said, 'Man to man the world o'er shall brithers be for a' that'. Except for them heidbangers o'er in Auchinleck and Cumnock toons, of course.

FOOTNOTES

1. If Ayr had accepted a takeover offer in the mid-'80s, they could have been playing in this season's Champions' League section of Ajax, Auxerre and Zurich Grasshoppers. Instead the quartet was completed by Rangers, where rejected would-be investor David Murray found a more amenable investment opportunity for his Murray International Metal millions; £6 million bought a 74 per cent stake in the sleeping Glasgow giants, and today the Ibrox institution is worth approximately £200 million.

DENS PARK
Dundee v Greenock Morton
First Division, 24.8.96

'There is nothing wrong with your TV set. We are controlling transmission
. . . Aberdeen 1, Zalgiris Vilnius 3 . . . Barry Town 3, Budapest Vasutus 1 . . .
Alania Vladikavkaz 2, Glasgow Rangers 7 . . . This is your sportscaster Rod
Serling signing off from the fifth dimension of Twilight Zone Television
News, brought to you by the official sponsors of the Jeux Sans Frontières
Outer Limits Euro-Disney Cup – Kimberly-Clark, makers of low-tar, low-
nicotine tampons. Remember: *You're never alone with a Lil-let!* And: *Other
sanitary products may be a real drag, but a Tampax is a good smoke!* Goodnight and
good bleeding . . .'

Such midweek footballing madness was almost as bizarre as feminine
hygiene commercials dripping with blue 'blood', and if Dundee had been
renamed 'Juteopolis', as the next stop after Leuchars, I couldn't have been
more amazed (the Lithuanians had arrived at Pittodrie after a 12-hour
coach trip from London at four o'clock on the morning of the match, the
League of Wales champions had a ground capacity of 2,500 and the best
team in Russia went out 10–3 on aggregate). Almost as incredible to
contemplate is the fact that in 1962–63 Dundee beat Cologne, Sporting
Lisbon and Anderlecht in the European Cup before narrowly losing to
eventual winners AC Milan in the semi-finals, a run they repeated in
1967–68 in the old Fairs Cup.

'Surely Nick Hornby isn't that bad?' I urbanely enquired of the blonde
beauty sitting across the aisle, after she had laid aside *High Fidelity* on page
91 in favour of the ScotRail magazine *Horizons*.

'Not at all,' said Heidi (25) from Lancaster, 'it's just not as laugh-out-
loud hilarious as the promotional puffs would have you believe.'

Crivvens and help ma boab! 'Don't you think it shows what being a New
Man in the '90s is all about?'

'Self-pity, you mean?'

Wow! Blonde, 20-something, ex-medical student, friendly, funny and
intelligent enough to see through the hyperbolic blurb-speak that all pub-
lishers insist on plastering their products with – both bad and quite good
books. Her only obvious imperfection was a Wimbledon-supporting
boyfriend called Alex. I'm sure I impressed her greatly with my zoom lens,
fully extended, when taking a picture of her reading Hornby's best-selling
novel with RSS *Discovery* in the background. Having a good hair day,
'researching my *second* book' and with a flashily whirring camera round my
neck, I felt like a psycho-combo of Davids Cassidy, Hume and Bailey.

45

Scotland's fourth city (out of . . . well, four, really) grew on the profits from jute, jam and journalism, but is now trying to market itself to tourists as the 'City of Discovery' (although an advertising agency got into trouble when a photograph taken from the south bank of the River Tay and incorporating the road bridge was 'morphed' so that Dundee itself became uncannily like Manhattan by Night; also, before the Cold War ended, Scottish Screen Locations were forever touting Dundee as a cinematic dead-ringer for Communist Moscow, especially if scenes required to be shot using stand-ins for the Soviet workers' public housing projects which ring the Russian capital; but attempts to sell the City Square and the Caird Hall as alternatives to Red Square and the Kremlin only ever succeeded with Grampian Television productions, who normally ended up having to use phoney back-projection techniques anyway).

Discovery Quay cost almost £50 million to redevelop and the visitor centre Discovery Point has the *Discovery* moored alongside. Using the usual heritage industry tools of interactive displays, video docu-dramas and blown-up grainy photographs, the 1993 New Tourist Attraction of the Year celebrates Captain Scott's suicidal second place to Amundsen in the race for the South Pole and Antarctica's splendid scenery and spectacular wildlife (i.e. snow and penguins).

Bet you didn't know that Robert 'Old Mooney' Scott was born in Dundee and that he only lost out to Amundsen because Scott preferred Manchurian ponies 'with immortal human souls' to the Norwegian's 'devil-dog huskies' and because he insisted on loading his sledges with kitchen sinks. Well, he wasn't (he wasn't even Scottish) and he did. So what's the connection between Dundee and the South Pole? There isn't one. Although the Antarctic exploration vessel *Discovery* was built in the Tayside city, and Scott did sail aboard her, she was *not* the ship used for the South Pole expedition of 1910–12 – that was the *Terra Nova* (built in one of South Korea's government-subsidised yards). Nevertheless, the Angus and City of Dundee Tourist Board continues to extol Scott's highly debateable virtues (psychologically he was more than a few miles short of One-Ton Depot) and Dundee's highly tenuous connections to him.

'Four quid fer an effing auld whaling boat!' wailed an aggrieved local to his girlfriend, after seeing the admission charges to the hexagonal Discovery Point (obviously not a man keen to impress on a first date). Not wishing to part with £4 either, I limited myself to the free toilets and expensive gift shop – stocked with Captain Scott and Discovery memorabilia and other tacky trinkets commemorating Dennis the Menace and Gnasher, Desperate Dan, Oor Wullie and the Broons (comic-strip creations from the pages of the *Beano*, the *Dandy* and the *Sunday Post*). Copyrighted by the publishing giants D.C. Thomson, these cartoon characters espouse more right-wing sentiments than their superhero counterparts in DC/Marvel Comics, such as Superman, Judge Dread, Captain America or the Fantastic Four.

The *Dundee Courier* has quite phenomenal market share and penetration in Tayside, Fife and Grampian, even though it still serialises books on a daily basis without any abridgement, so that its readers get lengthy extracts from titles like *Flower-Pressing Was for Sundays*, *Portrait of a Perthshire Parish* and *The Wooing and Winning of a Wartime Widow from Wick* day after day for months on end. Most anachronistically none of the non-NUJ journalists get by-line credits for their stories – not even when a 'North-East man' connection can be made to mud-slide or volcanic-eruption disasters in South America. (In combination with coverage from the *Aberdeen Press and Journal*, a North-East man anywhere in the world will be located and quoted if he comes within a 20-mile radius of an international news story – e.g. *NE Man in DC-10 Crash-Landing Nightmare at Djakarta Airport*, despite the fact that he was in the Departures' Lounge waiting to take off on a different airline's Tri-Star – and his wife in Hilltown thought he was attending a sales conference on treatments for sheep scrapie and worm infestation in Worcester.)

Dundee itself used to be a hotbed of radical politics, however, with Communists on the local council (a fact which *Fodor* thought was shocking enough to merit reinforcing with an exclamation mark for its largely American readership). In recent years striking pickets at the entrance to the Timex factory managed to get themselves on *60 Minutes* (with subtitles) and one of the few manufacturing multinationals in the area to close down completely.

The most famous living Dundonian is probably the actor Brian Cox, who made a much more believable Hannibal Lecter than snorting and sniffing Anthony Hopkins, and although Dundee is reputed to have the most beautiful women in the country – due to a preponderance of female offspring in the last century and the resulting increase in standards of physical pulchritude necessary to attract the relatively low ratio of available males – the Wellgate shopping mall didn't exactly seem to be teeming with too many would-be supermodels on high-fashion shopping expeditions.

Tramping up Dens Road, I half-managed to convince myself that I was on a quasi-religious, medieval-type pilgrimage. Having skipped lunch for reasons of economy, I bought ten Benson and Hedges to stave off hunger pangs during the match. (As a freelance match-reporter I used to bomb up this steep hill in a taxi, after having enjoyed a three-course lunch, both on expenses. Oh, happy fucking days.) Feeling light-headed, footsore and wheezingly breathless, I reached the turnstiles to the South Enclosure, where I handed over £8 to sit on a bench protected overhead by a corrugated-iron roof. The *Eh Mind O' Gillie* (?) fanzine was okay reading for 50p, but even at a pound *It's Half-Past Four and We're 2–0 Down* sounded better value.

By three o'clock the Enclosure was almost full, while the refurbished Main Stand, costing its patrons a tenner, was almost empty. Despite the fans' obvious preference, only the Main Stand had been open for the previous two home games against Stenhousemuir and Dumbarton, another worrying sign of Dundee's precarious financial position – and the cash-strapped directors must have been grateful for the colourful presence of at least three hundred Morton fans congregated under *half* a roof in the Provost Road End (in a total crowd of 3,561). The opposite end was sealed-off weed-strewn terracing without any cover. The only major changes since my last visit in 1994 had been the installation of a greyhound racing track, with all the improvements in the Main Stand designed to accommodate the needs of the betting fraternity. (In 1944 local businessmen had attempted to buy out the football club entirely, in order to concentrate solely on greyhound, cheetah and dromedary racing!)

Although absentee Canadian chairman Ron Dixon had undoubtedly saved the Darkers from financial disaster in the early '90s by buying the club and its debts for £600,000, two seasons in the highly competitive but remuneratively disastrous First Division have turned Dundee from a yo-yo up-and-down outfit to an established mid-table team who are happy to avoid relegation into Division Two and relieved to survive each yearly auditing of the club accounts. (To save money, the reserve team were disbanded for season 1996–97.)

Player-manager Jim Duffy may have led them to a Coca-Cola Cup final appearance in 1995–96 – where they lost predictably but pathetically to Aberdeen 2–0 – but after that their League form collapsed dramatically, leaving them in fifth place. Before the start of this season they haemorrhaged most of their best players – for example, Morten Weighorst, Neil McCann, Dusan Vrto, Michel Pageau and Cornelius 'Neil' Duffy – who didn't fancy a third straight season of lower-grade football and whom Dundee were willing to let go for woefully inadequate but desperately needed sums of hard cash. (When they hit clubs like Dundee, the after-effect ripples of the Bosman ruling have grown to tidal-wave proportions.)

New sponsorship deals with Olympic Boots and AVEC kit manufacturers (who?) only provide free boots and strips, and the ditching of previous shirt sponsors Auto Windscreens in favour of the Edinburgh-based Firkin Brewery was prompted by the need for a 'five-figure' cash injection – £10,000?

With a good atmosphere in the 'shed' but the Dees facing promotion-hopefuls Greenock Morton, what could stylishly bald Duffy expect from his patched-up team of journeymen pros and inexperienced youngsters? Answer: a goal in two minutes from Chic Charnley, when a blocked free-kick was thwacked diagonally across goal and in via the far post. Charnley has the same outrageous football skills as Gazza (well, sort of), but puts on weight faster and is even more mentally unstable. Imagine Colonel Gaddafi summoning the US ambassador to his bedouin tent for a diplomatic dressing-down after F-14s had bombed Tripoli and you've got some idea of how Charnley communicates with referees. In the second half he was booked for a horrendous stud-exposed tackle on Alan Mahood – who required seven stitches in a leg wound – but Charnley still had to be restrained from pushing Mahood off the pitch for treatment. Charnley may be able to hit defence-splitting 60-yard cross-park passes and bend free-kicks past the best of goalkeepers, but he is generally regarded as a psychologically volatile on-pitch time-bomb (with a Scottish record of 15 dismissals to his name). With each new transfer and promise to change his ways, he promptly marks each début with further violent conduct or foul-mouthed backchat.

In 17 minutes Morton's Derek Lilley sprang Dundee's offside trap and calmly lobbed Billy Thomson in goal. Ten minutes later the home side went back in front when Paul Tosh stretched out a foot and volleyed home an overhit cross with his studs. It remained 2–1 at the finish, despite Dundee playing most of the second half in their own penalty box. If Finnish striker Marko Rajamaki, blond and pony-tailed, could have forced Thomson into making a save or two, Morton would probably have equalised, since whenever stick-insect Thomson is forced to make a save or two, he is likely to let at least one in. Duffy at 36, in the centre of the Dundee defence, looked as if his ageing legs or dodgy knees could give way or pop out at any minute, but he marshalled his fellow defenders with impressive authority.

Sadly for Dundee, once a top club in Scotland and capable of mixing it with the best in Europe, the three points in the bag from this game may prove to be a much-needed insurance premium against relegation later in the season, and one must fear for the long-term future of the Dark Blues.[1] Compared with Dundee United's revamped Tannadice Stadium – literally no more than a stone's throw away in the same street – Dens Park is an embarrassing anachronism. Three sides of it need demolished and rebuilt, and the same could be said of three-quarters of the current side. Cash-rich and relatively successful neighbours United might even consider taking them in as tenants, leaving Dens Park to the dogs. (But even as a temporary measure for a season, any groundsharing proposal while Dens was rebuilt would probably flounder on Arab memories of Dundee's attempt to corner the market in United shares as recently as 1991.) The loudest cheer of the day came after the final whistle, when the Tannoy announcer confirmed that United had lost 1–0 at Ibrox.

FOOTNOTES

1. In mid-June 1997 businessmen brothers Peter and Jimmy Marr paid £1.3 million to buy out Ron Dixon's majority shareholding. With vacant ground with real potential for housing development located behind the dilapidated south terrace, this may prove to be a future financial windfall that the new owners – Dundee fans and Dundonians – will be able to use to upgrade the stadium and strengthen the playing pool. Dixon probably won't be missed – since no one normally knew where in the world he was on any given day – and because during his five-year-long, fax-length stewardship Dundee FC fell out of the Premier League and were forced to sell a series of star players for well below their market value. On the other hand, Dixon did save the Darkers from disappearing under a sea of debt in 1992 – and through the on-site intercession of long suffering vice-chairman Malcolm Reid, he did leave the club in a largely debt-free position.

CLIFTONHILL
Albion Rovers v Cowdenbeath
Third Division, 31.8.96

'You are a right heart-scald to your mother. What does it take to get you to screw the nut?' asked Sheriff Sandy MacPherson. Chic Charnley was in the dock a few days after the Dundee v Morton game, where he denied failing to give a breath test while driving erratically near his home in Balornock (an area of Glasgow that buses refuse to drive through without rear-gunners after the pubs close on Saturday nights). After pleading not guilty, his trial was set for January. The above quote was reported in the *Airdrie and Coatbridge Advertiser* (28.8.96), but in relation to a knife-wielding youth who had been caught carrying a concealed four-inch blade. (The 'Crimebeat' column also reported an abducted 'two-foot-tall Jamaican with curly hair, fruity hair-clasps and a nylon floral dress' and a bystander being hit on the head by an iron bar outside the Whinhall Mini-Market – which, if perpetrated by the same man, is a worrying indication of the propensity of *doll*-stealing sex perverts in Monklands to carry, and use, lead piping as an offensive weapon.)

In the week leading up to this top-of-the-table clash between the Wee Rovers of Coatbridge and the Blue Brazil of Cowdenbeath, Jimmy Thomson of Raith Rovers had become the second managerial casualty of the season. Elsewhere during his last game in charge on Saturday, 24 August, Ayr's keeper Henry Smith had almost ended up in casualty after a home fan at Brechin had thrown a brick at him. Clydebank's goalie Gary Matthews, however, was prevented from turning out at Boghead against Stirling after being charged with *allegedly* assaulting a former Bankies steward prior to kick-off. Falkirk's Albert Craig had sprinted across the pitch and up the Brockville tunnel in order to give Partick's Gareth Evans a cauliflower ear – after both players had just been red-carded by referee Rowbotham. At Stark's Park itself, Peter Duffield and Shaun Dennis (who'd just failed to turn up in court for sentencing after a pub brawl) squared up to each other in the tunnel at half-time, after the two *Raith* players had fallen out during their side's 3–0 home hammering by visitors Motherwell. As for sex scandals, Dave 'Psycho' Bowman of Dundee United and Davie 'Elephant Man' Dodds of Rangers had been caught playing away from their wifely homes . . .

Just another Saturday of gratuitous violence on the park, with binge boozing and sleazy sex off it for days afterwards? No, not quite. Even for 'soccer Scottish-style' it had been a very bad week on the public-relations front.

With no Premier fixtures because of Scotland's World Cup qualifier in Vienna against Austria – which ended 0–0 but which provided plenty of potential footage for the keenly anticipated video compilation provisionally entitled *Craig Brown's Thousand Greatest-Ever Corner-Kicks* (Cameron Williams, 600 minutes, £129.90) – the fairy-tale start by Albion Rovers had captured the imagination of the largely Celtic-supporting town (with six points out of six without losing a goal). A victory against Cowdenbeath would take them to the top of their division for the first time since 1988 and set them up for their biggest game since facing Rangers in the League Cup in 1978: the 1,238 all-ticket home tie against Hibernian in the Coca-Cola Cup.

Having a few hours to kill, I wandered the mean and prudent and generous streets of Coatbridge, which is only a few miles east of Glasgow and which is pretty much a microcosm of the Big G – re-clad council tower blocks with 'concièrges' notwithstanding. The town's main 'tourist' attractions are the Sumerlee Heritage Centre, the World Championship-hosting Indoor Bowling Club and the Time Capsule (a theme-park of water flumes and an ice-rink, full of plastic plesiosaurs, plexiglass pterodactyls, rubber foliage and *faux* fauna).

'Protestant' Airdrie believes that it has lost out unfairly on such lucrative attractions because of a conspiracy of 'Catholic' Coatbridge councillors on the old Monklands District Council, and in the aftermath of various media and Labour Party investigations, Airdrieonian community-charge payers certainly appear to have some legitimate grievances.

Nevertheless, Airdrie FC now have planning permission for a new multi-million-pound stadium at Craigneuk, to be completed in 1997. But even before the horrendous planning problems had been resolved, the old Rovers board in 1995 agreed in principle to become tenants of the Diamonds wherever the latter ended up, selling Cliftonhill in the meantime and decamping temporarily to East Stirling's Firs Park. This 'sell-out' prompted a boardroom reshuffle and timber-merchant David Shanks as chairman promised to redevelop Cliftonhill while continuing to service what were in football terms Third-World-country-crippling-type debts. A commercial director was appointed, along with new player-manager Vinnie Moore (who sold office equipment during the week). Despite an impressive improvement from January 1996 onwards – which included beating League leaders Livingston in the first game under the new régime – Albion still finished bottom, for the fourth time in five years.

They would have disappeared down the plughole if the Scottish Football League's hermetically sealed structure had not saved them from free-falling any further – for example, into the Castlemaine XXXX Ayers Rock Amateur League. (In the English Third Division, 92nd-out-of-92 Torquay

United only avoided demotion to the Vauxhall Conference because Stevenage failed to satisfy the stadium requirements necessary for their deserved-on-merit elevation.) The new commercially circumspect board and Kirby-vacuum-cleaner-motivated management team had transformed the Wee Rovers from wooden-spoon certainties (40-1 against for promotion) to title favourites (10-1) in the most unpredictable and downright bloody awful of Scotland's four Leagues.

Climbing up the hill behind the stadium, I found that Shanks had been true to his word in threatening to erect two 50-foot-high wooden advertising hoardings, presumably using his own timber, to try and prevent the Behind-the-Wall Gang of 60-odd locals from gathering on the grass bank of the so-called 'Aberdeen Gate' for totally unrestricted and *free* views of the pitch. But to each side of the *advertless* hoardings, onlookers could still see most of the playing area. Would the 'free-loaders' be deterred by the visual obstacles or the chairman's moral disapprobation?

Spotting the neon signs of civilisation – a McDonald's drive-thru and a shopping mall (the Quadrant) – I strolled along Main Street, surprised by the number of Celtic tops and Eire jerseys being worn as 'smart-casual' daywear and gobsmacked by the amount of conspicuous consumption that these naffly attired shoppers were indulging in. Bulging carrier bags of new clothes and brown cardboard boxes containing electrical goods were being cheerfully humffed towards August-registration BMWs, Volvos and Renaults. Where does all this disposable income come from? Credit-card companies, I suppose, because most of the people I know keep their first-class-cabin *Titanic* lifestyles afloat on a sea of debt.

I only saw one charity shop on Main Street, an indication of local-trading health (unlike the plethora of second-hand retail outlets in Kilmarnock or Arbroath, say). In Imperial Cancer Research I shopped until my wallet dropped anorexically from £60 to £47. For 12 quid I got a pair of Atlantic boxing shorts, an Adidas T-shirt, a sweatshirt from the Sweater Shop, a long-sleeved Striker polo top and a Torino jersey (complete with Beretta sponsorship name, kit manufacturer ABM's logo and club insignia – made in Italia of *poliestere* and not clinging *bri-nyloni*). Plus, for a pound, William Golding's *The Paper Men* and Tim Parks's *Italian Neighbours*. The clothes looked unworn and the books unread. Brilliant bargains or what?[1] (Clotheswise, I'm like Vinnie Moore trawling 'Ayrshire and Lanarkshire like something from *The Magnificent Seven*, hunting down non-League talent and old playing colleagues who were looking for a move or had fallen out of football',[2] but if I'm ever reduced to buying shoes or – God forbid – underwear from charity shops, I'm tendering my resignation from the rat-race of life.)

Still on a shopping adrenalin high – I mean, a genuine XL red Torino top for £2.50! – I backtracked to Cliftonhill to beat the expected rush. My perforated to-be-retained ticket stub for the tiny wooden stand was stamped 'No. 1' but by three o'clock the stand and covered terracing paddock below were nearly full. Kick-off was delayed by 13 minutes to let the crowd of 906 in. (For this fixture a year before, 300 would have been an excellent turn-out and as recently as 1994 a game against Montrose attracted all of 112 paying customers.) The covered terrace opposite the Main Stand is structurally unsafe and both ends are weed gardens. The Behind-the-Wall Gang numbered about a hundred and although warned by a policeman not to lean on the 'collapsible' wall, an ice-cream van provided better catering than the paying fans got.

The pitch used to be a potholed jungle, but because Hamilton Accies are tenants their rent has been used to upgrade it to the smoothness of a billiard table. With new dressing-rooms, a gym and a sauna, the infra-structure is slowly improving, but my £7 seat forced my knees up into my breast-bone and one of the stanchions blocked the 'Aberdeen Gate' goal from sight almost completely.

In their snazzy new Lotto-supplied-and-designed strip, Albion played neat but powderpuff football (except for Moore who rattled the *square* crossbar with a long-range shot). Approaching the half-hour mark, winger Tony McNally sucked in four lumbering Cowdenbeath defenders, slipped the ball inside and watched contentedly as ex-Aberdeen pro Tommy Walker poked home the easy chance. Top scorer Dougie McGuire, ex-Celtic and now a social worker, looked like a class player and he helped create the move which put McNally through one-on-one with the goalkeeper in the second half. However, McNally took so long to round keeper Neil Russell that the oil-tanker Cowden defence had time to turn, semi-shoulder-charge him off balance and allow Kenny Munro to clear the feebly hit shot off the line. Munro then got himself sent off for another in a string of clumsy tackles. With three minutes left, Albion moved the ball smartly across the pitch and opened up a gaping space for Walker to blast in his second goal.

Cowdenbeath? Crap – with old warhorse Sammy Conn being 'sacked' in central defence more often than *Paris Review* editor George Plimpton when he played quarterback for the Detroit Lions. A final score of 2–0 was no less than Albion deserved, putting them on top with a maximum nine points, two ahead of Forfar. Cowdenbeath were the first team I'd watched who hadn't scored a goal, and a total of two in the game brought August to an end with my spectating goal average down to 3.2 (from six games). At the final whistle everyone filed out smiling and happy, and I for one never noticed the incident which would dominate the sports headlines on Monday (nor did any of the unusually large contingent of press match-reporters) – for example, 'Keeper in rock horror' (*The Sun*, 2.9.96). Apparently the Behind-the-Wall Gang had been pelting Cowdenbeath keeper Russell with bottles, wood and stones throughout the second half, with a half-brick allegedly hitting the crossbar near the end.

With 60,000 residents in and around Coatbridge, a successful Rovers side would have a larger potential support than Motherwell, Falkirk or Airdrie. As I write, Hibernian are setting off from Easter Road to face the Wee Rovers in a Tuesday-night Coca-Cola Cup Third Round clash, with 'cops set to guard hell hill' in soaraway *Sun*-speak.[3] Will the fairy-tale continue? Whatever the result against the Hibees (Albion were outclassed 2–0 but the swollen ranks of freeloaders apparently behaved themselves) the Wee Rovers will definitely avoid bottom spot this time. And if they gain promotion, who knows? Come the 21st century they could be mixing it on a weekly basis with the big Rovers of Raith (even if only in Division One). Whatever, I'll certainly go and watch them again – and I look forward to the first English commentator/presenter to forecast 'dancing in the streets of Albion tonight'.

FOOTNOTES

1. Oblique digressions into bargain-shopping experiences like this can very easily slide into otiose triviality and I'm probably guilty of having crossed the line here. By admitting so in a footnote, I hope I've spiked the reviewing guns of Johnny Dee, unlike the author of *An Irrational Hatred of Luton*, one Robert Banks. Banks was taken to terrible task for banging on about preferring a sandwich and a rest while 'Janet' persuaded him to get a cab into town, where they had a 'superb' pub lunch. 'Did you really?' asked an incredulous Dee. 'How fascinating!' (*Goal*, January 1996) Ouch. Absolutely hilarious critical analysis, I thought, but I'm not Mr Banks and I wasn't on the receiving end of a dismissive 3/10 rating. Great title for a West Ham fan's autobiog, though.

2. Jonathan Northcroft, 'Moore arrives to make a virtue of perfidious Albion', *Scotland on Sunday* (18.8.96).

3. I think it was Nick Hornby who first pointed out that broadsheet newspapers fail miserably in catering for that part of their ABC1 readership obsessively interested in the 'trivia' of how favourite players are recovering from anterior cruciate ligament, torn cartilage or compound fracture injuries. In the Scottish *Sun*'s case, I'm heartily sick of non-soccerati acquaintances who look at me as if they've just spotted the scar from a frontal-lobotomy op when they first see me buying or reading this tabloid. Yes, its support for the SNP was a Murdoch-inspired ploy to try and undermine the Labour vote. But its football coverage – of all four Leagues and not just the Old Firm – is superb. (The *Daily Record*'s footie coverage is also very good, because like their main

rivals, who they still outsell, they invest serious amounts of money in a plethora of reporters solely devoted to digging out stories and covering the sport at all levels.) And it's not as if I just buy *The Sun* — I jump promiscuously around all the Scottish and English broadsheets. If buying *The Sun* and *The Independent*, say, on a Saturday morning seems an oxymoronic combination, what about the middle-aged Morningside matron I saw coming out of a newsagent's with copies of the *Sunday Post* and the *News of the World*? (See Antizyzygy, Scottish).

EAST END PARK
Dunfermline v St Mirren
Coca-Cola Cup, Third Round, 4.9.96

If Andrew Carnegie were alive today – aged 161 – the financial support for his home-town team would make Messrs. Murray, McCann, Walker and Hall look like stingy Sweetex-daddies (not to mention the new co-owner of Chelsea FC Matthew Harding, sadly now deceased, whose £1 million dona-tion to the Labour Party prompted Union Jack and season-ticket-burning protests outside Stamford Bridge by celebrity Chelsea fans John Major and David Mellor). The misconceptions surrounding the multi-millionaire, philanthropist and author (but not of books like *How To Win Friends and Influence People*) are legion, and he's a difficult character to either whole-heartedly defend or unequivocally condemn. His benefactions included the purchase of the beautiful Pittencrieff Glen Park for the people of Dun-fermline (where peacocks still brighten up the auld grey toun) and the provision of almost 3,000 free public libraries across Britain and America. (Carnegie was a depressingly 'systematic reader' and worryingly worthy writer of 'self-improving' literature.)

In succinct summary a few striking steelmen in Pittsburgh were murdered and tens of thousands endured exploitation wages in order for Carnegie to make his massive fortune – $400,000,000 – which from the age of 65 he started to give away with enormous generosity and impressive effectiveness.

Dunfermline Abbey proudly displays its Caithness Glass Award for Church Tourism – for being Scotland's most welcoming church – but the grave and brass-rubbing plate of Robert the Bruce are probably what pull the punters in. The carved lettering of 'Robert the Bruce' on the high parapet tower is quite breathtakingly, gobsmackingly vulgar, however. I had to look twice – in puritan disgust – to make sure I wasn't hallucinating such stonily sacrilegious runecraft. What next – flashing blue and white light-bulbs? I'm not sure if the tasteless stone lettering dates from the early-19th century, when the Abbey was restored in an attempt to recapture its medieval glory (it suffered a bit of interior-design vandalism during the Reformation, when John K lead his Ku Klux Knoxers inside, took one horrified look at the crucified Christs and beatific Madonnas, and growled 'Do I not like those!'), but it put me into a spiritual spiral of scepticism even when confronted by beautiful stained-glass windows backlit by a low sun. However, I managed to resist the temptations of signing 'Stuart Adamson' (the Pars' most famous fan, as frontman of Big Country, and who now runs the Tappie Toories bar) and writing 'U2 and Riverdance are

57

agents of the Antichrist' in the comments column.

The sight of the Main Stand on Halbeath Road immediately thawed deep-frozen memories in domino-tripping and spine-tingling sequences: like drumming the steering-wheel — a plastic toy attached by a big black sucker to the dashboard of my father's Hillman — as a road-raging six-year-old, as fans exiting from East End Park caused the traffic to grind to a halt. Some years later I attended my first game away from Celtic Park here with my older cousin from Glenrothes, when the Pars thrashed Raith Rovers.

Three sides of East End Park are still terracing, with the visitors' end uncovered, but it is a wonderful experience in retro-'60s footballing nostalgia to stand on the North terrace on a beautiful late-summer's evening. When the old-fashioned pylon floodlights had to be turned on for the second half, however, the dim illumination this produced suggested the niggardly use of 20-watt bulbs, abnormally low voltage or specially reared fireflies. Simon Inglis once again perceptively puts his finger on the heart of a football club's dilemma when he describes East End Park as being in a state of limbo: 'too good to jettison, yet still some way behind the standards to which the club aspire'. If not for the requirements of the Taylor Report, Dunfermline would have a perfectly adequate stadium for the 21st century; but to meet the legislative criteria, the Pars will probably be forced to install benches or bucket seats on the terracing rather than erect properly designed stands, to make East End Park an all-seater stadium, because they are £2 million in debt. (At its annual meeting in September 1996, the Scottish League ruled that by the year 2000 all Premier Division clubs must have stadiums with a capacity of at least 10,000, with all supporters seated and under cover; otherwise automatic promotion will not be permitted or Premier status necessarily retained.) And whereas extensive ground improvements in the late '50s and all through the '60s were financed by an extraordinarily successful team on the pitch — which competed with great distinction in Europe for seven successive seasons, won the Scottish Cup twice, and twice finished third in the League — the present Dunfermline squad will do well to defy the odds and not go straight back down to Division One. (Before the season started the Pars were 2,500-1 against winning the title, compared to Raith's 1,500-1, Kilmarnock's 750-1 and Motherwell at 250-1.)

As a Premier club prior to relegation in 1992, the Pars had a genuine world-class(ish) player in the form of Hungarian Istvan Kozma. The current team are so stretched for talent that lumbering old warhorse Craig Robertson has been converted into a frighteningly ineffective sweeper-cum-*libero*. The death of club captain and frighteningly effective centre-half stopper Norrie McCathie in season 1995–96 — of carbon-monoxide poisoning from a faulty gas heater – almost cost the Pars promotion for a third cruel season running. Manager Bert Paton was in the team that won the Cup in 1968, but Premier and financial survival is all he can realistically hope for. Jock Stein may have helped awaken this sleeping giant of Scottish football when he took over for four successful years in 1960 but even he would have been hard pressed to make an impact at Dunfermline with the club in its present parlous state. For a team like the Pars, treading the mine-field between Taylor and Bosman is akin to navigating a ship between Scylla and Charybdis.

Interestingly, most of the 4,202 crowd preferred to pay £10 to stand on the terracing rather than cough up 13 quid to sit in the stand – and in the outstandingly good match programme I jotted down an estimate of 500 for the numbers in the Main Stand (most of whom were presumably season-ticket-holders). Dunfermline deserve real praise for a 50 per cent reduction for the unemployed (unlike the old Celtic board who, in the early '90s, gave a £1 discount to UB40-holders but who had to be in the ground an *hour* before kick-off).

Disappointingly, though, First Division St Mirren's two black players, Junior Mendes and Chris Iwelumo, suffered the only serious racial barrack-ing I'd heard all season – albeit mostly from the section of hard-core youths who congregated beside the fence segregating them from the travelling away support. The steel-and-wire-mesh fencing took some real punishment as it was rattled and battered from both sides of the supporting divide. A taciturn 20-something guy beside me suddenly exploded with a shout of 'clout that fuckin' coon' – and spineless as it may have been, I wasn't going to say anything because of my West Coast accent and backpack, which had already attracted some suspicious looks (along with photographing the ridiculous Sammy the Tammy mascot, who turned out to be ex-pro Graham Robertson in a bear suit). A middle-aged man in front of us handled the situation with skilful diplomacy, I thought – he turned round shaking his head and 'tut-tutted' in wryly smiling condemnation. 'No need fir that, son, ken?' he added.

Technically Dunfermline were playing in their traditional black and white stripes, but kit supplier Le Coq Sportif's 'football authentique' slogan was hardly justified by some horrendous design changes, which included the dark stripes being broken up into black and light-grey alter-nate squares, with occasional red triangles. The shirt's classic design was further defaced by the Landmark Home Furnishing's logo on the chest, along with the French company's rooster trademark and the home club's emblem. As if this wasn't cluttered enough, both arms had to carry the SFL badge.

The Pars took the lead in 30 minutes through Gerry Britton, whose side-facing, on-the-turn shot was either a complete mis-hit or a goal of Brazilian brilliance. (NB: Britton scores more goals with his nose than with his hydrocephalic forehead.) Although the pitch and playing conditions were perfect, caretaker manager Tony Fitzpatrick's young side were the only team trying to play football at ground level. The excellent Mark Yardley equalised before half-time when his initial shot was poorly blocked by keeper Ian Westwater – the rebound ricocheting off Yardley's shin and in. Before the break, Dunfermline left-back Derek Fleming was clear through on Allan Combe, but his attempt to emulate Davor Sukor's famous chipped lob over Peter Schmeichel was the equivalent of an 18-handicapper's topped tee-shot. 'Yer bad enough in yer ain half, Fleming – so stay the fuck oot ah theirs!' commented an unamused Pars fan. 'What's it like to follow shite?' chanted the Paisley supporters.

In the second half referee Martin Clark from Edinburgh started to lose control of the match, as the tackles got cruder, the players more churlish and the fans increasingly captious. When assistant linesman Elmslie flagged Clark to clipe on Yardley for a slightly late but innocuous tackle, the St Mirren forward had to go for a second bookable offence. All hell then broke loose as the Paisley youngsters started scything down the autumnal boiler chickens of Dunfermline (who were beginning to do headless-chook impersonations themselves). In 65 minutes David Bingham side-footed a shot through a forest of spindly legs to give the home side the lead again. Two minutes later the grey head of Hamish French nodded home the killer goal. At 3–1 down and reduced to ten men St Mirren knew it was all over, but they were still lucky not to lose another player or goal.

Yardley's dismissal turned the game in Dunfermline's favour, but even for notoriously competitive Cup-ties this was a gratuitously violent and incomprehensibly bad-tempered affair.[1]

If Dunfermline FC were on a par with Dunfermline the town, they would easily retain top-ten status every season. Dignified and decorous, Dunfermline isn't somewhere I'd move to if my six lottery numbers came up, but if the unforeseeable tides and twisters of life ever deposited me there, I'm sure it would be a very pleasant place to live. If the Carnegie Trust, which has done so much for the town already, could divert some of its funds into East End Park, Fife could have a team and stadium to rival the best in Edinburgh, Dundee or Aberdeen.

Not being on the main East Coast line which serves these three cities, I had to wait nearly an hour for a train, in a creepily isolated and – at that time of night – unmanned station. Take away the plastic ScotRail signs and Dunfermline could be a branch-line station 'in the shadow of the Carpathian mountains', straight from the picture-painting pens of M.R. James, W.W. Jacobs or H.P. Lovecraft (if not the cameras of Val Lewton, Tod Browning or any Hammer house-style director).

Thankfully there were half-a-dozen morose St Mirren fans waiting on the platform for the 10.20 Fife Circle service to Edinburgh, because it was almost literally a ghost train with only one female passenger aboard when the two Sprinter carriages pulled in. Sitting across the aisle from 'Nadja' I noticed that she had no reflection in the looking-glass mirror of the train window – but only after she had initiated conversation with me. After a quick pint with this emotional vampire I made some tired excuses and walked home where, after triple-locking the front door, I fell asleep bushed in my windowless study/bedroom. I awoke feeling, and looking, like death warmed up – but at least I didn't have a massive hickey on my neck . . .

FOOTNOTES
1. Dunfermline drew Partick Thistle at home in the quarter-finals, opponents who beat ten-man Airdrie the night before when the Diamonds' Kenny Black was red-carded *twice* in a double sending-off. The day after the Pars' victory SFA chief executive Jim Farry issued one of his regular papal encyclicals warning of the consequences if the early trend of violent and abusive conduct were to continue. Namely: 'A player is on his way to jail.'

SHIELFIELD PARK
Berwick Rangers v Queen of the South
Second Division, 7.9.96

'Berwick Rangers 1, Glasgow Rangers 0' is a scoreline that still raises nape-hairs, one of the rare giant-killing feats that the Scottish Cup almost never provides (unlike its more romantic English equivalent). Although only just having turned six years old, I find it incredible – and a bit depressing – to think that I was *alive* when the mighty Glasgow institution from Govan was humbled by a single Sammy Reid goal in the first round at tiny Shielfield (28.1.67). When the Wee Rangers finally go bankrupt or relocate, the only English club to play in the Scottish League will live on forever in people's memories because of this single 'monumentous' result.

Having made a pretty memorable 0–2, 0–4, 1–2, 0–6, 0–6 start to their season, I decided to hop the two miles across the border to see if that semi-mythical but well-documented beast – 'the 6–0 thrashing' – was about to gorge itself on the hapless Borderers for a third successive Saturday (though in predicting a result I'd pencilled in a 2–1 home defeat as the most likely outcome, with trauma-case manager Ian Ross surely liable to play an ultra-defensive formation, even at home, in order to avoid a triple whammy of six-goal hammerings – even if this would have attracted a feeding frenzy of national media attention).

Off the park and in the boardroom, directorial disputes were making front-page news, albeit only in the *Berwick Advertiser*. Chairman Roy McDowell had just resigned and the official supporters' club was question-ing his right to sell all his 70,000 shares, arguing that a disputed buy-back clause gave them first option on 53,000 of the main shareholder's stake. Vice-chairman Tom Davidson was so disgusted by average home gates of 240 in season 1995–96, when Berwick finished third, that he was in favour of relocating to East Lothian, where the council were apparently willing to build an all-seater stadium near Tranent if Berwick gained promotion to the First Division. The 'relocation man' said of the supporters: 'They have pressed the suicide button by not turning out to watch the team.' Up to May 1996 the club were £222,000 in debt, and this season's hoped-for promotion push was seriously undermined when they lost most of their defence under freedom-of-contract during the summer.

Berwick almost went bankrupt in 1992, during a period of turmoil that saw the greyhound racing company which leased the ground from the council locking-out the football team (who were sub-tenants). With a his-tory of financial mismanagement, the successive boards have used up most of the reserves of goodwill that the townsfolk of Berwick may once have had for their football team. Those I talked to thought their local club had been run by 'geriatric clowns', 'quasi-criminals' and 'carpetbagging spivs'.

If ever an independent Scotland needs to distract attention from a plummeting Scottish groat, three-digit inflation and rioting dole queues – assuming Shetland and Orkney are allowed to secede with 'their' North Sea oil to become Norwegian protectorates – Berwick-upon-Tweed may well need to be re-occupied up to the natural border of the River Tweed, on the south bank of which the microscopic Shielfield Park lies hidden behind residential housing and overshadowed by the humungous Simpsons Maltings factory (thereby ensuring that the club's few hard-core supporters can still regard themselves as 'Northumbrian English' and that we get the historic part of the town, as delineated by the still-standing Elizabethan ramparts).

Seven pounds got me into the ground – terracing or stand – and speedway's replacing of greyhound racing was made obvious by the piles of rubber tyres strewn around the track. The £1 'Borderer's Review' programme was abysmally devoid of editorial content, most of the 20 pages being made up of local trade advertising. The 'Talk of the Tweed' introductory column began and finished: 'Let us not kid ourselves! Things have not been easy of late! . . . Keep cheerful.' Only the 'News on players' paragraph raised a smile from this jaundiced reader: 'DONATO D'AGROSA (Deano) is currently playing with Eyemouth United . . . We are also hoping to get GREIG ROBERTSON farmed out.' What! No exclamation marks!

Most of the 432 attendees avoided the Main Stand in favour of the covered terracing opposite – 'the Ducket' – and the Doonhamers' fans made enough noise to make it feel like a home fixture for the visitors from Dumfries. I lay on the grass bank to its left and enjoyed the glorious sunshine. (Like all the pitches so far seen, the Shielfield grass was gloriously green and a credit to the groundsman.)

The yellow-and-black kit of Berwick Rangers, supplied by AVEC of Peterlee, was a postmodern Picasso-taking-the-piss design, not made any easier on the eye by the shirt sponsor's name, 'Federation Brewery (LCL Pils)'; Queen of the South, however, looked terrific in their royal-blue shirts and shorts, with white socks, the Open University sponsorship logo adding to the aesthetic effect. For the first ten minutes Berwick played as if crates of bottled lager had been consumed during the team talk, while Queens played like Ruud Gullit's cerebral Chelsea. Berwick goalkeeper Neil Young, who'd kept his place despite losing 12 goals in two games, looked positively shellshocked as the Doonhamers' hitmen bore down on him from all angles. Six goals looked like the absolute minimum to expect, once the

Queens strikers had calmed down enough to form orderly queues, but instead Berwick went ahead after ten minutes when Graham Miller's totally mis-hit, and deflected, shot rebounded from the post and spun over the line before goalie David Mathieson recovered from the shock of having something to do.

Ex-Clyde striker Stevie Mallan equalised with a glorious header on the half-hour, and when centre-half David Lilley put the visitors ahead with an unchallenged header from two yards out just after half-time, another heavy tanking for Berwick looked inevitable. But Young started to make some competent saves as his side began to experiment with retaining possession in the opposition half. After forcing Mathieson to make three excellent saves, Berwick kept feeding the ball to Tommy Graham, whose darting dribbles into the box were finally rewarded with a stonewall penalty in the 79th minute.

When substitute David McGlynn placed the ball on the spot, the one Berwick fan who really seemed to care passionately began shouting: 'Oh no, not McGlynn . . . He's like Dougie Bader – nae shot in either foot.' McGlynn sclaffed the penalty with his instep, but the ball dribbled over the line via the base of the post (unlike a similarly hit penalty on the same day by Eric '15-out-of-15' Cantona, whose effort bobbled past the Leeds United post). After the Berwick player's fortuitous score, the excited skinhead roared: 'Come on, Berwick – escape to victory!'

It remained 2–2, however, which probably answered the pre-match prayers offered up by Berwick physio Glynn Jones (a vicar and P.E. instructor at a local prison). Although the single point failed to lift Berwick off bottom spot, it left Premier League Raith Rovers and Third Division Ross County as the only senior clubs in Scotland without any points after four games.

As for Berwick Rangers, relocation to Tranent may well secure their long-term future, but will East Lothian Council still want them if they slip back into the Third Division? Berwick-upon-Tweed may have turned its back on its local football team, but the town seems well equipped to prosper and survive without the Wee Rangers if need be. Because of its superb location, beautiful landscapes and historically important architecture, Berwick-upon-Tweed was chosen as a flagship site for 'Visual Arts UK' and the imaginative Ramparts Project displayed installation and conceptual artworks in and around the defensive walls of the old town. After having a quick shooftie at Siobhan Davies's safe full of video monitors, located in the lookout post of Coxon's Tower, I took the opportunity to wax lyrical about its 'lack of cognitive validity' to the newly graduated female art student whose summer job it was to sit outside in a director's chair with a walkie-talkie guarding it. So impressed was she with my critique of Davies's aesthetic sensibilities that she agreed to meet me at the Town Hall clock for a quick drink after she finished for the day.

To kill some sexually excited time, I wandered through the golf course and into the fixed-caravan-site holiday camp. The atmosphere was almost reminiscent of the motel complex in Philippe Djan's novel *37.2° le matin* (or the chalet resort as depicted in Jean-Jacques Beineix's movie of the book, *Betty Blue*). Feeling French and sophisticated, I sat on the steps smoking as seven o'clock approached. Feeling Scottish and stood-up as the hour came and went I sloped off, disappointed that my mentally pre-prepared discourses on 'the greenness of the colour green'[1] and 'the intrinsic worth and market value of works of art'[2] weren't going to get a bevvy-fuelled airing and babe-enthralled hearing.

Was I really a sportswriter, the next Alison Watt had asked? As if someone would lie about *that*. Talk about anoraaaghknophobia . . .

FOOTNOTES

1. Not only are all football pitches variable in verdancy, the 432 fans at Shielfield will each have perceived a slightly different shade of green, depending on the number and effectiveness of their retinal colour receptors. The first time I experimented with covering one eye at a time and comparing the difference in 'brightness' I almost had a hypochondriac's heart attack.

2. The only sensible answer to how much an Alan Shearer or a Michelangelo Buonarroti is worth can only be how much someone is willing to pay for the privilege of securing one. Strangely, however, the boom in transfer fees has coincided with the explosion in auction prices for Old Masters. Up until Sir Robert Hall's purchase of Shearer for £15 million, the most expensive footballer remained Gianluigi Lentini, who cost AC Milan £13 million to buy from Torino in 1992 (but who proved to be a not very good fake). In both markets the 'name' is what gets the punters in queues for season-tickets or entry to exhibitions, the inflated valuations in and of themselves increasing public interest. For example, if I found a grimy and stained oil painting of the Grand Canal in a skip, none of my friends would accept an invite to come round and see it if I hung it over the fireplace. If, however, it proved to be an undiscovered but authenticated Canaletto, valued at £25 million, I could sell tickets to half of Edinburgh to troop through the living-room (although it would still be the same bloody picture). The same principle applies to Tony Cottee, Dean Saunders, Chris Sutton, Andy Cole and Stan Collymore – who collectively cost over £25 million but who all turned out to be footballing forgeries.

9.9.96 – Alex Smith 'resigns' from Clyde, whose board don't protest. A case of jumping before being pushed?

10.9.96 – First migraine of the season, thereby missing Celtic's 2–0 home defeat inflicted by Hamburg. Retire to bed before noon with packet of frozen peas and a basin. Radio reports confirm Billy Kirkwood handed P45 by Dundee United, with Tommy 'Lack-of-loyalty-lamenting' McLean replacing him at Tannadice, less than a week after joining Raith Rovers as manager. Iain Munro agrees to 'come home' to St Mirren, leaving Sandy Clark to take over at Hamilton . . . First projectile-vomiting session during TV highlights of Celtic v Hamburg game, with Jock Brown doing the commentary. As I awake in the wee small hours to retch up black bile – so disorientated that I think the 1984 movie *DEF-CON 4* about survivors of a nuclear holocaust is a news programme – Brown (the lawyer for various Scottish managers, including McLean) is reassuring his client Munro, telling him that he is not yet legally bound to St Mirren . . .

11.9.96 – Despite the Kirkcaldy chairman Alex Penman's outrage at having his manager 'poached' by United, Raith Rovers announce that Munro will be the new manager of the Rovers, leaving 'scandalised' St Mirren to appoint the already-rejected candidate Tony Fitzpatrick. Rangers lose 3–0 away to Grasshoppers of Zurich . . .

12.9.96 – Munro's move to Stark's Park is off (if only temporarily).

13.9.96 – Ray Wilkins (aged 40) joins Hibernian to play football. Chris Waddle signs for Falkirk to play the Brockville club's version of football for £2,000 per week.

After this extraordinary week I was almost prepared to concede that there may have been some truth in the 'reliable rumour' relayed to me by a drunken acquaintance over the phone that Tommy Burns was to be replaced by either Kenny Dalglish, Graeme Souness, or Arrigo Sacchi, if Celtic didn't overturn their two-goal deficit in Germany . . .

GAYFIELD
Arbroath v Albion Rovers
Third Division, 14.9.96

> *For as long as one hundred of us shall remain alive we shall never in any wise consent to submit to the rule of the English, for it is not for glory we fight, for riches, or for honours, but for freedom alone, which no good man loses but with his life.*

The kicker conclusion to the Declaration of Arbroath (1320) may owe more to the sensational speech-writing skills of Abbot Bernard de Linton than to the pompous prose style of the excommunicated Robert the Bruce, but it remains the only example of fourteenth-century literature that this author is able to recite from memory (without it ever losing its ability to bring goose-bumps proudly rising to attention on a ravaged epidermis).

Today, however, Arbroath is more famous for a football scoreline, which far more people can quote, and fill in the background details of, than for the above piece of pure poetry – namely 'Arbroath 36, Bon Accord 0' (the most one-sided rout in the history of first-class British football, run up in 1885 during a Scottish Cup first-round tie when the visitors had to use an outfield player in goal and the Red Lichties' keeper never had to touch the ball once while sheltering from the rain under a spectator's umbrella).

In a depressingly similar vein south of the border, Kenneth Wolstenholme's 'There's people on the pitch . . . They think it's all over . . . It is now!' has superseded the likes of Winston Churchill's 'Never in the field of human conflict . . .', Rupert Brooke's 'There's some corner of a foreign field . . .' and William Shakespeare's 'Once more into the breach, dear friends . . .' as the definitive sound-bite in the English popular imagination and sense of national identity.

Pre-personal-birth events are becoming ever more marginalised – unless vicariously relived through the Hollywood nationalism of movies like *Braveheart*, whose historical inaccuracies, sentimental scripting and cynical marketing still didn't prevent Craig Brown psyching up his troops for the Battle of Wembley '96 with a special screening (not that it made any difference to the outcome, with Gazza doing his 'Hammer of the Scots' impersonation after Gary McAllister's bottled penalty displayed all the character traits associated with Edward 'the Disinherited' Balliol, whose fatuous crowning at Scone and subsequent subservience to England's Edward III led to his being chased away with 'one leg booted and the other naked' in 1332).

Once in the fishing port of Arbroath, 17 miles north of Dundee, I made straight for the Abbey, where I was flabbergasted to find that Historic

Scotland were charging £1.50 for entrance to the red-sandstone ruins. I saw enough of them by walking to the Portakabin shop and ticket-booth situated within the crumbling walls, before waving a pound note and 50-pence piece at the capitalist and imperialist lackey behind the shatter-proof window and turning straight back round. Abbot Linton must be spinning in his grave with the centrifugal force of a tornado. Not only is Scotland no longer free but neither is entry to one of the country's most important historical sites.

Because the excellent Signal Tower Museum run by Angus Council does not advertise on TV, employ PR consultants or subscribe to newspaper-clipping agencies, entry to the 1975 Museum of the Year is free. The story of how Robert Louis Stevenson's grandfather Robert succeeded in building the Bell Rock Lighthouse is brilliantly told – a worthy testament to a fantastic achievement. Although now unmanned and fully automatic, the 115-foot tower had a well-stocked library on one level when it was completed in 1811. (What a great 'day job' for a struggling writer this must have been, being the lighthouse-keeper, right up to the modern era when the accountants insisted on automation. Lack of willing job applicants could never have been a problem, surely? If the post were advertised today, I'd be at the head of the enormous queue – and with me as live-in keeper the lighthouse would be visitable during the summer, drawing thousands of tourists into the town just to make the 24-mile round-trip to visit the romantic Inchcape Rock and the notoriously sex-starved employee of the Northern Lighthouse Board, whom American divorcees would pay good money to be locked in the observation bubble with, even if passing ships had to be warned that the noises emanating from the lighthouse were not amplified fog sirens . . .) The fishing, flax and lawn-mower exhibits were, inevitably, stupefyingly dull.

Gayfield Park lies between the Regency buildings of the Signal Tower and the ramshackle hangar of the Pleasureland arcade, a smoked kipper's throw from the North Sea. Once again, £6 gave me the choice of sitting in the Subbuteo-sized stand or standing on the terrace, and 90 per cent of the 525 crowd chose to lean on crush-barriers beneath roofed cover (except for the four corners which were unprotected). Gayfield is a great wee stadium on a sunny September Saturday, but when exposed to howling sea gales and horizontal rain in deepest January it must be like spectating in an ice-box.

Managed by John Brogan, Arbroath were unbeaten in the League and a home win would have taken the Red Lichties to within a point of pace-setting Albion Rovers. Within three minutes Jamie McCarron had blasted Arbroath in front, but relying on Willie Watters and Mark McWalter for more goals was always going to be a forlorn hope. (In the programme's

'Player Profile', the latter's favourite things included 'any chicken dishes . . . Budweiser . . .*Highlander* . . . *Bottom* and *Cracker* . . . and Ibiza'; and although 'unemployed at the moment', there can't be many openings for rocket scientists in Arbroath, whose team are all part-timers.) Unfazed, Albion equalised within seven minutes through the diminutive John Dickson, and in the 20th minute Tommy Walker put the visitors ahead – much to the delirious delight of the Coatbridge fans who, if slightly outnumbered, certainly weren't out-shouted.

Toothless up front, Arbroath were suffering from oral cancer in defence, with experienced left-back Steve Florence and centre-half John Ward missing (without managerial approval) on foreign holidays, the latter's mother having booked him on a surprise flight to Denmark because she thought he would be suspended for this fixture, having been booked twice but not sent off in a game against Ross County. Without Florence and Ward, the makeshift back line left keeper Craig Hinchcliffe horribly exposed, like a canine tooth with its neighbouring lateral incisor and first premolar extracted. Albion tortured him with gentle probing thrusts rather than subjecting him to full-metal-jacket drilling attacks.

In the second half Arbroath's goalscorer McCarron was sent off for 'play-acting' by Inverness referee Kevin Bissett, although David 'Budgie' Byrne appeared to attempt removing McCarron's amalgam fillings with the jarring force of his tackle. Substitute David McKenzie took advantage of the increased space to sidefoot a third coolly past Hinchcliffe. At 3–1 up Albion just kept possession arrogantly, waiting for further gaps to appear, which they duly did after Mike Waters was red-carded for subjecting the stand-side 'assistant' to foul and abusive language. This dismissal prompted a dozen or so irate Red Lichtie supporters to gather behind Mr Mack from 'Newton Meams' (*sic*) – as the programme described him – and the linesman was subjected to some further foul and abusive language. Arbroath's most famous fan, Sye Webster, didn't appear to be amongst them, if only because he obviously didn't want to risk another year-long ban (which he earned for running on to the Gayfield pitch to kiss a hat-trick-scoring Red Lichtie). Albion prudently started to play out time, as the Arbroath players were beginning to resemble their maroon-shirted counterparts at Ibrox, as Hearts were in the process of getting four sent off in a 3–0 defeat. It ended 3–1 to Albion, with no more red cards (somehow).

Arbroath the town? A bit of an armpit, really, but not a totally unattractive oxter if working fishing ports turn you on. Arbroath FC? They stunk. And Albion Rovers? Admirable and restrained under pressure.

Winning a tenner on the Lottery, and having found an extract from yours truly in a giveaway-magazine paperback of football quotations, I felt pretty good and I used my winnings to sink a couple of pints before watching the Rangers v Hearts farce on *Sportscene*. Inspired by the nearly abandoned match, I rewrote the Declaration of Arbroath for the football-obsessed '90s:

> *For as long as seven of us shall remain on the pitch we shall never in any way submit to the rulings of referees intimidated by the Rangers, for it is not for points we fight, for win bonuses, or for silverware, but for third-force freedom alone, which no good Jambo loses but with his wife . . .*

PALMERSTON PARK
Queen of the South v Ayr United
Second Division, 21.9.96

On the Monday morning prior to this match, the East Fife board had convened in secret session to discuss the future of player-manager Steve Archibald, the ex-Barcelona striker who had guided the tiny Methil club to promotion from the Second Division in less than two years. Were they meeting to hammer out a 'golden handcuff' deal to keep him under contract for as long as possible? No, of course not. Football club directors move in mysterious ways, quite possibly directed by radio receivers for listening to God implanted in their dentures, and they agreed to sack Archibald instead, citing 'irretrievable [sic] differences' as the reason. With five managerial departures by mid-September, out of 40 initial incumbents, this made for a casualty rate of 12.5 per cent (without any club yet having become totally detached at the bottom of their particular division). If this Bomber Command rate of attrition was set to continue, the handful of original managers left at season's end come 10 May 1997 would probably resign en masse to 'sit out the war in neutral Sweden'.

If getting to Berwick-upon-Tweed from Edinburgh by train was like riding for 40 minutes on a French TGV, reaching Dumfries was more like participating in a film for Great Railway Journeys of the World – in other words, the scenery eventually became stunning but the time taken, physical discomfort endured and appalling infrequency of service, via Glasgow Central, was reminiscent of travelling on a narrow-gauge switch-back line by steam engine across the roof of the world in the Andes (and poor Peruvian peasants couldn't have been uglier than the purblinded souls who embarked and alighted at every godforsaken station in Ayrshire and Dumfriesshire, looking as if conceived in petri-dish experiments which involved putting the newly fertilised eggs through fast-spin wash cycles in laboratory Zanussis). The penultimate stop was Sanquhar, where I once drove in drunken desperation to get some relief from a nightmarishly wet September weekend holiday in nearby Wanlockhead (Scotland's highest village, despite not being in the Highlands), looking for somewhere to buy a half-decent paperback (the sub-post office in Leadhills, Scotland's second-highest village, only stocking a few Barbara Cartland romances but shelf-loads of Dennis Wheatley novels and occult etiquette non-fiction). All Sanquhar offered was titles such as Silos and Silage, Double-Entry Book-Keeping for Ghillies, Foresters and Cattle Abortionists and The Witch Cult in South-West Scotland: Worshipping the Divine Monosyllable From Cumnock to Cairnryan.

Dumfries has about 35,000 inhabitants and a crowd of 1,813 were inside

71

8,352-capacity Palmerston Park for the 'derby day' visit of the men from Ayr (pop. 50,000). Sitting in my £8 seat in the new East Stand, I was mightily impressed. Just over a year before this £500,000-plus structure, with unrestricted sight-lines for almost 2,200 fans, replaced a covered terrace called the 'Coo Shed' or 'Jimmy Jolly's Bull Pen'. Opposite, the smaller and quainter Main Stand has been refurbished, using the £50,000 rent per year generated by the Tesco pyramid visible directly behind it (although Simon Inglis suggests that if Walsall and St Johnstone were able to sell their prime-site retail space to supermarkets for £4 million, Queen of the South were naïve not to have done the same). The covered Glasgow Street End terracing has a decorative but working clock in the centre of its roof, below an advert cleverly suggesting 'Time to Visit the Hole i' the Wa' Inn'. The other end is uncovered, but clearly superfluous, terracing.

Since he took over in 1994, chairman Norman Blount has transformed the club, even if the team have yet to match the developments taking place off the pitch. Last season the Queens were almost relegated, finishing three points above demoted Forfar despite spending a club record fee of £24,000 on a goalkeeper named Butter. Signed from Alloa, Jim 'Budgie' Butter almost took the Doonhamers down single-handedly, losing 18 goals in six games before being replaced by young Rab McColm for the final three-game run-in. Butter walked out in the huff, his 30 appearances having cost his employers £800 a game. Queens now have the reliable David Mathieson in goal, one of 14 full-time professionals on their books. They also have two co-managers (Rowan Alexander and Mark Shanks) plus a match analyst, an education officer, a careers officer, two physios, 14 coaches (to help run their numerous and far-flung soccer schools) and four club doctors. Programme editor Bruce Wright has five main contributors, which helps to explain the excellence of the publication, and the club runs regular buses to all away games, charging what must be subsidised prices for Travel Club members (e.g. £6 for an adult to Brechin and back). Of all the clubs so far visited, Queen of the South appeared to be making the biggest effort to involve the local community, and, after Livingston and Ayr, they are the best-supported team in their division.

With everything about the club geared towards First Division football, the team would have remained in third place if they could have avoided defeat against fourth-placed Ayr. But within 15 minutes an obscenely off-side Isaac English was allowed to play on by linesman Mr Andrews, and the Ayr forward scored with guilty ease. Running backwards in the proscribed manner along his specially astroturfed linesman's lane, young Mr Andrews was becoming increasingly nervous as the Queens fans in the East Stand berated him, mischievously but without mercy: 'Hey you, *assistant referee* —

get yer mither ship tae beam ye back up fir laser eye surgery, *ya blind bugger!*' He obviously wasn't hard of hearing, because his face flushed beetroot red like a spinster aunt confronted with a teenage nephew beating his meat with the inside of her high-heeled slingback. Even giving Ayr offside — *when they weren't* — resulted in a stream of non-complimentary invective from the home support.

Both teams played passing, pitch-level football which flattered to deceive, because the few scoring chances went farcically unconverted. Ayr's Steve Kerrigan missed three sitters, one of which involved failing to make any contact with the ball whatsoever, while at the other end Craig Flannigan shot ten yards wide from ten feet out.

Approaching half-time, a trench-coated gentleman in his mid-60s passed along Row A with the supremely confident air that only TV celebritydom can confer. Although I thought he'd died years ago, I could still summon up eidetic recall of his performances on *Glen Michael's Cartoon Cavalcade* (an STV show from the '70s in which a grown man sat in a studio introducing cartoons and conversing with a disembodied voice — 'Palladin' — which supposedly emanated from a lamp on his desk).

Three minutes into the second half, English flighted over a superb cross from near the corner flag and a totally unchallenged Kerrigan redeemed himself by heading home. Before the hour mark, player-manager Alexander came on for Queens to replace Alex Nesovic (from Bradford not Belgrade). Within two minutes the ex-Morton man's moaning presence up front helped the home side secure a penalty, which Flannigan buried past Henry Smith. Ayr, however, continued to defend their reduced lead comfortably. To wile away the remaining half-hour or so, two teenage Doonhamers beside me rocked with (Class A?) laughter as they made fun of ex-Queens midfielder Darren Henderson, a crew-cutted and scrofulously-complexioned 29-year-old who was having a bit of a nightmare down the left flank. 'Genghis, yer an oot-a-control google-grump! . . . Aw God, naw — it's Genghis chargin' up the pairk again . . . Archie Macpherson's huvin' an affair wae yer best freend's fridge-freezer in Girvan!'

The Doonhamers never looked like they believed they could beat Ayr, and after the match co-manager Shanks was quoted as saying: 'Ayr think they're one of the best teams in the division. If that's the case we have nothing to fear.' Hmmm . . . You lost 2–1 at home, Shanksie. Maybe chairman Blount ought to consider adding a personal motivation guru to his burgeoning backroom staff, because although promotion to the First Division is a reasonable and achievable goal, Queens' management team really should be aspiring to Premier League status. Just look at Auxerre's dramatic rise in France — another provincial club from a rural area who decided the footballing sky had no limits. Winners of the League and Cup double in 1996, the town of Auxerre has a population only 5,000 or so in excess of Dumfries.

With 90 minutes to spare before the last train for Glasgow departed at 6.25 p.m., I wandered the historic and attractive streets of Dumfries. *Fodor* revealed some surprising historical connections. In 1306, for example, Robert the Bruce had chibbed John Comyn to death in Greyfriars Monastery to secure his succession. Also, the well-known writer J.M. Barrie had gone to school at Dumfries Academy, where his arrested development fantasies about Peter Pan were supposedly fleshed out in the beautiful gardens of Moat Brae House.

Having visited the birthplace cottage of Robert Burns in Ayrshire about a dozen times – 'Mystery Tour' bus trips run by my old primary school and bible class invariably alternated between Alloway and Alva – I decided to get my first look at the Bard's resting-place in St Michael's graveyard. (Alloway may have given birth to Burns, but Dumfries killed and buried him at a cruelly early age in 1796.) Amidst the sound-stage collection of toppling tombstones and weather-beaten crypts, the dazzlingly white mausoleum where he is buried pulls the visitor up short with volitionless admiration. Two hundred years before, Burns had already been dead for a few months, but my attempt to force maudlin tears (of self-pity?) were abandoned when I became aware of being watched – by a man cutting his hedge (which overlooked the mausoleum). Jesus dead at 33. Me alive just now, aged 35. Burns dead at 37 . . .

Resisting the urge to run amok with the householder's electric hedge-trimmer, I rushed to make the train connection. Two centuries ago Burns had joined the Dumfries Volunteers, realising that the French Revolution had thrown up a murdering megalomaniac in the short, stocky shape of Napoleon (although fears of an invasion were probably unjustified). As the train drew out of Dumfries station, the Crown Defenders of Cumnock were gathered on the north bank of the River Nith to take part in an Orange Walk. Burns definitely lived in more interesting and romantic times.

At Kilmarnock the train idled for 25 minutes, waiting to become the 19.51 service to Glasgow. I felt like a reforming radical spy for France when two dozen Rangers fans piled on board; 1–0 down to Killie at half-time, what were they so damned drunkenly delighted about? A 4–1 away victory as it turned out . . . Ignoring them as best I could, I buried my head in a paperback copy of Tom Paine's *The Rights of Man* that I had picked up second-hand in Dumfries.

With ten games ticked off and 34 goals seen, my spectating average was a pretty healthy 3.4 per game. Worryingly, though, I was beginning to care about completing my Holy Grail travels without the average falling below three. As if I didn't have more important matters to be anxious about . . . But that's part of the attraction of arbitrary averages, I guess. And according to a surprisingly complicated and authoritative health questionnaire in *The Sun* about individual life expectancy, I'm scheduled to keel over at the relatively tender age of 58! Would I accept this allotted span or choose to 'open the box'? I think I'd open the box . . . 35! But I am thirt-. Cause of death: Anaphylactic shock. (Eurrr . . . Someday someone could be reading this, and calling out to his wife, say, 'When did Bennie die? What age? . . . 57, is that right? . . . Jeez, the poor bastard must have miscalculated. Or lied about his consumption of coffin nails, chocolate and coffee on the survey. Fuck 'im — this book isnae worth 200 Ecus anyway, not even second-hand. No wonder it's out of print.' Out of print? Dead and out of print? Oh shit . . .)

FIRHILL
Partick Thistle v Clydebank
First Division, 28.9.96

Like any marathon runner, I expected that sooner or later I'd hit the wall —
but having to force myself through the pain barrier as early as Game 11 was
a major disappointment. Laid low by a dose of the flu and an attack of
ennuitis, my intended itinerary had contracted in ever-decreasing incre-
ments of driving mileage — thanks to another one-day rail strike — from
Montrose initially, through Plan-B Cumbernauld (home of Clyde), to the
final last-minute destination of Firhill. Having already driven 333 miles
from Glasgow to Aberdeen and back on Thursday night/Friday morning,
without any sleep to break the eclipse-of-the-moon witnessing journey, I
eventually arrived in Maryhill on Saturday afternoon sprawled in the back
of a taxi.

Shivering and saturnine, I sat in the new Jackie Husband Stand cradling
my polystyrene cup of hot brown sludge, aching to be back in the musky
unmade bed, and enveloped between the pendulous breasts of Yolanda from
Port Said, a hitch-hiker I'd picked up on the A9 near Auchterarder,[1] sipping
hot toddies and listening to the Rangers v Celtic game on the radio (and
although both clubs had been humiliated by Auxerre and Hamburg,
respectively, a few days earlier, it did not stop over 50,000 turning up to see
the home side's eventual 2–0 victory).

Thistle managed to attract 1,974 fans, most of whom were hoping to
witness the Jags' first home win of *1996* (never mind the season), and by
common consensus Murdo MacLeod's team had not yet recovered from the
trauma of relegation in May, when in the second-leg play-off against Dundee United at Tannadice they had been a mere 36 seconds from aggregate
victory in normal time. Brian Welsh equalised for the Tayside club — less
than a minute after referee Les Mottram had refused to award a stonewall
Partick penalty — and Owen Coyle sank the demoralised Jags in extra-time.
After four years of dour defensive doggedness in the Premier League, the
attacking attrition of Thistle's play-off opponents had finally resulted in a
deserved denouement.

Thistle won the Scottish Cup in 1921, but more famously they beat Jock
Stein's all-conquering Celtic side 4–1 in the League Cup final of 23 October
1971; 4–0 up within 30 minutes, the 'Maryhill Magyars' of manager Davie
McParland were setting a one-off standard of fantasy football that no Jags
team which followed will ever be able to match — unless the winning 50-year
cycle repeats itself in 2021 with Thistle bringing the UEFA Cup back to the
north side of Glasgow by beating Castel di Sangro, Go Ahead Deventer,

Larvik Turn, Stinta Cluj, Red Boys Differdange, Boldklub and Barry Town (all of whom Partick Thistle are presently on a pathetic par with).

Like Conservative supporters who lie to opinion pollsters about their voting intentions, the number of Glaswegians who profess allegiance to Thistle pose severe statistical sampling problems. They certainly never vote with their feet or bums. Most of the regular attenders live, or were born, locally in Maryhill, which used to be an overcrowded but colourful working-class district. But as the sandstone tenements have been demolished, to be replaced by low-level red-brick terraced housing developments, the area has become increasingly soulless and characterless. First bulldozed, then Bauhaused. The hand-on-heart fans, who almost never progress to bum-on-seat supporting, tend to be bourgeois 'intellectuals' from various parts of the West End, who justify their lukewarm preference for the Jags because of the close geographical proximity, non-sectarian status (true) and reputation (totally unjustified) for dramatic inconsistency on the park (in reality Thistle are appallingly average).

Standing up and stomping my feet to keep warm, the uncomfortable plastic seats were definitely not filling up with would-be Havels from Hillhead, Hockneys from Hyndland, Kerouacs from Kelvinside, Wittgensteins from Woodlands – or even a solitary Pinter from Partick.

In early September club secretary and ex-assistant headmaster Robert Reid published *Red and Yellow – Forever!* (GD Records, £8.99). A personal 50-year-history of Thistle, it fails to merit a place in the Pantheon League of modern fan autobiographies – just like Bert Bell's *Still Seeing Red: A History of Third Lanark*, which was published at the same time. Both books are meticulously researched, and in the former's case competently written (although as a retired modern languages dominie, Reid should realise that ending three sentences in a row with exclamation marks is poor prose style in any lingo), but to get any real reading pleasure out of them, you have to be an obsessive fan of the club concerned. Concentrating on dry football facts and descriptions of on-pitch action, the attention span of disinterested or neutral readers decreases in inverse but direct correlation. If old-fashioned authors can recognise the attractions of individually unique footballers – like Gazza, Cantona or Charnley – why can't they realise the need for a singular and distinctive tone of voice – like Hornby, Kuper, Pete Davies, Harry Pearson or Jim White – in the highly competitive world of soccer's *belles lettres*? Still, according to the programme notes Reid's magnum opus was already 'selling like hot cakes' . . . Ah, the joy of clichés. Sorry, I mean of course the epiphany of shibboleths.

Surprisingly, however, Thistle have inspired a genuine work of literary art – in short-story form. 'Scotfree' by Patsy Thomson, first published in

Scottish Short Stories 1975, brilliantly captures the atmosphere of both Maryhill and Firhill during the mid-'70s, in a game against Falkirk 'shiftily wearing their pseudo-Scotland strips'. Written by an English (!) woman, its artistic worth can partly be summed up by its avoidance of the phrase 'wearing red and yellow', Thomson preferring the more poetic 'resplendent in gold and scarlet'.

Having been relegated, plans to build stands behind both terraced goals have been shelved, because without four Old Firm visits a year their additional seating capacity will not be required (commercially or legally). As it is, the ability to seat over 9,000 punters is unlikely to be tested this season. The Jackie Husband Stand replaced the old enclosure in December 1994, and with the usual cantilevers on the roof this decorated shed affords unrestricted sight-lines for 6,263. Sitting towards the south end, my £10 paid for a wonderful view of the Trinity College Tower (which some lucky yuppies now get to live in), the University Tower and the spires of Park Church – a vista that could have been transposed all the way from Florence were it not for the looming presence of steel-grey clouds and horizontal rain. (Lallygrad however is becoming more and more like Savonarola's Firenze, and a fortnight or so before this game the City of Glasgow Licensing Board banned the consumption of alcohol in all public places – including streets and parks! – with anyone caught in possession of an open can of Special Brew or an uncorked bottle of Château La Tour '66 liable to an on-the-spot fine of £500.)

The smaller Main Stand has been spruced up, but the jarring presence of what I first mistook to be three levels of executive boxes under the southern lee of the roof turned out to be a self-contained mini-towerblock of offices, with the players' changing-rooms in what would otherwise be the foyer/reception area. This prefabricated-looking monstrosity even has one of Firhill's new neo-brutalist floodlight poles embedded right in front of it. (According to Simon Inglis, these French-manufactured 'masts', like 'giant telegraph poles', cost £120,000 but in my opinion they look like the kind of concrete phallic symbols that the French authorities would install in high-security state mental hospitals.)

As three o'clock approached I found myself surrounded by Asians and Eskimos, while sitting beside me was a one-eyed black lesbian saxophone player, all of whom had taken to attending home matches at Firhill after chairman Jim Oliver had issued a statement in 1995 denying allegations of racism. As part of his denial Oliver had promised to deal fairly with anyone from either of these two racial groupings and he went out of his way to stress that even someone with the remarkably unusual combination of visual disability, non-Caucasian skin pigmentation, inverted female sexuality and musical ability would not be discriminated against in his boardroom. Previously, in case you're wondering, Oliver had responded to a potential takeover bid by a consortium of Asian businessmen with the following – undoubtedly bullish rather than bigoted – statement: 'If anyone thinks we're going to give away a company which we've built up over six years at a personal loss to satisfy the wishes of some Indian with a curry shop, they'd better get real.'

An injection of capital from the sub-continent and the provision of additional business expertise from Glasgow's successful Asian community would be one possible lifebelt for the current Thistle board to grab at. Having been relegated, the reduced revenue projections have necessitated the demise of the reserve team, the sale of goalkeeper Nicky Walker and midfielder Ian Cameron, and a clutch of free transfers. Further stadium development is impossible without regaining Premier status. And winning promotion looks like a forlorn hope with a small squad of ageing journeymen and inexperienced youths.

Within ten minutes, however, Easter Road reject Gareth Evans (5ft 7in) had headed home a cross by ex-St Johnstone right-back Tommy Turner (aged 32). For the next 80 minutes Clydebank poked, prodded and finally piledrived forward in search of an equaliser.

In the glossy match programme, the 'Gilmour's Garbage' column exhorted the Firhill faithful to give the team 'that special, noisy, humorous, raucous backing that became our trademark throughout the early '90s'. (What? – *Thistle, yer fuckin' shite?*) Gilmour was 'firmly of the opinion that the distinct apathy (never mind the severe criticism) of Jags fans towards the team this term can only have a detrimental effect on performances'. As the second half wore on, the Jags in the stand had moved on from their initially raucous backing, through apathetic silence, to stinging criticism of all their players, except for goalkeeper Mark Cairns, who was keeping his team on course for a slender victory.

Murdo MacLeod's cash-strapped Catch-22 dilemma – no promotion = no new players; no new players = no promotion – is glaringly illustrated by the fact that centre-half Jim Slavin had played in 16 straight games prior to kick-off (including the pre-season tour of Ireland). At 14 stone, with the stomach of a Sumo wrestler and the thighs of a prop-forward, Slavin is a ponderous carthorse who would not look out of place in a Sunday pub team. A waddling slag-bing, rather than an intimidating man-mountain, he actually made three consecutive first-team appearances for Celtic in early 1995, before manager Tommy Burns saw sense and dropped the lumbering liability. With no pace, tactical awareness, ball control, passing ability, heading technique or tackling skill, his ever-present place at the heart of the Thistle defence was a damning indictment of the current player pool at Firhill.

Approaching the hour mark, Slavin latched onto a loose ball in the centre-circle and hoofed it skyward – in the direction of his own goal! As keeper Cairns back-peddled, a spectacular o.g. – or free-kick on the goal-line for handling a pass-back – looked inevitable. Instead of emulating Columbian goalkeeper Rene Higuita's 'scorpion' back-flip clearance, Cairns timed his jump to perfection and glanced the ball away with his bald head for a corner. At 21, Slavin can only get fatter, and if he doesn't have a heart attack he's going to end up playing for *Largs* Thistle.

MacLeod must have been eyeing ex-Jag Davie Irons enviously, as the 35-year-old coaching assistant strolled through the game for the Bankies. Sweeping up at the back when necessary, he sprayed passes around with laser-guided precision. Clydebank manager Brian Wright is another popular ex-Thistle star, and although his team lost 1–0, the scoreline bore no relation to the way his young charges had dominated the second half.

This season Clydebank are tenants of Dumbarton (whom MacLeod led up to the First Division in May of 1995, before departing for Firhill three days into season 1995–96). Slumming it in the DSS bed-and-breakfast accommodation of Boghead was supposed to be a short-term measure, while the new £3.5 million Davie Cooper Stadium was under construction away from the crowded town centre of Clydebank, but the refusal of planning permission for the property developers who bought Kilbowie Park in 1995 has meant that the company were entitled to withhold full payment of the previously agreed £2 million price. Therefore, the decision to dismantle and abandon Kilbowie Park became somewhat precipitous. At the start of this season, Bankie fans phoning Boghead for season-tickets were told by Dumbarton officials to try elsewhere. The old Kilbowie Park number treated callers to a disconnected humming noise. (The Clydebank officials and office staff were in fact operating out of a Portakabin in the grounds of the West of Scotland Rugby Football Club.) What the Luftwaffe failed to do during their blitz of Clydebank – namely destroy Kilbowie Park (then home of Clydebank Juniors) council red tape and boardroom miscalculation have managed to achieve. Kilbowie currently stands derelict, a theme park for vandalism.[2] And although pop group Wet Wet Wet started to sponsor the Bankies in 1993, Marti Pellow *et al* can't be relied on for any more financial investment – because they're really all true-blue Rangers fans.

Maybe Clydebank should try relocating somewhere like Oban, since they have no real traditional following or sense of history (they only formed as a League side in 1966, after a forced merger two years earlier with East Stirling had been overturned by the courts – but not before the Shire's enclosure roof had been spirited away and reassembled at Kilbowie). If Dublin City FC are still interested in playing in the Scottish League, after having their takeover bid for Cowdenbeath knocked back in 1989, it would be ironic justice if Clydebank disappeared in a similar manner to their original carpetbagging formation.

As for watching Partick Thistle, in her short story Patsy Thomson ends by suggesting that there are 'worse ways to spend your Saturday afternoon'. Apart from being a solitary Celtic fan trapped in the Clockwork Orange tube train which got stuck between Ibrox and Govan just after the Old Firm game, I can't think of one.

FOOTNOTES

1. Yolanda from Port Said is of course fictional – and even if she isn't, the topography of her topless nudity is definitely imaginative description rather than straight reporting/boasting.

2. Early in July 1997 six of the Steedman family, who owned 88 per cent of the Clydebank stock, 'agreed in principle' to sell the club to a mysterious overseas businessman – but only after the money from the sale of Kilbowie and the new site earmarked for development (estimated in total at £2 million) had been transferred into the account of a new company called Kilbowie Retail Ltd. The expatriate buyer would simply inherit membership of the Scottish Football League and a playing pool worth a pittance. With speculation rife that some of the Steedmans would invest in Partick Thistle, assurances were made that adequate funds would be made available to ensure Clydebank's continued financial viability. Hmmm . . .

IBROX STADIUM
Rangers v Dundee United
Premier Reserve League, 5.10.96

Alex Miller's resignation as manager of Hibernian on Monday, 30 September, following an embarrassing 3–1 defeat at home to Hearts, probably had Walter Smith and Tommy Burns reflecting on whether they too would be required to do the 'honourable' thing and fall on their own swords come the end of the season. With both Rangers and Celtic having suffered European humiliations, winning the Premier League was going to be the only outcome that would guarantee Smith and Burns continued employment as managers of Scotland's two biggest clubs. With Rangers going for nine successive championships, and Celtic equally determined to stop them from emulating their nine-in-a-row record, the stakes could hardly be higher.

From a personal point of view, the possibility of Rangers making it nine, even this early in the season, induced waves of physical nausea and periods of dry-mouthed anxiety.

If not for another one-day rail strike, I would have made it up to Inverness for the last-ever game at Caledonian Thistle's Telford Park. And if Stirling Albion versus St Johnstone had not been postponed because of players involved with the Under-21 squad in Latvia, I would have ended up at Forthbank. But a last-minute, spur-of-the-moment decision resulted in a detour to Govan. With the Premier card blank because of the World Cup qualifiers in Latvia and Estonia, the Rangers reserves got a rare run-out at Ibrox (they normally play at Bathgate's Creamery Park). With established stars like Erik Bo Anderson, Ian Durrant, Ian Ferguson, Derek McInnes and David Robertson in the team, the Govan Stand was over a third full, with 4,000 fans taking advantage of the £2 entrance charge and relishing the opportunity to get into Blue Heaven without having to be a debenture investor, season-ticket-holder or credit-card customer. With the other three stands eerily empty, Ibrox was even more impressive than I remembered it (my last visit being for the 1994 Coca-Cola Cup final between Raith Rovers and Celtic).

If a football institution is greater than the sum of its parts – including the stadium, the squad and the support – where do Rangers come on the pecking order of 'greatness'? Taking eight key categories – including number of League championships, ground capacity, most expensive player, and number of season-ticket-holders – journalist John Kelly rated 16 teams in an attempt to objectively arrive at the world's number-one team (*Goal*, October 1995). A year on, even after updating his figures for Rangers – who now have 46 League championships (a world record), a ground capacity of

50,500, a £4.3 million player in Paul Gascoigne, and almost 40,000 'socios' – they would still be rated tenth in the world. On this basis the Ibrox club would just make it into a World Super League, behind Boca Juniors (Argentina), Flamengo (Brazil), Ajax, Barcelona, Penarol (Uruguay), Benfica, Juventus, AC Milan and, *numero uno*, Real Madrid. (For the record, Celtic's parameters were statistically skewed so that the Parkhead club came last out of 16, despite having won the European Cup – unlike Dynamo Kiev or Rangers – but with their recent financial resurgence they're surely now above São sodding Paulo.)

Rangers, and to a lesser extent Celtic, are rumoured to be seeking a way of floating off to join some kind of European Super League, possibly leaving behind their reserve outfits to lord it over what remains of Scottish football. If Kelly's listed 16, which also included Bayern Munich, Liverpool, Manchester United and Kiev, actually constituted themselves into the 'Mondial XVI Scudetto', Rangers FC would either have to add dozens of extra tiers to Ibrox or start accepting house deeds as down-payments for season-tickets. Or introduce the first £100 match-day tickets. If they can well-nigh sell out the stadium for fixtures against the likes of Dundee United, Raith Rovers, Kilmarnock and Motherwell, just imagine the media hype and fan frenzy surrounding a final series of home games against Real Madrid, AC Milan, Flamengo, Manchester United and Celtic, with the chance to become World League Champions in the last game, while at the same time relegating their arch-rivals from the élite.

Twenty years ago, however, Rangers still clung tenaciously to the club tradition of playing only Protestant professionals (or non-Catholic carpet-baggers), and in 1976 they went out of the European Cup in the first round to FC Zurich. Like an élite handful of Scottish clubs, though, their European record prior to, during and just after the swinging sixties was – in retrospect – stunningly good, climaxing in a European Cup-Winners' Cup final win against Moscow Dynamo in 1972 (3–2 in Barcelona, *en route* to which they disposed of Rennes, Sporting Lisbon, Torino and Bayern Munich!). But for generations also, Ibrox had been an old-fashioned and dilapidated death trap, where sardine-sandwiched supporters endured constant spectating discomfort and intermittent injury and death – culminating in the infamous crush on Stairway 13 in 1971, when 66 home fans died.

After 1978, however, the dangerous embankment terraces behind both goals were replaced by the identical Broomloan and Copland Road stands. Two years later the rickety Centenary Stand was demolished, to be replaced by the Govan Stand running the whole length of the north touchline. In season 1981–82, when Rangers finished third behind Celtic and Aberdeen, rumours began to circulate about terrible design flaws in all three new stands . . . namely that they had been erected facing the wrong way – over-looking the pitch. Having spent £10 million on the stadium, inevitable economies were made with the playing squad, and at one point crowds plummeted below the 5,000 mark.

In 1986 new chairman David Holmes recruited Graeme Souness from Sampdoria as player-manager and gave him a blank cheque-book with which to play the transfer market. English internationals like Chris Woods, Terry Butcher and Trevor Francis reversed the flow of star players southwards and Rangers immediately began to reap their rewards in silverware. The first success came in the Skol Cup of 1986, in the final of which Celtic's Maurice Johnston 'Glasgow-kissed' Rangers full-back Stuart Munro. After being red-carded, 'devout' Catholic Johnston blessed himself as a sign of contrition, directing the inflammatory gesture at the Rangers support. Afterwards, Johnston transferred to Nantes. On his departure one irate but anonymous Celtic fan wrote to him, 'I don't know how you will be able to speak French, because you can't even speak English properly. All the worst . . .'

The Ibrox revolution gathered momentum in 1988 with the appointment of David Murray as chairman. Having made his fortune in steel tubing, and having lost both legs in a car crash, maverick Murray combined elements of Roosevelt, JFK and Nixon (while across the city Celtic were being run into the ground by directors who displayed all the most indecisive character traits of Ford, Carter and Bush). With demand for seats outstripping supply, Murray still knew that radical change was required if his invest-ment was to generate ever-increasing returns. Not only was the pie-and-bovril image of Rangers Football Club becoming increasingly unwanted, attracting corporate sponsors and achieving European success with a team of 11 Protestants, as club tradition demanded, was likely to prove night-marishly problematic as time went by – not because of practical problems posed by any paucity of proficient Proddy players, but because UEFA were becoming increasingly impatient with the sectarian recruitment policy (with some EC bureaucrats from Catholic countries like Spain, Portugal and Italy even less disposed to turn a blind eye to the situation). Potential sponsors who operated across Britain, Europe or the world were not queuing up to associate themselves with a club that could soon have found itself being banned from European competition and getting itself hauled through the European Court of Human Rights in the Hague.

Murray saw the commercially damaging writing on the wall, and Souness had only accepted the manager's job on the understanding that he would be allowed to sign anyone he wanted. He did attempt to recruit Welsh Catholic Ian Rush from Juventus – and although Rushie passed the medical, his IQ rating conceivably frightened Rangers off as much as his salary demands, as evidenced by his famous irony-free quote about life in Turin being like 'living in a foreign country'. Other high-profile Catholics reputedly turned Rangers down.

Having failed to recruit a Continental Catholic – which would have side-stepped the normal knee-jerk association of west-of-Scotland Roman Catholicism with Irish Nationalism in the minds of many Rangers' supporters – Souness stepped in to snatch Johnston away from returning to Celtic in 1989. Despite having acquired *grandes passions* for fine French wines, back-list classics from the Parisian Olympia Press (in translation, alas) and Art Disco architecture, Mo Jo arrived back in Glasgow still wearing an earring and no socks, having learned just three French phrases: '*Je suis un soccer star*', '*Cherchez la femme*' and '*Il faut d'argent!*' ('One must have money!') Before his departure, Mo Jo had admitted that he might be persuaded to become Rangers' first Catholic signing if they paid him a million pounds in cash and bought him Stirling Castle to live in. Rangers provided the money, but because the castle was a security risk Mo Jo took up residence in a fortified farm near Edinburgh.

Mo Jo's quote (even if inaccurately attributed) – 'Rangers are the only team I ever wanted to play for' – incensed a large body of the Ibrox loyalists, but rather than burn or return their season tickets the vast majority 'tholed' Johnston for two years, some even refusing to acknowledge his many goals when recounting match scorelines.

A combination of terrific footballing skills and worrying personality defects, Johnston was probably the only high-profile Catholic star who would have risked running the gauntlet of becoming Rangers' first Fenian forward. Although particularly inflammatory at the time, because of the circumstances, it meant that subsequent Catholic recruits who hadn't stuck the head on Rangers players while playing for Celtic could be integrated into the team without causing too much damaging controversy. Today, the religious affiliations of potential players don't even get mentioned in the press, and Rangers have raised a Catholic through their youth system in the form of John Spencer (who became a Scottish international after moving to Chelsea). This year Rangers paid £2.4 million for Jorge Albertz (a Catholic from SV Hamburg).

By the end of 1994 a third tier had been added to the South Stand, the salubrious facilities of the Club Deck attracting the 'Ibrox gannets' (famous for hitting the buffet tables before the half-time whistle). A new white roof was also put in place. Today the demand is such that every opportunity to install additional seating is acted upon – from lowering the level of the pitch (to allow new rows of seating around three sides of the ground) to filling in the corners at both ends of the Govan Stand.

Having spent over £40 million since 1978, Ibrox is now an all-seater stadium endorsed by UEFA as suitable for hosting European finals. Having retained Leitch's red-brick façade on Edminston Drive (which in 1980 became a listed building), Ibrox is now an aesthetic delight, a superb example of modern architecture in which design follows function, but whose design deserves all the architectural awards it has presumably won. Even when 'empty' 13 days a fortnight, rented-out offices, booked-up restaurants and oversubscribed guided tours generate large revenues. And like Manchester United, less than half of Rangers' massive turnover – estimated at £30 million for 1996 – comes from 'gate money'.

On the field over the same period Rangers have invested a net £25 million in transfer fees, but because of Bosman the necessity to maintain such expenditure can be expected to decline. The Bosman ruling also means Rangers are no longer restricted to a maximum of three foreign players in European competition. The spine or backbone of the current squad is undoubtedly Andy Goram, Richard Gough, Paul Gascoigne and Brian Laudrup. (If not employed as footballers, two of this quartet would have succeeded in normal professional occupations, while the other two would have been in and out of various buildings with dormitory sleeping accommodation and/or solitary confinement.) If Rangers can discover, or import, a world-class striker, European Cup success could be a real possibility. As long-serving manager, and part-time sleeveless cardigan mannequin, Walter Smith has marshalled his vast resources competently rather than spectacularly, although the clock is definitely running down on his permitted timescale for European glory (Scott Symon was unceremoniously sacked after just one bad result in Europe). As 'No. 2', Archie Knox is a chip off a very old and gnarled block. The appointment of Davie Dodds as first-team coach, according to a contributor to the Rangers *No. 1 Fanzine* (Issue 43), had his old boss Jim McLean rolling up and down the aisles of Tannadice's George Fox Stand in paroxysms of uncontrollable mirth. (Dodds, as well as being a real uglie-buglie, was the kind of player who couldn't have trapped a ball playing on the moon with a butterfly net.)

Comparing the aforementioned fanzine with the official *Rangers News* (which sells a phenomenal 30,000 copies a week), the latter only comes out ahead in terms of club propaganda, statistical analysis and glossiness of paper. Like its better-known counterpart *Follow, Follow*, the *No. 1 Fanzine* contains nothing but libellous allegations, vulgar obscenities and scurrilous rants. Yes, you know what's coming – it can also be very funny. Fanzine contributors all over Britain kept original and honest football writing alive long before the publishing Big Bang.

With 'Sellik Bhoys Club' having been at the centre of child-abuse allegations in the tabloid *and* broadsheet press, and Bishop Roddy Wright having run off with a divorcee from his parish (but not the woman who gave birth to his unacknowledged son 15 years earlier), anti-Celtic material was not in short supply. For example, suggested phrases to avoid while waiting upon diners at Brother Walfrid's restaurant at Celtic Park included: '3. Can I push your stool in a wee bit, sir?'

Sitting near the back of the Govan Stand (Rear), no Rock Steady stewards or policemen intervened to stop a large group of supporters singing 'The Sash', using 'fucking' as a constantly repeated adjective, lobbing paper projectiles or throwing themselves head-first over seat-backs – at least not until one of the unaccompanied six-year-olds required to be taken away in a folding chair for medical treatment to a gashed knee. Otherwise, the atmosphere was relaxed and festive, and the air of unreality was added to by a Corinthianly competitive game in which the normal flurry of yellow cards failed to appear. Complex moves were allowed to develop without defenders sliding in from behind with two soles of exposed studs. Having lost 1–5 to Kilmarnock and 2–0 to Celtic, the Rangers reserves were obviously responding to an unusually large, if high-pitched, support.

Surprisingly it took until the 75th minute for the first goal to be scored, and it was counter-attacking Dundee United who scored it, courtesy of a diving header from David Mitchell. 'Aw naw,' flashed the electronic scoreboards at either ends, amusing many of the adult supporters around me who obviously didn't get to attend Ibrox regularly, if at all (the financial distress caused by unemployment, invalidity, parenthood, low pay, further education or retirement preventing them from possessing the next best thing to a season-ticket: a credit card). After going behind, Rangers played through a spell of paralysing panic, as the first team would do more often if not for the reassuring presence of the unstoppable match-winners Gazza and Laudrup. Darren Fitzgerald scrambled an equaliser from three feet (and an OAP and lifelong fan assured me 'excellent prospect' Darren was a 'left-footer signed from a Catholic school in Belfast'). Right-back Jaswinder 'Jazz' (*Jeezuz*) Juttla – the first Scottish-Asian footballer I had seen in my travels – was involved in the move which led to Erik Bo Anderson's last-minute winner (a powerful header): 2–1 final score.

Rangers had churned out a slender victory through extreme determination and ruthless efficiency, and this *modus operandi* accusation is often levelled at the star-filled first team – Celtic supporters in particular insisting that although the playing personnel may alter Rangers' general style of play never does. At least one journalist has iconoclastically questioned whether clinical organisation and brutal consistency can be said to characterise Rangers teams of whatever era, and whether Celtic are entitled to rejoice indefinitely in their reputation for cavalier flair, as summed up in the nickname 'Green Brazilians' (which, to be honest, is not in any kind of common usage and which was apparently coined by 'brainwashed' Rangers fans).[1] Historically true in my prejudiced opinion, with last-minute winners for the Celts being due reward for 89 minutes of relentless and entertaining attacking, and late penalties for the Gers being indicative of desperate late surges and superhuman stamina, the media's current and continuing acceptance of these stereotypical soccer styles must grate with Rangers fans who are privileged enough to see Gazza and Laudrup destroy five-man defences week in and week out. Currently Celtic may be more attractive to watch as a collective unit, but in the aforementioned duo Rangers have the two most explosively exciting individual talents in the Scottish game (even if lumbering Scottish defenders lie down and play dead in front of them).

'Despite Rangers' recent domination, Celtic still have the "name" on the Continent,' noted Kelly in his *Goal* article. This is probably fair comment, largely based on Celtic winning the European Cup in 1967 with such attacking imagination, but if Rangers were to emulate the feat in similar flair-filled fashion, with a non-sectarian squad, other liberal-humanist-intellectuals all over the EU would be won over — in both hearts and minds — to the Teddy Bears' cause.

The club motto, depicted high up on both ends of the South Stand, is 'Ready'. The stadium certainly is and an increasingly non-sectarian and glamorous squad of players is getting there; and although a genuine if *massively hyped* clamp-down on loud-mouthed bigots by operations executive Alistair Hood has improved the atmosphere and behaviour of fans inside Ibrox, too many Rangers supporters still see every goal scored as a blow for Presbyterianism, Unionism, the monarchy and other such nonsensical connections. At the extreme ends of the sectarian spectrum, Celtic have just as many pig-ignorant numpties as Rangers, as any viewer of Channel 4's admittedly sensationalist *Faith, Flutes and Football* documentary will have seen, but Celtic avoid the worst excesses of religious hatred by having thousands of ostensibly Protestant supporters (even if they are a smallish minority). If they only amount to between 50 and 500 (a very conservative estimate) in a capacity crowd of 50,000-plus, their very existence and attendance has an impact on the club's character out of all proportion to their number. Only when christened Catholics from Clarkston, Cork and California start filling up the Copland Road end will Rangers have become a 'global brand name' that all of Scotland can be, without qualification, proud of.

In *Football Against the Enemy* Simon Kuper suggests that the Rangers–Celtic rivalry has outgrown religious hatred, a dead God for both sides being no reason to ditch enjoyable secular competition. Rational rivalry between two big city giants, free of religious and political baggage, is still a long way off, but hopefully the process will continue to accelerate.[2] Writing as a Celtic-supporting 'Protestant' atheist, I'd happily pray for Rangers making it nine-in-a-row if an omnipotent God would guarantee that their run of success ended right there. And P.S., Lord, that includes next season's European Cup/Champions' League — because joint ten-in-a-row/European Cup celebrations in May 1998 would be my worst footballing nightmare writ large in rebarbative royal-blue life.

FOOTNOTES

1. The term 'Green Brazilians' was completely unknown to me until I read about it in an article in *Scotland on Sunday* by Graham Spiers (the Scottish soccerati's soccerate?) entitled 'Old Firm Style Council Debate' (24.3.96).

2. The religious differences which supposedly separate Old Firm fans, theologically speaking, would definitely amuse — and appal? — cynical but civilised aliens sent to study the phenomenon undercover, one of whose report back to the mothership might read as follows:

'The "Hun" homo sapiens belong to a branch of Christianity which subscribes to the view that the word of God is to be found *only* in the Bible (a series of books written by some notoriously unreliable narrators long after the events described). The "Taig" terrestrials, however, believe that one ordinary man in the form of a Holy Pontiff is God's *sole* representative on Earth, and whose *ex-cathedra* statements are supposedly infallible. This schism might be regarded as leading to two separate routes up the same mountain, at the peak of which resides the same God, but although the founder of the Christian religion Jesus preached in favour of faith, love and charity, a large number of "Prods" and "Tims" never venture out above their base camps — Queen Elizabeth II and Pope John Paul II — preferring to fight it out with each other in the shadowy and satanic foothills. This could be described as secular sectarianism, with religious observance not even requiring attendence at church or Mass (except for births, deaths and marriages). Teddy Bear One ending transmission, but before signing off with telepathic love, please inform Hooped Bhoy One that if he starts boasting about Lisbon in '67 again, I'm going to "Glasgow kiss" him right on his middle eye. Over and out!'

Signs of increasing tolerance are definitely to be found, however, mainly because of Rangers dispensing with their 'What school did you go to?' signing policy. Although I initially thought that live satellite transmission of Old Firm games in public bars would be an alcohol-fuelled recipe for Wild West saloon-type rammies, I have 'sat' through at least half a dozen, as part of a mixed clientele, without there being any trouble (although the potential is always there). In all seriousness, Rangers fans are a combination of braying bigoted bullies, ordinary flawed but funny folk and pseudo-intellectual soccerati sophisticates. Just like Celtic supporters, really (even if you could argue about the percentage make-up). The latter two categories can cope with the paradox of 'hyper-criticising Huns/thundering-against Taigs' in a footballing context, but without letting such *abstract* animosity leak across the divide at work, in social situations – or even in 'mixed' marriage. (Personally I'd happily walk down the aisle with a Teddy Bear bride, although if she was a Tory Teddy Bear we wouldn't get past a first date.) Sadly, however, a significant number of fans on both sides are unable to draw the distinction in *real* life.

CENTRAL PARK
Cowdenbeath v East Stirlingshire
Third Division, 12.10.96

Hard-line communism and *laissez-faire* capitalism, although ostensibly at opposite ends of the political spectrum, are so extreme that the red- and blue-shifted ideological dead-weight at both ends of their supposedly straight-line separation results in a downward bending, which eventually leads to a closure of circular completeness. At the point of indistinguishable connection, the same (or similar) victims get crushed and exploited.

After the Second World War a newly nationalised coal industry gave hope to towns like Cowdenbeath, which depended on buried 'black diamonds' for their financial future. After the Second World War Estonia was forced to become a satellite republic of the expanding Soviet empire, along with the other Baltic states. In 1956 Russian tanks rolled into Budapest. In 1960 Cowdenbeath's last working pit, No.7, was closed down, its winding wheel left to overshadow Central Park. In 1968 Celtic were the first visitors to Central Park to play under Cowdenbeath's new floodlights. In 1968 Russian tanks rolled into Prague. In 1988 privatised British Coal shut its workshops in Cowdenbeath, cutting the town's last link with mining. In 1989 Estonia's football club supporters, who had become increasingly vociferous in voicing nationalist sentiments, celebrated as the 'Velvet Revolution' brought the Berlin Wall down and looked forward to their own independence (which was declared the following year).

On Wednesday, 9 October 1996, Craig Brown's Scotland side kicked off at three o'clock against a non-existent Estonian team playing a 0-0-0 formation in protest at the abrupt rescheduling of the start time. (The previous evening Scotland had informed FIFA that the temporary floodlights were 'absolutely abysmal', even though the hydraulic cat-cradle supports imported from Finland had not yet been raised into final position for the training session, and Italy and Turkey had both played at the Kadriorg Stadium in Tallinn at night without complaining.) After three seconds of 'play' the referee abandoned the game, and John Collins and Tosh McKinlay had the embarrassing brass-neck to raise their arms in celebration (assuming that Scotland would be awarded the fixture 3–0). But if the Kadriorg Stadium had remotely resembled run-down Central Park when I visited it, Jim Farry of the SFA would have turned his team around and refused to let them, or any supporters, set foot inside it – and quite rightly.

Imagine an Albanian Second Division ground in Korce, say, where the only concession to capitalist enterprise is a stock-car racing track. To stop the souped-up Wartburgs, Moskviches and Volgas careering all over the pitch, giant rubber tyres from Chinese-made giant tractors surround the inside of the cracked concrete track.

Current chairman Gordon McDougall used to rent the track for his stock-car racing company, but after being invited to join the board he eventually took control after an acrimonious share battle. Under his controversial leadership, Cowdenbeath won promotion to the First Division in 1992, immediately parted company with manager John Brownlie, went 101 weeks without a home win and saw a large part of the Main Stand gutted in a fire. But for all his autocratic faults, McDougall obviously isn't afraid to get his hands dirty, because he's listed in the *Scottish League Review* as both chairman and groundsman. (Some supporters suspect he'd like to prepare the pitch by doing handbrake turns in a Land Rover hitched to a wheelless caravan, thereby obviating the need to run a cash-draining football club at all.)

It's only 400 yards from the railway station to the football ground but by the time I'd sprinted this short distance I was so wet that I could feel a rivulet of rainwater beginning to form a puddle between the cleft of my buttocks. Incredibly, a dozen or so cheapskates preferred to save a pound by standing forlornly on the tiny terrace on the far side as Typhoon Kelty passed overhead. The proverbial one-umbrellaed-man-and-his-dog stood at the uncovered, *unterraced* railway end. As I held the damp match programme, its flimsy paper disintegrated between thumb and forefinger.

During the first half I sat in the new Alex Menzies Stand, all plastic seating, concrete aisles and corrugated steel roofing. At half-time I switched to what remains of the wooden Main Stand, after deciding against queuing outside in the rain for a pie or washing my hands in the men's room sinks, which were black with engine oil. Of the 206 crowd (Britain's lowest of the day), at least two dozen were East Stirling fans, supporting the team rooted to the bottom of the Third Division.

The match was turning into the worst I'd yet seen, its rank awfulness not even enlivened by late tackles, suicidal defending or outrageous misses in front of goal. Only my Walkman was keeping me awake, as Radio Scotland commentator Chick Young desperately attempted to inject some hyperbolic life into the dull on-pitch proceedings at Celtic Park, although being somewhat undermined in his efforts by the more realistic assessments from Charlie Nicholas as match summariser.

After Cowden keeper Neil Russell was forced to make his first and only good save, the Blue Brazil – an ironic nickname if ever there was one – went straight up the park and scored, substitute Brian Malloy hammering home from a few yards. For the remaining eight minutes the man with the dog edged closer towards the exit. As did I. Final score 1–0 to Cowdenbeath.

I sprinted past the Job Club, housed in the new stand, leapt in the air as Pierre van Hooijdonk rose superbly above the Motherwell defence to head home a last-minute winner – which Chick Young memorably described as 'Van Hooijdonk!' – and caught the 16.56 train back to Edinburgh.

Two Rangers fans sitting morosely in Waverley Station, after watching their team go down 2–1 to Hibs at Easter Road, were ranting to each other that Brian Laudrup should have had a second retake of his penalty (Millen having encroached the first time when the Danish winger hit the bar and Leighton supposedly having moved when he saved the retaken attempt). '1–0 to the Blue Brazil, but,' I said, trying to cheer them up, grinning and circling my head like a mental retard.

'Who gives a fuck?'

'Not me, pal,' I confirmed.

A hundred yards further on I shouted back: 'Pierre's the name, and scoring's my game!' Up the steps two at a time to Princes Street like a bat out of hell. Home just after six o'clock. Drookit but delirious.

Having spent a mere £12.50 all in to visit Central Park, I bought half a bottle of whisky and settled down to finish *Black Diamonds and the Blue Brazil: A Chronicle of Coal, Cowdenbeath and Football* (Northern Books, 1993). Written by the Revd Ronald Ferguson, this combination of social history and diary-of-a-season reminiscence is probably Cowdenbeath's greatest ever PR and publicity coup for both town and club. HarperCollins turned it down, even though they had published the author previously, and if such a major publisher had marketed it aggressively it could have sold a lot more than a cultish 5,000. Ferguson baulks at the suggestion that he has now joined the 'football literati', and good as the book undoubtedly is, it does have too many one-line, one-sentence paragraphs (a style quirk acquired from the author's days as a reporter with the Edinburgh *Evening News*?). Nevertheless, its writing was obviously a labour of love – and as well as being an interesting and enjoyable read, it should serve as a beacon of inspiration for would-be fan biographers of other small unfashionable clubs.[1]

As for post-match analysis, Cowden's Tom Steven boosted the tarnished reputation of managers when he was quoted as saying: 'We are joint top of the League [with Montrose] and they [East Stirling] are bottom, but they're no worse or better than us. We're just carrying a bit more luck.' In the worst senior League in Britain, this was not false modesty but fair reflection on a brutal reality.

Halfway through the bottle of booze, I switched on *Sportscene* hoping for highlights of Celtic or Rangers. Instead BBC Scotland had chosen to cover Dundee United's boring 0–0 draw against Kilmarnock. After watching the end of *The Silence of the Lambs* and a late-night documentary on British porn star Mary Millington (dead at 33!), I fell asleep drunk under the kitchen table. When I awoke the portable TV had been moved into the kitchen – where it was hissing white noise – and all my laundry had been immaculately steam-ironed. Ah, the humiliation. Cowden's legendary striker Hooky Leonard or nearby Hill o' Beath-born Jim Baxter would undoubtedly have woken hungover and bleary-eyed to be confronted by discarded silken underwear and/or a part share in a racehorse (in the form of a severed head). God knows in what state Berwick Rangers boss Ian Ross must have woken up on Sunday morning, after leaving his post by 'mutual consent' on Saturday night after a 2–1 home defeat to Stranraer.

FOOTNOTES

1. In *The Absolute Game* (Aug/Sept '96), No.49, Archie MacGregor describes *Black Diamonds and the Blue Brazil* as being 'within that admittedly minor sub-branch of the publishing industry which goes by the heading Books-on-Scottish-football-that-are-actually-worth-reading'. This unarguable observation will make a better jacket puff for any future edition than one of the quotes which adorns the back of Hunter Davies's novel *Striker* (Bloomsbury, 1992), from ex-England manager Graham Taylor: 'Hunter Davies writes the sort of book you even take to the loo.' Any swithering buyer would have put it back on the shelf after reading that, surely; hence my picking up a hardback copy for £1 in Bargain Books prior to my visit to Ibrox (RRP £9.99). Football novels are always problematic to write, because of the legal necessity to invent teams like Melchester Rovers. Davies gets round this problem by having Joe Swift play for real English teams, but thereby has to pussyfoot around because of legal man-marking. He solves the problem of a main character closely resembling Gazza by giving the real Gazza a small walk-on part in the narrative. The novel only achieves some Norman Hunterish bite towards the end, when the action moves abroad, and Swift plays for a German team called 'Eintracht Hamburg'. In 1989 they beat Glasgow Celtic in the third round of the UEFA Cup, despite the fact that in reality Celtic had gone out of the Cup-Winners' Cup in the first round to Partizan Belgrade that year. Swift finally moves on to 'AC Sporting Venice' rather than Venezia. *Striker* is nevertheless an inherently poor piece of fictional drama/humour (for which Davies can be forgiven, since he wrote the seminal football classic *The Glory Game* back in the early 1970s – and with a new fourth edition currently on the bookshelves it must be one of Mainstream's most lucrative, and admired, cash cows). Someday, somewhere, somehow, someone will probably succeed in overcoming the legal and plausibility problems inherent in the task and manage to write the Great Football Novel (the last unconquered genre of the Western literary canon).

FORTHBANK STADIUM
Stirling Albion v St Johnstone
First Division, 15.10.96

If watching Cowdenbeath had left a bad taste in my mouth, I was left
smacking my lips with pleasure after this midweek encounter. Having
endured a two-mile walk from the railway station in pouring rain, however,
I hadn't been looking forward to my third visit to Forthbank. Situated
amidst a sprawling business and retail development at Springkerse, I could
only agree with the writer of the 'Travelling Reds' column in the excellent
match programme who, referring to Airdrie's old ground being Safeway-
ised, railed against the 'relentless tide of so-called progress towards the
urban peripheralisation of football in the retail park era'. Quite.

Without any spectators the stadium is almost as soulless as the commercial estate which surrounds it. When Stirling Albion first moved into
Forthbank in 1993, only the East and West stands alongside both touchlines
had been completed. But as every stadium architect now realises, 'atmosphere' leaks out of undeveloped ends, no matter how many fans are going
mental in the middle, and two small uncovered terraces were soon built to
try and make Forthbank 'four-sided'. Simon Inglis notes that they cost
£500,000 to construct, which seems an incredible amount, but maybe they
have *trompe l'oeil*/Tardis-like qualities, because if my arithmetic is right
each one must hold almost 700 people when required. Neither was open for
the visit of St Johnstone.

Stirling Albion are famous for the circumstances surrounding their formation, in 1945, after King's Park FC's Forth Bank Park had been bombed
to bits by a skelly-eyed Luftwaffe bomb-aimer (which didn't please Field-
Marshall Goering, who had convinced his Führer that Rudolf Hess had set
up home with the Duke of Hamilton in Stirling Castle and had promised to
blow the impregnable fortress to smithereens with a single shellburst of
pin-point accuracy). Annfield Park became notorious in 1987 when the
local council, by then owners of the ground, insisted on the installation of
an Astroturf pitch (Stirling District accountants having been impressed by
the increased number of goals that visiting goalkeepers conceded when
playing on the artificial surfaces at Queen's Park Rangers and Luton Town).
The experiment was not a success, one visiting manager promising to play
a return fixture 'on the biggest bloody bouncy castle money can hire'.

The crowd of 1,432 was almost equally divided between home and away
supporters, the former housed in the West Stand and the latter in the East.
Having won promotion and the Second Division Championship by scoring
83 goals, Stirling went into this game with only seven goals from eight

games, a scoring drought which saw them propping up the First Division with six points. Manager Kevin Drinkell was having to operate with ten full-time professionals and ten part-time players – unlike fully professional St Johnstone. (Historically, the Saints have always been a much bigger club than the Albion, and although Perth has a slightly larger population than Stirling – both towns having populations slightly over 40,000 – the difference does not explain the gulf that divides the two football clubs.)

After a ferocious opening from both sides, one player was beginning to stand out – a tall, long-haired Austrian called Attila Sekerlioglu. A skilful midfielder for St Johnstone, he opened the scoring with a swerving free-kick that banana-bent round Stirling's wall and soared into the top corner of Mark McGeown's goal. (Although only half-an-inch shorter than 5ft 11in tall Andy Goram, McGeown has somehow earned the reputation of being a brilliant shot-stopping midget, a day-job draughtsman who needs an extra cushion on his swivel seat at the office, but he's a damn sight more effective dealing with high balls than Celtic's Gordon Marshall.) At the other end, St Johnstone's Alan Main (just under 6ft) was managing to keep his goal-kicks in play, despite the Stirling supporters 'Ooooooo-ing' during his run-ups and then shouting 'Shite!' in unison as he made contact with the ball. Charming. As was their chanting directed at the visitors from Perth in the opposite stand: 'Nice to see you, nice to see you – *fuck off.*'

Before the first half ended, the ball had to be replaced three times as the original soared out of the stadium behind McGeown's goal. Seven minutes into the second period, Leigh Jenkinson prodded home a second goal for the visitors. Although being outclassed, Stirling were fighting for their lives, and in 63 minutes Craig Taggart emulated Sekerlioglu's strike – but from open play and further out. With chances coming and going at both ends, referee Jim McCluskey decided to earn his £200 match fee by incurring the outraged wrath of the home support, giving a highly dubious penalty against Ronnie McQuilter for tackling John O'Neil in the box. Roddy Grant made it 3–1 for St Johnstone from the spot.

Although O'Neil had been sent sprawling, McQuilter had made contact with the ball first, and decisions like this must drive professional players to the edge of despair. An excellent centre-half, McQuilter at 25 must wonder why clubs like Celtic will splash out £3.5 million on a stopper like Alan Stubbs, when he could be snapped up for one-hundredth of the outlay. Signed from Ayr, McQuilter has played abroad for APOP Paphos of Cyprus and he turned down a move to Turkish club Besiktas in the summer.

With more than a few promising young players and a manager committed to an attacking style, Stirling are probably doomed to go straight back down (as richer clubs cherry-pick their talent under the Bosman ruling and their more cynical opponents pick them off on the break). A Clydebank collapse is probably their only hope of survival. At the end of this game, a small but amazingly foul-mouthed section of the support were already advising their manager to collect his P45.

Walking away from the stadium, still gloriously floodlit against the dark sky, it struck me as a shame that no Scottish club in the process of relocating or rebuilding has yet had the imagination or the funding to commission a top architect like Norman Foster or Richard Rogers. With a remit to put East Fife FC, say, on the architectural and footballing map, surely such individuals could be persuaded to do for Bayview Park what they have already done for Stanstead Airport, the Lloyds Building or the Pompidou Centre. Functional as Forthbank undoubtedly is, it's no more than two undecorated sheds in the middle of an architectural desert.

Having missed the 21.33 train by three minutes, and the Edinburgh coach by three seconds, I left the depressing modern shopping streets and climbed the steep braes to Stirling Castle. On my only previous visit I had parked on the esplanade and turned my libidinous attentions to my female companion. Heavy petting sessions were obviously going on behind the steamed-up windows of the few parked cars, but with the rain having relented I was able to enjoy the panoramic view of the neon-lit streets and the Wallace Monument.

If the SNP sweep to power in 1997 and Stirling Albion get relegated, I thought, there's no way the Scottish capital will be moving to Stirling. Can you imagine the unsubtle digs from English supporters?

'What division do Albion play in now?'

'The second.'

'Just like the independent country, eh?'

If St Johnstone gain promotion to the Premier, maybe the capital could go back to Perth? (I know, I know – Stirling Albion have more chance of securing the First Division title and winning the Scottish Cup in '97 than the SNP have of forming a government after the next election. Depressing, innit? Wallace, Bruce and McGregor *fought* to retain their freedom on battlefields visible from the castle ramparts; today Scotland's whining electorate won't even *vote* to regain their independence. And what can you do except weep with frustration when snooker player Stephen Hendry's manager warns that a devolved parliament with tax-raising powers would force his client out of the country, and whose only comments about the town of Stirling concerned the amount of litter thrown up in the slipstream of his Rolls-Royce.)

After a double malt whisky in the Portcullis Bar, I wandered into the open but pitch-black graveyard next door. Ignoring warning signs about toppling gravestones, I felt sad for my so-called country and slightly scared for myself. My heartbeat dropped back into the low hundreds after a high-pitched screech and two red eyes in the foreshortened distance proved to be a hard-braking car on the castle esplanade.

The next evening Scottish confidence took another knock when Ajax hammered Rangers 4–1. But apparently Gazza only retaliated and got sent off after Winston Bogarde had shouted in his ear: 'Have you stopped beating your wife yet?' Eleven matches in the Champions' League without a win . . .

STATION PARK
Forfar Athletic v Albion Rovers
Third Division, 19.10.96

Forfar or Brechin? Since the Beeching cuts in the 1960s neither of these Angus towns has been served by a rail link, but because my sister was travelling to Aberdeen from Glasgow in her new Micra (via Edinburgh), hitching a lift allowed me to avoid the privatised nightmare of local bus services from Dundee, Arbroath or Montrose (the tourist map for which simply gave routes and frequencies – e.g. 'occasional' or 'twice daily' – rather than times). Despite the name of the ground, Station Park is the British senior stadium furthest from a rail station (14 miles away from both Arbroath and Dundee). I opted for Forfar because they were the Third Division's highest scorers, lumbered along with the League's leakiest defence, had won 4–3 at Alloa a week previously and whose last home game had resulted in a 5–2 defeat against Cowdenbeath. Ah, those crazy goal-scoring and goal-gifting Loons . . . And although the Wee Rovers had gone four League games without a win, they hadn't failed to score in any of them.

'Are we going slower and slower because we're breaking down or because you're going up this hill in fifth gear?'

'Shit! . . . Hey, why didn't you visit Forfar and Brechin, as well as Inverness and Dingwall, while the weather was good at the start of the season?'

'Oh, I dunno . . . Just couldn't be arsed, I suppose . . . What's so fucking funny?'

'Put that in the book. Sums up your late-rising, underachieving character in a sentence.'

'Of course, you'll be a full fucking professor by 40 – *our kid*.'

'When you'll be 47! . . . Groundhopping round . . . the Irish League . . . on a pogo-stick made for one!'

Getting out of the car in the massively bomb-cratered Market Muir carpark beside the ground, a colleague from Lynn's academic department at work appeared. Anders was a fledgling groundhopper from Sweden who supported Sunderland. Six-fifty got each of us into the 739-capacity stand, whose squat structure, steel stanchions and horizontal hawsing-wire were designed to keep the roof in place during high winds (all the previous roofs having taken off in the direction of Brechin in the past).

The total attendance was 393, with most of the Coatbridge contingent congregated beneath the cover opposite the stand. The majority of Loon fans stood directly beneath us on the concreted terracing (and even when promoted to Division Two two years ago, the capacity of over 8,000 remained ridiculously underutilised).

As the teams kicked off, Anders was kitted out in a blue Forfar baseball cap, with five programmes in his lap and a stopwatch in his hand. Having foregone the pleasure of a Forfar bridie (a pastry filled with minced beef, onion and spices), Lynn was regretting not stopping at the McDonald's at the turn-off to Forfar on the A94. Some sort of vegetarian, she could still have permitted herself a carton of Chicken McNuggets, apparently. I therefore urged her to have a bridie or one of the 'delicious' pies that I'd bought from the refreshment kiosk.

Albion had the best of an abysmal first half, with Forfar's Iain Lee doing well to knee a goal-bound deflection up onto the bar. The home manager, silver-haired Tommy Campbell, kept leaping out of his dug-out to swear like a Tourette's Syndrome sufferer. (His board had just informed him that desperately needed new defenders would only be coming to Forfar if other clubs could be persuaded to accept a lamentable Loon in a swap deal.) Since the ladies' toilet was underneath the stand beside the home changing-room, Lynn got a choice earful of references to sexual activity, illegitimate children and female orifices during her half-time squat.

In the second half the piss-poor pattern of play turned round in Forfar's favour, but it still took until the 70th minute before an attacking player forced a quality save – Loon Lee watching in frustration as Stevie Ross got a gloved stitch to a well-struck free-kick. Another highlight came when the lewdly latitudinous Loonatics below us managed to so rattle referee Sandy Roy that he felt compelled to consult both his linesmen purely because of the fans' hysterical overreaction to an innocuous tackle. But on both occasions after Albion's Davie Byrne and Colin McFarlane had been booked, an old woman from Coatbridge at the front of the stand barracked the *illegally* tackled Loon players for trying 'tae get a fellow professional sent aff'. The second time she got a volley of verbal abuse from the Loonatics that made Campbell sound as if he was minding his Ps and Qs.

With Forfar pressing frantically forward for a goal, the best chance of course fell to Albion Rovers. Player-manager Vinnie Moore just missed connecting with a diving header at the far post. The match ended, in slow motion like a nightmare, 0–0. Although no real consolation, visiting Brechin wouldn't have been any more rewarding, because they drew 0–0 with Stenhousemuir – the only two scoreless draws on the Scottish card that Saturday. Tantric footie satisfies no one, except for goalkeepers who have managed to retain their self-respect instead of being serially gang-banged.

Being driven to Montrose to get dropped off, I brooded on a goal average that had just dipped below three per game. 'If it drops below two, I'm jacking the whole thing in.'

'Aagh,' moaned Anders in the back seat. 'Sunderland beaten 3–0 by *Southampton*.'

'Crikey,' said Lynn. 'Chelsea beaten 4–2 at home by Wimbledon.'

'If you knew anything about football, you'd know that was their seventh straight win in the Premiership.'

'One more and they equal Manchester United's record,' Anders correctly pointed out.

Standing on the platform outside the ticket office of Montrose Station I was confused. Situated on an East Coast rail line, I presumed that the horizonless body of water before me was the North Sea. Since British trains 'drive on the left', why was the opposite platform signposted for Aberdeen and the North? As the 17.56 approached from my *right*, I was convinced that it must have been heading north. The only other passenger on the platform assured me it was 'the Edinburgh train' but when the doors whooshed shut behind me I concluded that he must have meant that it had *departed* from the capital. Certain that I'd arrive in Aberdeen before Lynn and Anders, I flushed bright red as I admitted my mistake to the conductor. I didn't even believe his assurances to the contrary until we pulled into Arbroath (rather than Stonehaven). Not until home with a map open on the kitchen table did I realise that the station faces out onto the Montrose Basin, a massive bay or inlet that only meets the North Sea south of the town. Instead of facing east I'd been facing west. With sanity restored, I decided to stop brooding on my first no-score draw.

Instead I brooded about the 83 supporters crushed to death in the Mateo Flores Stadium during the Guatemala v Costa Rica World Cup qualifier, the abandonment of the Portadown v Cliftonville match because of safety fears for the visiting Catholic fans, and the fact that I started down the pay-cheque paper mines once again come Monday morning. No goals to write about, lack of recognition as a writer and low remuneration that would make winter fuel bills a real worry . . .

I may not be a significant member of the soccerati but, boy, do I make up for it in sensitivity.

McDIARMID PARK
St Johnstone v St Mirren
First Division, 26.10.96

Although provided with an excellent photocopied map by the Tourist Office in the High Street, I still managed to take a seriously wrong turning on my way to McDiarmid Park. The 'Fair City' of Perth is a nightmarishly confusing grid system of one-way streets at its congested centre, and on my only previous visit to cover a St Johnstone match as a reporter I simply took advantage of an expense account to hire a taxi from the rank at the railway station.

My fellow pedestrians included foreign backpackers scratching their heads outside Irish theme pubs, schemies who would have instantaneously combusted if the cigarette butts hanging from their lower lips had fallen down the inside of their non-flame-retardant shell-suit tops, and young couples dressed in either Cotton Traders rugby tops with the collars turned up or waxed green Barbour jackets (the Alastairs eventually loading the back of their Shogun 4WDs with tackle and ammo and the Fionas throwing saddles and picnic hampers over the open tailgates of their mud-splattered Range Rovers). Perth has become a magnet for moneyed incomers, who are attracted by the amenities offered by a big town and the scenic beauty spots in surrounding Tayside. Whisky, insurance and twee speciality shops offer local employment for young marrieds who do not wish to commute to Glasgow or Edinburgh. Instead of roadsweepers, Perth has those Parisian-patented street-cleaning buggies with mechanical brushes and compressurised water cannons (and the one that almost ran me over on the pavement of South Street had *two* grinning Perth and Kinross Council employees crammed inside).

Having reached the top-left corner of the map, I had to choose between the green-marker-highlighted Crieff Road and Football Stadium arrow or the actual road signs at the roundabout indicating that the 'Football Stadium' was to be found somewhere down Dunkeld Road. Foolishly following the road sign, I soon passed the Asda store which had replaced the old Muirton Park (the supermarket group agreeing to pay the £4.9 million bill to build McDiarmid Park in 1989). Dunkeld Road soon became a never-ending stretch of dual carriageway, a pavementless thoroughfare lined by expensive car showrooms for dealers such as Mercedes, BMW and Volvo. In the Jaguar forecourt an amused father-of-two said I was miles away on the wrong road but that I would be as well continuing since I had gone that far. Directions were duly given. 'Next time remember to walk down Crieff Road, son.'

Being called 'son' at 35 years of age might be flattering, in a patronising sort of way, but it drives me nuts and I exploded in footsore pedestrian rage. 'Next time I'll take my Jag-*war*! XKSS. With D-type racing car body-work.' Pretty snappy retort, huh? I regretted adding: 'It's a rollover week on the Lottery tonight, don't ye know?' the moment I said it. People with money intimidate me, but when my numbers come up – either literally or metaphorically – I'm going to cut quite an intimidating figure myself.

Eventually I reached 'the second roundabout after the bridge' and turned left, only to find myself trudging along beside a fully fledged fuck-ing motorway. After half a mile or so the first sign on the Perth City bypass appeared, indicating an upcoming slip-road back into Perth. Although this comes out at McDiarmid Park I wasn't aware of the fact and I decided to ignore it and follow a muddy footpath off the hard shoulder instead. Up hill and down dale on my arse (twice) I went until all signs of inhabited civilisation disappeared. Except for a trafficless road behind an iron fence and closely planted trees. I twisted my right ankle jumping the fence and got horribly snagged on the low branches flailing through the trees.

Limping bipedally (I also had a massive blister on the sole of my left foot), rubbing a staved wrist and bleeding slightly from my left cheek, I could hear pre-match announcements on the Tannoy. Where the fuck was I – a private park? Turning right – wrong, wrong, wrong – I soon came to a low, modern building made of ochre-coloured bricks. Christ, I thought, it's a bloody crematorium. The black-tied attendant in the foyer eyed me suspiciously as I rapped on the glass door. I asked for directions, politely but in a somewhat bug-eyed manner, and the man told me to go back the way I'd just come along the driveway to the main entrance on Crieff Road. It was ten to three.

'You're not a new Saints signing, are you?'

'No, I'm the fucking St Mirren coach driver.'

I could now see McDiarmid Park to my right, but the sweeping driveway of Heavenly Glades was gently curving away to my left. If I'd been match-reporting I would probably have had a heart attack at this point. Sprinting out of the main gates, I joined the fast-moving flow of late-comers (whose wary glances in my direction would have been more appropriate if I'd just escaped from a booby-hatch or sanatorium rather than a crematorium).

After handing over my £11 at the turnstile, I was in my seat at the back of the West Stand with two minutes to spare. What should have been a 15-minute stroll from the A85/A9 roundabout had turned into a 55-minute obstacle course.

McDiarmid Park, situated on the periphery of Perth, may only be four decorated sheds with the old floodlight pylons from Muirton Park transplanted into each corner, but as the first purpose-built all-seater stadium in Britain it preceded the recommendations of the Taylor Report. Any lack of atmosphere is largely due to the failure of crowds to approach anything like the 10,169 capacity (the attendance of 3,567 for the St Mirren game being close to what the home club have been averaging since their relegation from the Premier League in 1994). An unopen North Stand may have been a discouraging sign, but the South Stand's family section designation resulted in most of its seats being filled.

The pitch was in perfect condition but defaced by not-quite-painted-over rugby markings. St Mirren totally dominated the first half, the powerful running and exciting dribbling of winger Junior Mendes not only embarrassing left-back Allan Preston but also the other St Johnstone players who were dragged out of position to try and nullify his runs. Arsenal-target Ricky Gillies hit the side-netting with a spectacular volley and the McDiarmid Park home support gave him a sporting round of applause. From six yards out Mark Yardley not only blasted over the bar but almost cleared the South Stand's roof.

At half-time St Johnstone's much-admired decision to adopt continental training methods, including having the players back in for afternoon training sessions during the week, didn't appear to be having anything like the desired effect. Manager Paul Sturrock must have felt his blood pressure rising all through the first half – in October 1995 he had collapsed at Tannadice with chest pains caused by stress and angina. After recuperating in Spain, Sturrock had decided to introduce the nine-to-five schedule for the players. And although sensibly delegating minor tasks and taking an occasional afternoon off himself, Sturrock has put on two and a half stones in weight through comfort eating. If a family bereavement and moving house are two of the most traumatic events experienced in everyday life, managing a football club must be like losing a loved one every few weeks and having to do moonlight flits every month – with the job security of an American film-studio head of production executive. In what other occupation do you have to satisfy the (often conflicting) demands of financially parsimonious directors, money-grabbing players, crazily expectant fans and cynically hypocritical journalists? Satisfy all of these groups, in a precarious balancing act, and you could well be staggering home in the small hours to find that your dinner's in the dog and your wife and children are at your mother-in-law's.

Press match-reports of this game suggested that St Johnstone re-appeared after the interval like a team transformed, but for the first five minutes they were unable to get the ball off the one-touch-passing Paisley Buddies. Then Saints' star winger Leigh Jenkinson put over his first decent cross and Patrik Berger lookalike (from a distance) Attila Sekerlioglu bulleted a header past a rooted-to-the-spot Alan Combe.

A minute later Andy Whiteford came on for Danny Griffin, the 19-year-old Northern Ireland international who had dumbfounded neutral observers earlier in the season when he had turned down a million-pound move to join Derby County in the English Premiership. By staying at St Johnstone Griffin was foregoing a guaranteed £500,000 over four years. Although as anonymous as any of his team-mates before the substitution, I sincerely hope that he regains the form that prompted Derby's original offer — otherwise equally lucrative deals in the future may not materialise and he could become a journeyman footballer *who once turned down half-a-mill*. (To St Johnstone's credit they didn't pressurise him into accepting the offer, even though they would have benefited from an equally large transfer fee.) And, although attacking St Mirren aren't one of them, there are a few teams in the First Division who could cripple Griffin for life if he doesn't get out soon.

Jenkinson was now running riot down the left and another excellent cross in the 70th minute led to a second headed goal, Roddy Grant nodding home. Three minutes later Jenkinson swung in a free-kick from the right and, with the St Mirren defence sleepwalking, Sekerlioglu glanced another header past Combe. In the 88th minute substitute Ian Ferguson broke through the middle and scored the fourth and final goal. St Johnstone's 4–0 win left them second top, one point behind Dundee.

Before following the home fans down Crieff Road back towards the town centre, I had a quick stroll round the council estate of Letham — the original home of the Saints most famous follower, Stuart Cosgrove. Controller of Arts and Entertainment at Channel 4 and presenter of Radio Scotland's fanziney *Off the Ball*, as well as the author of *Hampden Babylon*, Cosgrove excites extreme reactions amongst Central Scotland's cultural cognoscenti. I once sat gobsmacked in a pub and watched as a female friend almost choked on her gin and tonic when his name was mentioned. Being Scottish herself, her ire stemmed not from any justifiable opinions about how good or bad Cosgrove was as a commissioning editor but from his allegedly 'phoney persona'. The case for the prosecution, as she sprayed it, was based on the fact that like many Scottish professionals in the arts and media, Cosgrove supposedly exaggerates or embellishes his working-class background. Letham, for example, is a perfectly respectable housing estate, rather than a run-down scheme, but the only negative comment about it that I could find in my Cosgrove clipping file was 'bleak and wintry' (which it certainly is in late October). His current abode in Dennistoun came in for further criticism, since this area of Glasgow is largely regarded as an East

End sink-estate of council tenements. But having been born there myself —
in a really bad bit — I know that there are exclusive pockets of residential
respectability. As a socialist committed to minority and special-interest
television (including themed sex evenings), Cosgrove has written amusingly about football, doesn't have an irritating on-off broad Scots/mid-
Atlantic accent (unlike Lulu, Miss Marie Lawrie actually coming from
Dennistoun), and is a funny and polite host on his radio phone-in show. In
America he'd be a role-model and hero. In Scotland he's a class-traitor and
pseud. So what if he winds people up by describing himself as a 'schemie'?

Multi-talented as Cosgrove is, managing St Johnstone might be a
possibility after Sturrock's current three-year contract is up. Sturrock was
a marvellous player for Dundee United and Scotland, and he has given the
St Johnstone set-up a real shot in the arm, but like a former boss of the
club, Willie Ormond (who has a stand named after him), Sturrock's
obviously an introvert and a bit of a 'worrier'. Hopefully, however, the
Saints will get back into the Premier League, keeping Sturrock in a job and
Cosgrove in supporting clover. And if Cosgrove is ever appointed chairman,
he ought to arrange for a directional sign to be erected for pedestrians at
that bloody roundabout.

FIRS PARK
East Stirlingshire v Inverness Caledonian Thistle
Third Division, 2.11.96

With British Summer Time having ended, this 0–0 exercise in footballing futility heralded the onset of yet another seemingly endless soccer winter, with Scottish supporters wrapping themselves up to endure haemorrhoid-throbbing privations on the terraces and players preparing to practise six months of pagan primitivism on increasingly heavy pitches. Since my long-detour short-cut to McDiarmid Park the clocks had gone back an hour, the long-johns had been passed fit to wear (after a crotch-sniffing test) and Firs Park had been looked up on the map.

As the train approached my destination of Falkirk, I spoke for the first time to the two final-year honours students who had been discussing what degree classification would be required to get them into 'advertising' on starting salaries of '18k min'. 'Settle for a 2:1,' I advised them, 'and end up in your mid-30s covering East Stirling versus Inverness on a wet and windy Saturday afternoon.' Although the guy and girl both laughed with youthful indulgence, I think I managed to scare them pretty good (or at least unsettle their sensible, but not unattractive, 4-4-2 mental patterns for a few moments). In the competitively cut-throat League of Life I hope they get off to a flying start; if not, they still shouldn't succumb to any managerial approaches made by a paste-jewellery-wearing artistic Muse who doesn't know her big spotty arse from her funny-bone-jarring elbow and who will never appreciate the well-nigh insurmountable gap between creative conception and commercial completion. Whether as 'creatives' or 'suits' I hope they never get lumbered with the Firs Park account or East Stirling as a client.[1]

Firs Park and Brockville are almost equidistant from Grahamston Station, but in opposite directions, and although not as incestuously close in proximity to each other as Dundee's two League grounds, the case for Falkirk being big enough to support a pair of senior football clubs is even more difficult to put forward with any conviction. Frankly, it's impossible.

Battling in the wind to keep my baseball cap on, my cigarette lit and my raincoat closed, I splashed along outside Tesco. Deploying a defensive psychological formation along the lines of 6-3-1 to try and keep negative circling thoughts from running up a cricket score, I was desperately hoping for an exciting game that I could lose myself in.

Walking round Firs Park to reach the single entrance turnstile, I decided to actively support the Shire, since I could empathise with their anonymously abysmal position and sympathise with their dire financial circumstances. Lying 40th out of 40 since 21 September, and having just declared a trading loss of £40,000 up to the end of May, East Stirling have done almost nothing of note in their 115-year history (or 114 if you don't include their acrimonious one-year merger with Clydebank in 1964, after relegation from their only season in the top flight in 1963–64). Formed as long ago as 1881, the Shire have nearly always been floundering flotsam since they moved to Firs Park in 1921, especially when compared to the relatively buoyant Bairns about 600 yards away at Brockville.

The previous Tuesday there had been something of a boardroom *coup d'état*, director Alex Forsyth being 'sensationally' voted out at the 'stormy' AGM in the Thornhill Road Community Centre. 'If the Shire goes down the swanny now, it will have nothing to do with me,' he declared with magnanimous dignity. Chairman Bill Whyte, however, had managed to convince the auditors of the club's financial viability, conceivably eliciting the 'true and fair view' stamp of approval by letting the tame accountants run riot at the Falkirk offices of the Angus Williamson Therapy Clinic, the Shire shirt sponsors, whose services include 'Aromatherapy, Reflexology and Massage'. Could you resist the blandishments of a blonde bimbo called Trish dressed as a French maid who gives you a whiff of bottled sweat and linament, knees you in the testicles and then shoves an ice-cold sponge down your boxer shorts? In reality the massage service is definitely depressingly respectable. Run by the proverbial mix of local butchers, bakers and candlestick-makers, East Stirling only survives because of SFL hand-outs.

A fiver got me into the terracing, which makes up one end and one touchline (with a small cover). The Lilliputian stand of 297 plastic seats cost an extra quid to enter, and although the total crowd of 398 almost filled it, at least 150 Highlanders had travelled south to support their ambitious team. The only source of architectural interest was the two two-seater press-boxes at the back, plastic and glass constructions like the sealed compartments in which headphoned contestants used to be given the answers in televised 1950s US quiz shows. Behind the railway end goal, a wall of concrete slabbing rose from the grass not more than three feet beyond the goal-line, with the result that off-target shots rebounded on to the pitch instantaneously. In addition, any wingers haring towards the line to get their crosses in before the ball went out of play ran a real risk of knocking themselves out cold by colliding with the wall. Only once did the match ball soar over its barbed-wire top and according to Simon Inglis – who shall henceforth be referred to by genuflecting surname only, as when citing the likes of Gibbon, Fowler or Partridge – ballboys receive 25p for each one retrieved.

The Shire hit the post in the first half, or maybe the wall, and had a goal-bound header cleared off the line in the second, but that was the sum total of the goalmouth action. Caley Thistle were even more tactically and technically incompetent. Playing the last of four away games in a row, they were obviously looking forward to their move into the new £3.5 million Caledonian Stadium in a week's time. Billy Little, the long-suffering Shire manager, had nothing similar to look forward to (unless Falkirk accept the Shire as tenants in their new stadium) – apart from the dubious probability of receiving Scottish football's wooden spoon at the season's end.

Division Three has its own brutal micro-climate, of course, and early November's contracting isobars on the weather front were reflected in the brutal bunching at the top (the six interchanging pace-setters being separated by only five points). Although not exactly stranded, the Shire were still bottom at 4.45 p.m. despite having won a point, one behind Queen's Park and Arbroath on the ten-point mark. Forfar were the only team not yet pigeonholeable as either promotion contenders or hopeless also-rans. Having seen every team in the division except Alloa, was it too early to predict the final pecking order after a mere dozen games? No, because the Third Division results had already established scientific 'reliability' at the foot of the table.

One advantage of working in a press-clippings agency (part-time but pre-dawn) – *again* – is a constant source of interesting articles.[2] For example, in Nigel Hawkes's 'Science Briefing' column (*The Times*, 4.11.96), a research paper in *Nature* was summarised. According to one Dr Nicholas Christenfield of the University of California, the length of sporting seasons is merely a function of the need to roughly balance the determining effects of skill and chance. Therefore the US baseball season requires 162 games to produce a worthy winner, while grid-iron football only needs 16. Hence, the World Series is played over the best of seven games and the Superbowl decided during a single final. 'Reliability' refers to the predictability of individual games, based on a study of previous results in the same league. Baseball requires lots of fixtures to equalise the effects of skill and luck, while rugby union on the other hand needs very few to balance the role of talent and chance in determining winners (as in the Five Nations Championship, with only four games required to see the gaping chasm that separates the English and French from the Scots, Welsh and Irish).

Bearing in mind the American extremes of 162 and 16, the Scottish League's 36-game season means that skilful teams will rise to the top, with chance only playing a part in separating the leaders. After 12 games it was obvious that either East Stirling, Queen's Park[3] or Arbroath would be replacing Albion Rovers as the worst team in Scotland. (In the Scottish Cup, however, these teams could ride their luck over a mere six games and conceivably win it.) For 40th place my money is on the Shire, whose continuing existence as a *senior* team would then become even more questionable.

On Saturday night manager number eight joined the dole queue, Jim Fallon of Dumbarton resigning (so no Job Seekers' Allowance for him for at least 12 weeks). His team had just been thrashed 5–0 at Livingston. Stranraer manager Campbell Money, who had been at Firs Park prior to Sunday's Challenge(d) Cup final at Broadwood, saw his team beat St Johnstone 1–0 (even if this dire knock-out competition is restricted to teams outside the Premier League). The Saints' hapless Danny Griffin scored an own-goal, making his earlier decision to turn down Derby seem even more deluded.

FOOTNOTES

1. I do wish this couple on the train well for the future, but it's undoubtedly best not to know. A feature in the *Daily Telegraph* (5.11.96), by journalist John Whitley, brought readers up to date with the lives of the child actors who starred in Peter Brook's 1961 movie *Lord of the Flies*. James Aubrey, 49, who played moral but wimpish Ralph, is now a 'jobbing actor' in London. Hugh Edwards, 45, the overweight and picked-upon Piggy, manages pet-food factories in Russia. Tom Chapin, 48, the bully-boy thug, currently prospects for gold as a qualified geologist in Nevada. When I read this at work, I had to step outside for a calming cigarette. I was born in 1961. And never in a million years did I think I'd end up groundhopping round every Scottish League ground in a single season . . .

Only a leavening of non-football books is keeping me going, re-reading some ten-out-of-ten personal favourites, in one of which I found the basis for the following test question for soccerati/literati egg-heads: Which fictional footballer – with the initials JT – moved from Ibrox Park as a 23-year-old to Loftus Road for just under a million pounds in 1989 or 1990? Even if you, Dear Reader, have read this brilliant modern novel, narrated by 'Sampson Young', I really doubt if you'll remember this fleeting reference to footie in the narrative. Melvyn Bragg might, since he did a *South Bank Show* about the book, but Terry 'Hazel' Venables definitely won't. If you know the name, or can trace it – which will probably mean re-reading the entire book – write to me c/o Mainstream and you'll get . . . a return-of-post reply full of . . . admiration and respect.

2. The only literary figure I know of who used to work in a clippings agency is Ian McEwan, but he didn't need to go back after the deserved critical and commercial success of *The Cement Garden*.

3. Queen's Park boss Hugh McCann had been blaming his team's lowly League position on the black-and-white hooped tops that they traditionally play in (the same as East

Stirling's, except a lot thinner). Apparently because of the building site backdrop that had replaced the demolished South Stand at Hampden, the Spiders were having trouble picking out their own players on the south touchline. Aye, right, Hugh . . . Change to white-and-black hoops then. This is Alex Ferguson's risible excuse (remember the change from grey strips to blue at the Dell at half-time?), and the current Manchester United boss actually started his managerial career at East Stirling's Firs Park.

GLEBE PARK
Brechin City v Livingston
Second Division, 9.11.96

Kissing my stunning Scandinavian wife Sonja goodbye on the doorstep of our detached family villa, I turn and shoo our two child prodigies Marmaduke and Marzipanella down the tree-lined driveway (thereby giving Sonja an undisturbed afternoon to catch up on the latest research about laser-aided micro brain surgery, the medical journals propped open on the music stand of the Steinway enabling her to simultaneously study and practise her piano concertos for the charity Christmas concert at Nine-wells Hospital in Dundee). Non-identical but equally golden-curled, our precocious five-year-old twins are intrigued and excited about their first sojourn to 'the footie'. Hopefully it will tire them both out, so that they sleep through the dinner party planned for later in the evening – to celebrate the six-figure advance for my latest book – although with a deliberately provocative oil-and-water guest list and seating plan I won't be surprised if raised voices and flying fists awaken them from their sanguine slumbers.

Momentarily I feel a chasm of guilt opening in my chest, after thinking how glad I am that 'Eggo' is no longer with us. (Egbert Bergman Bennie was my father-in-law – who changed/extended his name by deed poll when I married his 'bourgeoisely beautiful but boring' daughter – and who came to live with us when he was forcibly evicted from a nursing home in Helsing-börg.) A cantankerous and evil old bugger, I somehow managed to cover up his death as arising from the 'natural causes' of a heart attack, despite find-ing him in the upstairs bathroom with his head rammed down the toilet bowl and his body suspended in mid-air. Marmaduke, meanwhile, sat in the bath absorbed by his plastic toy, a guilty smile playing across his angelic lips as he levitated 'Damien the Duck' over the churning blood-red bubble-bath water . . .

Maybe because of this family skeleton – Eggo is buried in the cemetery behind Glebe Park – redoubtable Brechin feels like a Scottish equivalent of Stephen King's 'Castle Rock' (i.e. Orono in Maine), with its larger neigh-bour Forfar resembling fictional 'Derry' (or real-life Bangor) – places where the decades have passed without inflicting too much post-modern progress.

'Look at the white horsey, Daddy. Is it a unicorn?'

'What? . . . Where? . . .'

My sister pointed again at the well-groomed beast galloping freely around a paddock, directly behind the small and wildly off-centre wooden stand. We were seated high up behind the west goal in the five-year-old

Trinity Road stand, an incongruously massive cantilevered structure that can accommodate . . . Well, take the day's *total* attendance of 401 and triple it – and you would still have 25 free seats. A traditional covered terrace occupies most of the opposite end. To our left a narrow walkway terrace runs the length of the pitch, but a tall privet hedge ran out of roots just beyond the halfway line, where a concrete wall becomes the boundary. From our crow's-nest vantage-point the russet and rolling hills of Angus were only slightly obscured by a spectral mist. Weird and wonderful as Glebe Park is, it looks as if it has been laid out and added to by a giant's growing child, Hornby Town-and-Country or Subbuteo-like life-size accessories being plonked down any old how.

With a population of 6,000, Brechin is the smallest conurbation in Britain to field a senior soccer side of its own; the City suffix and nickname arise from the presence of an episcopal see's cathedral. Almost two-thirds of the town's inhabitants could fit inside the 3,900-capacity ground, but in a Scottish Cup tie against Aberdeen in 1973 the record attendance was set at a mind-boggling 8,244. (In comparative terms Celtic would need to attract, and accommodate, a crowd in excess of one million.)

The match programme was a bizarre mixture, too. Adverts extolled the virtues of electric shepherd fencing, local lemonade and fly screens/blackout blinds. A 'spot-yourself-in-the-crowd-photo' ad offered as a prize 'a [*sic*] Electronic Metal and Voltage Detector worth almost £9'. Steve Kerrigan was sponsored by 'FT (Anonymous)' and James McKellar by 'Simmet and Drawers' (who hopefully don't expect the player to model their underwear in the company's mail-order catalogue, above the strapline 'Hello, Big Boys'). The main shirt sponsors are Rowco International, freight forwarders with offices in Aberdeen, Glasgow, Rouen, Singapore and *Baku* (but not Brechin). And according to the 'Guests of the Glebe' column, Livingston's Graham Harvey had been signed from Instant Diet (of Hong Kong). Weird or what?

Brechin had won promotion behind Livingston, but while Jim Leishman's poetastering management style had resulted in the Livvy Lions roaring ahead once more, the City were struggling to maintain a cushioned gap between themselves and crisis-ridden Dumbarton and Berwick. Manager John Young was having to draw on the Under-18 team and reserves for fresh blood, and 19-year-old McKellar was in the team, along with 21-year-old Gary Buick (whose fright wig of bottle-blond hair made him look as if he had just been dragged backwards through, not the famous Glebe Park hedge, but one of the electric shepherd fences advertised in the programme).

The large and loutish Livingston support surrounding us tried their bellowing best to put off 41-year-old City keeper Ray Allen during his run-ups, resulting in the shortest and most misdirected goal-kicks I have ever seen. Those that didn't fall woefully short of the halfway line either sliced or hooked straight out of play. (Imagine bandy Jim Leighton in callipers taking goal-kicks without his contact lenses in and you'll have some idea of the strange parabolas that the match ball was being launched on.) Livingston's left-back Stevie Campbell was just as bad at delivering his left-footed corners. In 30 minutes, after a series of air-shots, a Brechin forward finally made contact with the ball. Dougie Scott could only watch in frustration as his 30-yard piledriver rebounded off the underside of the bar.

Minutes into the second half the visitors' Grant McMartin hit the post, and Allen brilliantly blocked his follow-up effort. Although a gauche goal-kicker, he proved to be a synergic shot-stopper. Livingston looked far more likely to score, but it became increasingly obvious why Brechin are something of a bogey team to Livingston at Glebe Park. At 4.30 p.m. the temperature plummeted below freezing and I lost all feeling in my extremities. The City, however, responded by charging forward and 6ft 4in Robert Douglas (ex-Symington Tinto!) pulled off two fine saves to break Brechin hearts. The home fans remained impressively good-humoured, except for one young man – a farm labourer? – who kept standing up to scream at Leishman: 'Shut yer arse, Leishman, jist shut yer arse – ya verbal diarrhoea slurry sprayer!' The 0–0 draw left the home side 17 points behind Livingston, Brechin having played 270 minutes of football without scoring a goal.

Shouts of 'Git the bluidy heater oan' echoed round the carpark. Lynn had picked me up at Montrose Station and by the time I had her Micra bombing down the A94, the hot air blasting out from under the dashboard was beginning to defrost my fingers and toes (even if it helped harvest the first winter crop of chilblains – for which alcohol is the only effective emollient, taken orally every four minutes). They were fiery little fuckers by the turn-off to Forfar.[1]

Having walked round Brechin prior to the game, we had been surprisingly impressed – it even had a public library open at two o'clock on a Saturday afternoon. In the Old Bake House tea-room Lynn mused about the possibility of renting a house there for her next academic year, and over post-prandial cappuccinos it was enjoyable to have a rallying conversational knockabout instead of our usual point-scoring bickers full of verbal smashes. Outside a – the? – newsagent's she enthused about the friendliness of the locals. Not being able to resist the opportunity for a whorfing smash return, I countered with: 'Christ, how fucking nice is it possible to be when selling someone a *Guardian*?'

If my lift to literary fame and fortune ever stops being hauled up hand-over-arthritic-hand by hunchbacked dwarves, and transforms itself into an external glass express elevator, I'm sure I would enjoy living in Brechin and supporting the City every fortnight. Savills could arrange for the purchase of the detached family villa (with character), and possibly an up-market introduction agency like Drawing Down the Moon could put me in touch with a virginal but whorish Swedish neuro-surgeon called Sonja? Hey, why not? Men fall in love through their eyes and women through their nostrils (at the first whiff of bulging joint bank accounts). If Brechin City had a financial fortune invested in them by a Brechin-born billionaire, they'd soon be taking their Premier League status for granted . . . Come May, I hope they manage to stay up.

FOOTNOTES

1. Reaching Forfar or Brechin by public transport from Central Scotland is an uncomfortable and time-consuming nightmare, as illustrated by the experience of East Stirling fan Brian Stocks from Edinburgh, who needed to take four different buses to reach Station Park on the same Saturday as the Brechin v Livingston match. Sports journalist Michael Henderson talked to various Shire fans for a terrific article in *The Times* (11.11.96) entitled 'Warming to the winter wonderland', and Henderson obviously enjoyed himself at Station Park as the Loons of Forfar hammered their opponents 3–0. Sports writing such as Henderson's is often the best journalism that broadsheets have to offer, but my Monday-morning tea-break enjoyment of it was tempered by the fact that while Henderson was enjoying three goals I had been witnessing my second 0–0 draw in a row ten miles up the road (the third in four games). The previous week I had seen East Stirling playing out another scoreless draw at Firs Park. Forfar's rediscovered firepower was galling, because three Saturdays earlier I had arrived in Angus with Albion Rovers for the first no-score draw of my travels. If an airline's computer ever seats you beside me on a charter flight to Alicante, demand to be taken off the flight immediately – because the plane will undoubtedly crash into the high ground north of the Spanish airport if southerly winds are blowing after dark. I may have underachieved hideously in life because of inherent ineptitude and acquired laziness but ill-luck has dogged my footsteps in a one-forward-two-back fashion for as long as I can remember.

IBROX STADIUM
Scotland v Sweden
World Cup Qualifier, 10.11.96

When John McGinlay scored after only eight minutes, drilling a low shot past Thomas Ravelli, the Basil Fawlty of international goalkeeping, the Scottish support erupted in an orgy of glee. Tommy Svensson's team had been booed onto the pitch because of the supposedly sneaky Swedish role in persuading FIFA to decree that the abandoned Estonia v Scotland fixture would have to be replayed (the committee in Zurich which ruled against awarding Scotland a 3–0 victory being chaired by Stockholmer Lennart Johansson).[1]

After McGinlay's early goal, the sell-out crowd of re-recruited Tartan Army enthusiasts struggled to keep from falling silent as Sweden's combination of semi-professionals and Serie A superstars threatened to overwhelm Scotland. They were only prevented from doing so by the goalkeeping heroics of Jim Leighton (who wouldn't even have played if Andy 'The Flying Pig' Goram hadn't declared himself physically unfit – which made a change from 'mentally untuned').

At one point in the frenzied first half, the few thousand Swedish supporters segregated in the bottom level of the Broomloan Road Stand looked set to riot. They had just noticed the full-page ad in the glossy match programme which read 'Welcome to our Swedish friends to Scotland'. (The literate and largely bilingual Swedes buy ten times more books per head than the Scots, and although their hysterical reaction to SFA syntax may have seemed disproportionate, one must bear in mind that Sverige has the third-highest number of emergency admissions to mental hospitals in the world.)

Around my sister and me in the Govan Stand (Rear), about a fifth of the Scottish fans were wearing those tartan tammies with orange crêpe-paper hair attached. Half the Swedes wore plastic helmets with Viking horns. Guess which was the snazzier statement of sartorial style?

Live Sunday-afternoon TV coverage on BBC2 did not prevent 47,000 fans turning up at Ibrox, and although the atmosphere remained good throughout the game, it would have been goose-bumpingly brilliant if Scotland could have forced Ravelli into any kind of serious action (a fight referee would have stopped this contest because of the pounding Scotland were getting if a boxer had been on the receiving end of similar punishment). My personal highlight of the seemingly endless second half came in the 63rd minute when Jesper Blomquist bore down on an unprotected Leighton. The 38-year-old veteran keeper stood his ground to make a fine

116

one-on-one save, whereupon bug-eyed and muttering Ravelli started beating his bald head with his outsize gloves in furious frustration. This victory took Scotland to the top of Group Four and will hopefully see us qualify for France '98 (assuming we don't fuck things up against Estonia in Monaco in February 1997).

Was this game worth £14 to see? Yes, definitely – if only for the cathartic pleasure of being one of 45,000 fans rising together to cheer a well-worked Scottish goal. In the Sports section of *The Herald* (11.11.96), however, Brian Meek wrote: 'It was £10 to cheer on the Scottish football team, more than double that to watch our rugby failures' (who had lost to Australia 19–29 the day before at Murrayfield). Like politicians who never buy their own milk, and therefore haven't a clue how much a carton of cow-juice costs, sports journalists with press passes and expense accounts tend to lose touch with economic reality. The only adults who got into Ibrox for a tenner were those accompanied by juveniles and who were willing to sit in the high-pitched hell of the family section. Otherwise tickets were £13 and £14, with £1 booking fees for each ticket if purchased by telephone from TOCTA. Meek's inaccurate generalisation would have been less irritating if he had been filing a straightforward match report, but his column was supposed to be one of those fans-overview-and-atmosphere-assessment pieces. Neverthe-less, he presumably wrote it from the cocoon of the press box. Although laugh-out-loud funnier than most other fans with laptops, there's no way Meek made his way home via the Clockwork Orange Underground either, the congested Ibrox platforms at five o'clock resembling the Tokyo subway system during the rush-hour when terrorists have set cyanide bombs to go off all over the place.

FOOTNOTES

1. Lennart Johansson's reasonable decision undoubtedly had a political agenda, the Vice-President of FIFA needing the support of small ex-Soviet satellites in his attempt to succeed 81-year-old Joao Havelange as president. Following the Scotland game at Ibrox, the Swede hinted that Havelange was so senile that he was incapable of realising that he should retire. Havelange, whom some joke is an ex high-ranking Nazi given a new identity in Brazil after the war, hit back almost immediately when he, allegedly, authorised the breaking of an old story involving his challenger. Apparently the sprightly 60-something Swede had returned from a trip to South Africa and described a meeting held there as follows: 'The whole room was full of blackies and it's fucking dark when they sit down together. What's more, it's no fucking fun when they're angry.' (*The Sun*, 16.11.96) Forced to apologise and recant, in an attempt to retain the developing-world vote, Johansson had the gall to repeat the old chestnut about having 'many coloured friends'.

117

OCHILVIEW PARK
Stenhousemuir v Dumbarton
Second Division, 16.11.96

At some point in the recent past, Stenhousemuir started to become a fashionably chic minnow, up for adoption as a 'second team' by English fans with obsessive love to spare (like sponsoring a Third World orphan while pulling strings to get one's genetic offspring into Church of England schools and/or executive boxes at Old Trafford). The Warriors Abroad club now has hundreds of English members, dozens of Norwegian affiliates (who enjoy descending on Ochilview between October and March for a spot of sunbathing while lying on their inflatable herrings and chanting 'Come on, ze Vorri-Vorri-Vorriiiooors!'), and at least one Punjabi mystic called Ravindra Soni. Stenhousemuir certainly meet all the criteria necessary for inspiring a committed cult following – they're small, shite and have a fairly stupid name (but a memorable nickname). Viking visitors, southern-based seat sponsors and Scottish souvenir buyers help keep the club afloat, because Stenhousemuir the place is really only a large village which merges seamlessly into the small town of Larbert (with both almost subsumed by the military-industrial complex of Falkirk). With Falkirk FC and East Stirling within walking distance to the south, Stirling and Alloa a few miles to the north, Clyde at Cumbernauld to the west (and even Dunfermline just over the Kincardine Bridge to the east), the Warriors have an extremely narrow indigenous fan base from which to draw.

Their present-day popularity in places like Solihull and Stavanger may owe something to the unpredictable power of advertising, since a nationwide campaign for an insurance company in the early '90s played upon Stenhousemuir's footballing frailty and geographical anonymity. (The fact that Stenny are one of many clubs who huddle together for cold comfort in the Central Belt certainly surprised me before my visit, because I was half-expecting a trip to a frontier footie outpost somewhere in Ayrshire, Perthshire, Fife or Angus.)

Since 1992, however, Stenhousemuir have beaten St Johnstone and Aberdeen in the Scottish Cup (in 1995), have won the League Challenge Cup by beating Dundee United in the final (also in 1995), and have managed to erect a new half-million-pound stand (which was opened at the start of the current season). Managed by ex-Meadowbank Thistle boss and full-time headmaster Terry Christie (of lucky dufflecoat fame), they are now sponsored by Four-in-One, a fast-food chain serving diverse fare from around the world – e.g. Polmont, Linlithgow, Alloa and Rumford – with branches in America, Turkey, India and Italy (or possibly the other way round).

The one-mile walk from Larbert Station was footslogged through a bone-chilling wind and beneath leadenly gravid clouds. Main Street's shopping precinct could have passed for downtown Batumi, but with a wallet bulging with hard currency I lunched like a lord in Crawford's tea-room. Outside the window, empty crisp packets snapped at the thick ankles of unmarried mothers and wild dogs flew through the air like tumbleweed. Having developed a nervous facial tic prior to the Old Firm clash on the previous Thursday (which I watched on satellite in a spit-and-sawdust theme pub on Leith Walk), it was still convulsing away, intermittently but annoyingly after the nail-biting but nausea-inducing result (0–1). A fellow diner was reading a copy of *The Warriors* (1984) by Peter Moulds and as I mummified my neck and face with my Werder Bremen scarf ('Extra-Ultra-Long') he asked in a Brummie-ish nasal whine: 'Are you a German Warrior?'

'NawUmurnae; uryae?'

'Sorry, mate, I no sprakenzi Deutsch.'

'I vrite game report for *Vorld Soccer* on ze Vorriors, ja?'

Hearing him rabbit on was like listening to Talk Radio without any commercials. I made my Teutonic timetabling excuses and left in goose-stepping irritation. *Danke schön, Dummkopf.*

The cute and cheerful six-year-old who sold me my £1 programme got a 5 per cent commission. He was not pleased when I told him that little kids hawking Rangers fanzines outside Castle Doom received 25 pence per sale.

Most of the 450 fans in attendance chose to pay eight quid for a seat in the new stand (capacity 700), with the old wooden construction opposite reserved for dozens of under-12s (whose half-time penalties and seven-a-side games were a damn sight more entertaining than the dreadful adult dross served up before and afterwards). Those standing on the Tryst Road terracing held their bucking umbrellas two-handed and wide-stanced, like trainee Jedi knights struggling to control activated light-sabres. Yellow light blazed from a farmhouse on the horizon, beyond which pastoral purgatory beckoned. Even before kick-off my teeth were chattering because of the damp cold, and combined with the by-now furious facial tic, smoking a cigarette through a prised-open gap in my scarf proved to be a good trick (especially without setting my eyelashes alight).

In the opening minute the Warriors' strikeforce of Paul Hunter and Ian Little missed two gilt-edged sitters. Referee George Simpson from Peterhead, who'd officiated impressively at Glebe Park, again tried to let the game flow, but both sets of players were incapable of matching the *skill* standard exhibited by their under-12 teams. Played at 100 miles an hour, it was like watching 20 brass monkeys on motorised roller-skates. Stenhousemuir's best player was probably centre-half Graeme Armstrong, a veteran who will never again see the right side of 40. Although frighteningly fit and psychopathically committed, both sides cancelled each other out by constantly pushing up and congesting the midfield. But give enough brass monkeys enough Mitre footballs and enough unstopwatched time and you will eventually get a goal of Shakespearean superlativeness . . . However, I had to settle for a looping header from Dumbarton's Jim Meechan in the 73rd minute. Stenny keeper Steve Ellinson's head drooped in dismay at his failure either to cut out the cross or to stop the header.

Dumbarton's 1–0 away win was only their second victory of the season (and a week later they recorded their first home win in over a year). New manager and ex-Son Ian Wallace (for whom Brian Clough once paid over a million pounds) was obviously thrilled, as were the excited away supporters who congregated round the tunnel to give their team a standing ovation. The boys from Boghead were certainly the least awful of the two teams. Strip-wise, too, they were streets ahead of Stenny, the Sons reverting to their traditional and attractive all-white kit, apart from two black chest bands separated by a yellow strip. (Yellow hoop notwithstanding, this was the brilliant dog's bollix design I selected for my Subbuteo team as a young teenager in the early '70s.) Stenhousemuir out-barfed Berwick in the gestalt jeremiading of their jerseys. The maroon torsoes were okay, but with the upper arms patterned with a diamond patchwork and the elbow-to-wrist segments delineated by white stripes, the overall effect was gorge-raising.

After this defeat the Warriors were definitely out of the promotion race, having already been first-round casualties in three cup competitions (including a game against East Stirling). Indeed, Dumbarton's revival could eventually drag Stenhousemuir into a relegation dog-fight. Another giant-killing run in the Scottish Cup is all that Stenny supporters can realistically hope for, along with mid-table security.

Although home by 6.30 p.m., I had been bored rigid, wet through and frozen solid. Three days later, late-night sub-editors were rehashing their annual 'Scotland in Winter Snow Shock' headlines, and the Tuesday night East Fife v Morton game fell victim to the freezing conditions (along with the reserve fixture between Stenhousemuir and Arbroath). On the same day, Mintel published a report on consumer attitudes which revealed that Scotland had the most fanatical football fans in Britain, attending more games than their English counterparts and being more supportive of their local clubs (rather than glory-hunting with bigger and more glamorous teams). At £495 the dossier was designed for club commercial managers, keen for hints on how to exploit and cash in on supporters' loyalty.

For Stenhousemuir the arithmetic just doesn't seem to add up. Their few local fans may be loyal to the point of financial kamikaze-ism, but if they can all be accommodated in a 700-seat stand how can Stenny hope to survive, never mind prosper? A week after this game, Queen of the South chairman Norman Blount told Ken Gallacher of *The Herald*: 'I truly believe that it is crazy to have 40 clubs in a country of five and a half million people . . . By the turn of the century I believe that there will be just 20 to 24 senior clubs left in Scotland. The others will have been forced to shut up shop or will have been amalgamated with another team in their locality.' With Bosman deflating, if not destroying, transfer-fee income for clubs like the Warriors, off-the-field commercial activities become all the more important. Ochilview's new grandstand incorporates catering facilities, and the Saturday High-Teas advertised in the programme would probably have done great business after the match if they had not been served from six o'clock (over an hour after everyone had gone home!). The new souvenir shop may be part of the answer, but only if it supplies mail-order catalogues for the English, Norwegian and Indian Warriors.

Personally I get enough letter-box junk and I certainly wouldn't want to be on any such mailing list — although no doubt fawn dufflecoats and club-crested canned herring would be big selling lines for Norwegian subscribers.

VICTORIA PARK
Ross County v Cowdenbeath
Third Division, 23.11.96

If I hadn't been in possession of a free but date-specific travel pass, courtesy
of ScotRail, the Arctic conditions sweeping across Scotland would
definitely have persuaded me to switch destinations from Dingwall to
Dundee (Tannadice having the benefit of undersoil heating). Postponements in all the divisions had started being announced as early as Friday
afternoon. Although an official pitch inspection was scheduled for Victoria
Park at 9.30 a.m. on Saturday morning, I nevertheless telephoned the
ground at 8.10 a.m. from Perth (where I had to change trains). The Ross
County groundsman Dougie MacDonald, who used to tend the turf at
Murrayfield along with 23 assistants, had already walked around the
covered pitch and given his personal green-light opinion. Joining the late
Glasgow–Inverness train my hopes were rising, but by Dalwhinnie a white-
out blizzard was delaying the service still further. Through the FM static of
my Walkman, a moronic Moray Firth DJ warned about the possible closure
of the A9 to traffic because of the blanket snow cover. Convinced the game
would be off and/or that I would fail to make the Thurso connection at
Inverness, I cursed myself for lazily making do with Easter Road as far back
as Game Two in balmy August (Hibernian's ground being equipped with
undersoil heating and with Aberdeen scheduled to play an away fixture
there at the same time as the Ross County v Cowdenbeath clash). The
Thurso Sprinter was held back for ten minutes, though, and the 15-mile
journey through Ross-shire revealed a temperate miracle of micro-
climatology. Disembarking at Dingwall, green hillsides, blue skies and a
shimmering sun greeted my arrival.

With over three hours to spare, I climbed the hill with the Hector
MacDonald Monument at its summit. Above the crenellated parapet of the
high tower, cast-iron cannon protruded and a Saltire fluttered in the gentle
breeze. The Scottish vernacular architecture of the town nestled between
snow-covered peaks, with the still waters of the Cromarty Firth providing
a stunning backdrop. Victoria Park looked smartly modern but tastefully in
proportion, sandwiched – but only because of the perspective – in between
the train station and the expanse of water. Never having been further north
than Oban, Perth or Aberdeen – or out of them – I realised what I had been
missing all my life. Smoking a Marlboro in the well-tended graveyard, surrounded by '1995s', the scenery was beautiful beyond Central Belt belief.

Walking back down into Dingwall I felt sentimentally and seminally
Scottish, especially when a blue electrician's van in a carpark revealed the

self-employed sparky's name as 'D. Rennie'. Rennies, Benzies, Benvies and Bennies are common patronymics in the North-East, and I felt a satisfyingly *imagined* bond with my ancestors and forefathers whose short lives in this land of sempiternal stone and seasonal snow had resulted in my existence, in this present synapse of time and space, through a long series of slight deviations in double-helixed bacterial DNA. (The mad McMillans of Knap on my mother's side, from the Mull of Kintyre on the West Coast, I'll leave out of this ancestral equation, even if I carry the genes in my low-grade lunacy and the clan title in my middle name.)

Ah, all those mushroom-masticating jesters with pig bladders on a stick, shebeen-shickered foot sodjers and ricket-ridden, clapped-out crofters from whom I am descended . . . Not being a self-obsessed celeb or deluded nobody, if I were regressed through *risible* reincarnated lives, I wouldn't expect to have been Kenneth MacAlpin, Mary Queen of Scots' gynae-cologist or even Sir Alec Douglas-Home's mentally retarded wet-nurse.

Ravenous with a rushed cold-croissant breakfast still heavy in my stomach, even after seven hours, I swithered between a Wimpy and a 'tea shoppe' in the High Street. The latter also sold knitwear and was a big mistake. Everything on the menu came out of a microwave and my request for a cooked breakfast had the waitress tapping her size 12 Doc Marten's with ill-disguised impatience. 'Bridie and beans' turned out to be partly defrosted meat-substitute with tomato sauce so overheated that the beans in it bubbled like lava. I pushed most of it away uneaten. No wonder the ex-head of the Scottish Tourist Board, Alan Deveraux, used to get so upset at standards of Scottish service that he sometimes felt like knotting a long tartan scarf round his scrawny English neck and bungee-jumping off the Forth Railway Bridge.

Ross County were elected to the League in 1994, after Bobby Wilson had led them to their first Highland League championships in 1991 and 1992, years which also saw senior clubs Queen of the South and Forfar being turned over 6–2 and 4–0 respectively in Scottish Cup shocks. After two years without quite clinching promotion to Division Two, Wilson was sensationally sacked and the untried Neale Cooper appointed in his place. County's opening day defeat to Queen's Park, which I saw, was followed by five further consecutive defeats. Going into this game, however, County had gained 25 points from their last 11 games (out of a possible 33) and Cooper had been named Bell's Third Division Manager of the Month for October.

Americans can talk for hours about the 'personalities' of ball parks, and before kick-off Victoria Park would have to be described using adjectives such as pretty, pastoral, petite, smart, neat, scenic, bijou, cute and nautic.

After three o'clock a crowd of 1,832 – less than a third of the stadium's capacity – turned it into a passionate little spitfire of a ground. The fairly douce denizens of Dingwall were demanding no less than the complete destruction of League-leaders Cowdenbeath, and in a frantic opening period the visiting Blue Brazil were sweating aristocratically coloured blood and getting their nuts well and truly squeezed. Cooper 'directed' proceedings with windmilling arms and violently vibrating vocal cords, jumping up and down like an irate baseball coach.

The most popular viewing area was the six-quid Jail End, but I soon stopped leaning on one of this covered terrace's stainless steel crush-barriers because I could feel its cold surface conducting the life-heat out of me. The open Jubilee End for away fans held about a dozen matchstick men lifted straight from a Lowry canvas – like the rare Far North canvas entitled *Old Houses, Wick* (bought for £40 in 1947 and auctioned for £122,000 just after this match) – but when County's Derek Adams scored a 21st-minute penalty half of them leapt into celebrating life. The 320-seat Main Stand, a secateured-in-half metal cornflakes box, seemed to be full of sponsors, officials and other holders of complimentaries. The one-year-old East Stand was held up by the now compulsory cantilevers and it can seat up to 1,200. The pencil-thin grey floodlight poles were impressively invisible (unlike, say, Partick Thistle's Redwood tree-trunks). With plenty of surrounding room for further expansion and training pitches, County obviously haven't spent over a million upgrading their stadium in order to bounce around in the Third Division indefinitely. If the team's no-nonsense style fails to reflect the attractive surroundings, no one in Dingwall will be complaining if a kick-and-Highland-charge approach secures promotion. Cowden played some silky soccer before half-time, hitting the bar and having a perfectly good goal chalked off for offside by stand-side assistant referee I.G. Frickleton, but County were cynically confident enough to soak up the pressure and pile forward on the break.

In the second half Cowden improved further, almost living up to their ridiculous nickname. But while Steve Hutchinson in the County goal was performing heroics, his opposite number Neil Russell was undergoing a goal-kicking nervous breakdown, initiated by the cruel County fans behind his goal booing and hissing during every run-up. Perfectly audible shouts of 'Ee-aw, ee-aw' and 'Ya fuckin' donkey' effectively destroyed his distribution, to the extent that simple back-passes were necessitating nervous and acutely angled goal-line clearances. The Jail End jabberwockies even managed to so demoralise Russell that he dropped to his knees in frustration at one point.

In the final minutes County substitute Stuart Golabeck had the game's second legitimate goal disallowed by flag-happy Frickleton, whose gutless decision was probably rationalised internally as follows: *I've fucked up for one team in the first half so if I fuck up equally erroneously for their opponents in the second I'll maybe keep everyone happy* . . . Fat fucking chance. If looks could kill, long hard dagger stares from both County and Cowden players during the 90 minutes would have resulted in Frickleton's riddled corpse only being identifiable by post-mortem reference to his dental records (or by checking the name-tags sewn into his black thermal gloves).

A 1–0 Ross County victory may have flattered the hosts, but by grinding out another victory they rose to second place, one point behind Caley Thistle. I was delighted at having managed to get to a game that was on – one that even had a goal and which had been entertaining to watch – but I was ecstatic about having bagged Britain's most northerly senior ground on a day when the window of weather opportunity had seemed totally opaque and frozen shut. While the limp-wristed and concave-chested babies of the Bundesliga are preparing to close down from early December until February, the real hard men of Scottish football are just flexing their rippling muscles and girding their iron loins in anticipation of playing *two* games per week, in conditions that vary from physically unpleasant to brutally bone-breaking. Why the calls for summer soccer when Scotland doesn't even need a winter shut-down?

As I waited at the postcard-pretty but eerily deserted Dingwall Station, I imagined myself into the mindset of a character out of *Dr Zhivago* – although I struggled not to snigger at the thought of being exiled for writing poetry – killing time at a lonely station on the Trans-Siberian line. But with no Lara/Julie Christie to impress I wrapped my Werder Bremen scarf around my freezing napper and accompanied Sheryl Crow on air guitar as she sang 'Every Day is a Winding Road' on the Moray Firth Scottish Top 40. When the 19.11 from Kyle of Lochalsh failed to appear on time, I began to pace up and down while chain-smoking in a decidedly unheroic manner. With no later or Sunday services to Inverness I saw myself freezing to death right there on the south-bound platform. (Being real life, the waiting-room was of course locked, thereby preventing me from sheltering inside and burning the dot-matrix-printed pages of my manuscript in the fireplace page by page, minute by minute, in order to stay alive, which may have prevented publication of this book but would surely have persuaded any Julie Christie-lookalike to succumb to my increasingly hysterical requests for shared bodily warming and unsheathed penetration.) The train arrived ten minutes late.

The Glasgow train pulled out of Inverness on schedule at 20.02, and as the only passenger I had two carriages all to myself. A surprising number of human snowmen stomped gratefully on board between the winter-wonderland stations of Carrbridge and Pitlochry. Changing at Stirling, the cold air stung my face and seared my lungs as I waited a very long 15 minutes.

I was back in the ice-cold flat half an hour after midnight, where I jumped under my bedcovers fully clothed and watched the final sketch in Woody Allen's movie *Everything You Always Wanted to Know About Sex* (the skit about Allen's semen tadpole panicking about being launched into the hairy black anus of the love that dare not speak its name reducing me to hysterics once more).

I slept until well after noon, when I finally got to indulge in a lip-smacking cooked breakfast of bacon, eggs, tomato, toast, coffee and cigarette. Pleasantly full, I watched the Coca-Cola Cup final on BBC Scotland, live from Parkhead but presented by dead-eyed Dougie Donnelly. It was a terrific match and, with Rangers winning 4–3, it had the perfect outcome. As a Celtic fan, not rooting for the maroon Huns of Hearts may seem strange, but whenever these clubs meet I'm emotionally ambivalent about the result. Rangers have won so much recently I'm almost inured against their success, but as a Glaswegian living in Edinburgh, the Jambos defeat meant that I would still be able to wind up supporters of the supposed Third Force in Scottish football, who haven't won anything since 1962.

Even if Ross County don't progress to contesting cup finals or Premier League fixtures, I'll be back at Victoria Park at some point. The circled '21' on the wall-map of Scotland in my study looks splendidly isolated, and I know I'll get many hours of pleasure just from looking at it and remembering my seven and a half hours in sunny, if sub-zero, Dingwall.

LINKS PARK
Montrose v Albion Rovers
Third Division, 30.11.96

A crowd of 10,000 lined the Royal Mile to gawp mindlessly at the Stone of Destiny, encased in a bullet-proof perspex bubble, as it made the short journey from Holyrood Palace to Edinburgh Castle. As I walked along Regent Terrace high above the procession, I speculated on what James Graham, Marquis of Montrose (1612–50), would have made of the bizarre proceedings. Not someone to do things by halves, he would either have insisted on taking the wheel of the converted 'Stonemobile' jeep or he would have been in position beside me, hunkered down with carefully calibrated mortars. The only true hero to come out of Montrose, the 'Great Marquess' let loose thousands of drunken Irishmen and wild Highlanders, but led them brilliantly as a military genius in defence of the Catholic monarchy. In 1650 the handsome, cultured and liberal aristocrat was hung, drawn and quartered in the Old Town's Market Cross. More than 300 years after his death, not only are his beloved Stuarts no longer on the throne but his country has disappeared (even if it was an independent nation he was willing to subdue by force to keep rebel Covenanters and Cromwellians under royal yoke). Passing the old Royal High School – mothballed since 1979 as Scotland's designated site for a devolved parliament – my heart sank at the positive, puffed-up publicity the sandstone cludgie cover was generating, its return from London being no more than a calculated and empty gesture, a political PR stunt and sloppily sentimental sop.

By two o'clock I was sitting on beachfront steps at Montrose Bay, watching wild seahorses crashing against the rocky sea defences. To my right a lighthouse blinked reassuringly, while behind me the deserted and locked amusement arcade, toilet pavilion and gothic ice-cream parlour were closed for the winter. I felt like a character in a French art-house movie (set in an out-of-season Normandy resort like Deauville and directed by Eric Rohmer) or a Ray Bradbury cipher tele-transported to a winterish 'Brooklyn Beach'. Smoking furiously, I continued to re-read Richard Ford's novel *The Sportswriter*, second time around identifying more with successful suicide Walter Luckett than with jaundiced journo Frank Boscombe. Personally, I've always indulged in pseudo-sincere 'existential angst', but play head games like this for long enough and psychological trap-doors of real despair and genuine depression will open up. Since the East Stirling game at the beginning of November I'd been punishing myself with worst-scenario-won't-go-away trains of thought (which had been rolling past the downed barriers of cerebral crossing-points like never-ending, hitched-

127

together boxcars of Amtrak rolling-stock). Indeed, the rail network connecting external existence to personal perception isn't a fixed, fair and facilitating infrastructure; in the real lived world it operates a random, irrational and unpredictable timetable (including late, cancelled and crashed services). On our personal platforms we wait and fret about intimations of our own mortality, insignificance and inferiority. Solid structure, rigid identity and hard meaning are not stations where most of us alight or embark, even if our insatiable egos announce them as such over blaring internal Tannoy systems.

Free-floating-plus-event-specific anxiety and gargantuan guilt overwhelmed me. Aware of the *rational* inappropriateness of my feelings, what was causing my maudlin misery? Presumably the corporeal source of my consciousness – the amalgam of brain cells and molecules oscillating across my neocortex at 40 hertz – was still the same (or was it?). And although self-pity was the 'sole' object of my conscious attention, I did of course feel other things bubbling away underneath, or in the background, or in the wings of my psyche (including hope for an exciting game and happiness at being beside the seaside on such a mild day). Facing the North Sea of Faith, Montrose Bay could as well have been the Dover Beach of Matthew Arnold's poem – the incoming tide of alienation was pounding away at the molecular rocks of my mental defences.

'Are ye all right, son?' asked a tweedie old dear out walking her Highland terrier.

Psychologically disintegrating, Missus. 'Yes, thank you . . . Just allergic to my own bloody cigarette smoke!'

Plodding back across the sand-dunes, grassland and terraced streets, I was outside the entrance to Links Park within ten minutes (another five and I'd have been back in the sandstoney solid High Street). The positioning of the town is definitely strangely skewed, 'fronting' as it does the mudflats of the inland tidal basin rather than the four-mile-long beach.

A complimentary programme at the turnstile had me blocking the way in confused gratitude. At six quid for the terracing, admission prices hadn't been bumped up to compensate and the publication was glossily bound and full of well-designed pages. Local businesses advertised extensively and anything connected with the club was smothered in sponsorship – from players through ballboys to goals scored. The club shop advertised an impressive range, but after psyching myself up to ask for a pair of Montrose FC 'Ladies Knickers' at £2.50, I was deflated to hear that early-arriving Albion fans had already bought up the entire stock – and some were already wearing them (on their heads!). Duthies and Sons supplied the single

Ah, the romance of the Scottish Cup . . . Recreation Park minutes before the
Alloa Athletic–Hawick Royal Albert tie kicks off

A Swedish Sunderland-supporting soccerate at Station Park (Anders)

April in Inverness by the banks of the Caledonian Canal. Hilarious or what?...

The loneliness of the long-lensed photographer at Arbroath's Gayfield

Clyde's Eddie 'Snoop Doggy Dog' Annand gets substituted at Broadwood. Soon after, the lure of the Dens Park dog-track proved irresistible . . .

Scotland versus Sweden at Ibrox Stadium – one of the best European stadiums that money can buy. Rangers, however, have yet to live up to their refurbished surroundings

From the utterly sublime (high above Ross County's Victoria Park) . . .

. . . to the bloody ridiculous (locked inside Cowdenbeath's Central Park)

Henry Smith fails to prevent Hamilton Accies taking the lead at Somerset Park

Livingston's Almondvale Stadium's 'horseshoe' design . . . in other words, it's not yet finished. Note the attractive New Town surroundings . . .

The Behind-the-Wall Gang at Cliftonhill almost outnumber paying Albion Rovers fans

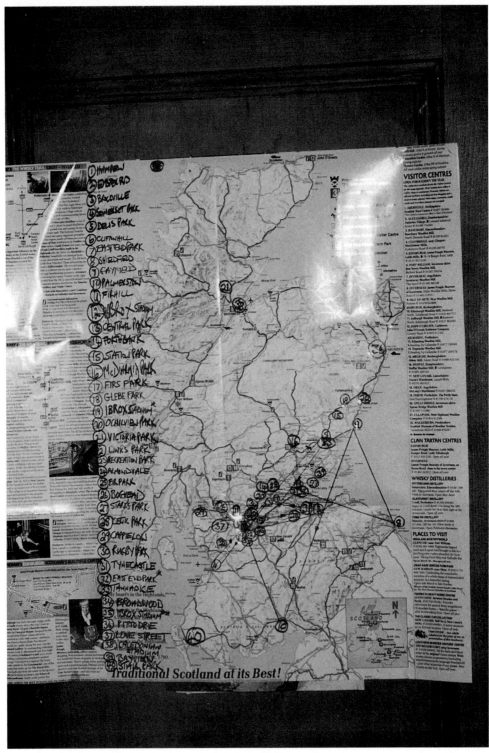

Mission accomplished. However this route was undertaken, it wasn't alphabetically (or with military planning)

'Montrose FC Club Car', while Angus Fertilizers Ltd's copyline read 'Covering Scotland in Shit' (well, almost).

Compared to tiny Brechin's Glebe Park, big Montrose's Links Park was a major disappointment. The cantilevered Main Stand went up in 1992, apparently designed by a Neo-Brutalist sadist. The exposed roof girders made the covering look like a bolted-on factory roof and neither end section had any protective side-walling to prevent howling winds from buffeting the seated supporters. Although it can accommodate almost 1,300 people, would not the old wooden stand have been more in keeping with the surroundings? The one million pounds that the new stand cost could have been used to improve the rest of the ground. (The Gable Endies' highest attendance for the season had been a mere 838, in September against Angus rivals Arbroath.) I stood under the covered Wellington Street terrace, while the Albion fans congregated opposite the stand on a grass verge. The Union Row end was a grassy knoll, too. The hideous concrete floodlight poles were topped by BhS lampshades lit by low-voltage fairylight bulbs.

Even with 634 fans inside Links Park, the atmosphere was apathetic in the extreme. A 50-something fan believed that the town was almost completely indifferent to the club's fortunes (and had always been so except for early in 1976 when Montrose looked like achieving promotion to the top flight for the first time in their history; eventually they missed out on the Premier League by one place). This die-hard fan had been at Links Park the previous Tuesday, when the game against East Stirling had been the only Scottish fixture to beat the freeze. 'Cauld enough tae collapse', he had nipped out at half-time to the next-door British Legion club 'fir a heat and a wee snifter'. Just over 300 had attended this 1–0 win.

Managed by Scotland's first black boss Dave Smith, who had turned Whitehill Welfare into non-League entrepreneurial winners, the Gable Endies threatened to overwhelm injury-hit and on-the-slide Albion Rovers. Veteran hitman Colin McGlashan walloped them ahead after only 11 minutes. (The Coatbridge side had been mooting the possibility of a name change, to incorporate the name of the town, but after a dire first-half performance any thoughts I had of writing in and suggesting 'Coatbridge Celtic' were completely dispelled; 'Perfidious Albion' would have been more appropriate.)

At 3.45 p.m. the temperature begun to plummet alarmingly and I walked round the low dividing wall made of light insulating bricks to try and keep warm. Caught at the exposed end after the re-start, the Montrose strikers were aiming for my head with the blue-and-white Mitre match ball. Self-consciously trying to avoid its flight path, I made my way back, ducking and diving. Back behind my crush-barrier I was just in time to see Montrose captain Mark Haro rise like a Greek gonk to nod the ball past a helpless Cammy Duncan, but McGlashan helped the goal-bound header over the line (eliciting the post-match comment from Haro that Glash the Bash was 'a greedy bastard'). With ten minutes left, Albion's Neil McKilligan shot home for a deserved consolation (turning this into the first game in *eight* where I had seen both sides score). Only David Larter in the 'Mo' goal prevented his dissolving defence and the visitors' pepped-up attack from combining to create an undeserved equaliser. Montrose's 2–1 win kept them second top on goal difference behind Caley Thistle (whose 4–1 victory at Gayfield prompted the Arbroath directors to sack John Brogan, the ninth managerial casualty of the season even without December having been reached; then three days into his family's advent-calendar-door-opening, Kilmarnock's Alex Totten got the old ho-heave-ho).

With half an hour to wait in the wonderfully warm Montrose Station, I spotted a hunched figure scribbling into a reporter's notebook, someone I correctly guessed to be a Dundee Press Agency stringer. Having covered the Tuesday-night game, tyro match-reporter Kenneth Stephen admitted he'd just switched from an existentialist-narcissistic overcoat like mine to a poncey-but-padded mountaineering anorak. I confirmed that certain *Scotland on Sunday/Sunday Times* (Scotland) match-report introductions – which often include gratuitous references to Wittgenstein, the Wombles or Welsh nationalism – are the result of personal side-bets and pre-match planning. Although I warned him that they are a bitch to write, because of ridiculously tight deadlines, he seemed determined and bright enough to succeed in his ambition to write a match report for one of the two Sunday broadsheets in Scotland. After Stephen's departure at Dundee, his place on the train was taken by two Dunfermline fans whose supporters' bus at Tannadice had left without them. It took until Leuchars for them to thaw out properly.

With talk of a breakaway Superleague and the enforced culling of 'parasitical' wee clubs surfacing again prior to the Montrose match, and with my having visited all four Angus clubs, it seems obvious to me that such a small district cannot expect to enjoy this over-representation at League level indefinitely. Who should survive? Arbroath? Yes. Forfar? Screw them (as manager Tommy Campbell chose to do when accepting the Arbroath vacancy after Brogan's departure). Brechin City or Montrose? One a tiny town but just off a main northerly road route and with a terrific little stadium; the other a medium-sized population centre served by the Edinburgh–Aberdeen rail line but with a ghastly ground. Hmm . . . Let them go into a *survival* play-off at Pittodrie, Tannadice or Murrayfield? (I'd definitely tune in if such a match were shown live.) Or are these four teams going to exchange places in the bottom two divisions for ever? (NB: only Arbroath have failed to gain promotion to Division Two.)

Inglis's summing up of Montrose, in the updated third paperback edition of *Football Grounds of Britain*, ends with a lonely 'the' – the word and full-stop 'future.' having slipped through a sloppy copy-editor's fingers. Fans of the Gable Endies will be hoping this isn't a prophetic sign or ominous omen. But maybe Montrose have already hit rock bottom and recovered, because in 1993 their involvement in an Albion Rovers v Montrose fixture went into the record books as the worst-attended senior match in British League history, having attracted a paltry 112 paying punters.

Back in Edinburgh by eight o'clock, I looked forward to visiting the Stone of Destiny in its new home. With a £5.50 entrance fee for Edinburgh Castle, it may cost £1.50 more to view than when it rested beneath the Coronation Chair in Westminster Abbey, but the savings in air/rail/coach fares to London make it one helluva bargain. And, unlike a devolved parliament, we Scots won't be paying an extra three pence in the pound income tax for the pleasure and honour of having it. Christ . . .

RECREATION PARK
Alloa Athletic v Hawick Royal Albert
Scottish Cup, First Round, 7.12.96

The rich get richer and the poor get poorer – in football as in life. If Alan
Shearer is successful in copyrighting his name, like Gazza, cash-strapped
but constantly name-checked Jean-Marc Bosman might be tempted to
follow suit. In August Alloa manager Tom Hendrie was gobsmacked when
a transfer tribunal ruled that four of his summer signings (from Berwick
and East Stirling) were to cost the Wasps £68,000. Although the players
had been able to move because of freedom-of-contract (introduced in the
1980s), Alloa still had to pay a transfer fee to the two clubs which retained
the players' registrations. Because the Bosman ruling was not adopted
internally within the Scottish game, the floodgates have opened to cheap
foreign imports – who, if out of contract, can be signed for the price of
personal terms alone. Alloa's early-season experience set a lot of Scottish
scouts scurrying to Scandinavia and the Continent (although none tried to
sign Bosman himself, despite this journeyman pro's experience of playing in
the Belgian second division).[1] Any possible financial crisis for Hendrie's
Third Division outfit was averted, however, when they drew Celtic in the
Coca-Cola Cup in September. But because Recreation Park holds a maximum of 4,111, the home tie was moved to 'neutral' Firhill (in Glasgow!),
where the crowd of 12,582 generated enough revenue to make up for the
inevitable 5–1 humping by the Hoops. Lying fourth in the League before
the visit of Hawick Royal Albert, the 'romance of the Cup' for Alloa meant
dreaming of masochistic humiliation at Parkhead or Ibrox in a later round,
any gang-banging goal orgy at their expense being worth enduring for a
multi-orgasmic pay-day.

With a bad overnight frost again playing havoc with the fixture list,
Alloa went to quite extraordinary lengths to get this game on (unlike
Stirling Albion seven miles up the road, whose First Division game was
postponed on the Friday). Five out of six Alloa directors joined supporters
in manoeuvring hired portable Calor Gas heaters in a successful attempt to
thaw out the pitch. So effective were they that the slick surface soon
resembled a soccer-school skid pan. Not to be defeated, groundsman Lachie
McKinnon sucked up excess water with an industrial carpet cleaner and
then deposited every available grain of sand, top-dressing and compost all
over the watery green swathe. For future fathers taking the field, it's only
to be hoped that McKinnon wasn't shovelling spare supplies of fertiliser,
fungicide, weedkiller and brewing yeast all over the shop (although the
surrealistic missed chances that were to follow, on a pitch that didn't cut up

and which took a stud, suggested that the Alloa forwards were high on either chemical fumes or DIF-118s from spiked Sweetex containers).

With a second pitch inspection scheduled for one o'clock, I sat in a shuddering Bluebird coach at Edinburgh's St Andrew's Bus Station waiting for it to leave at 12.45, and tuned into Radio Scotland on my Walkman. (If the game had been called off, I intended to pull the emergency-stop handle at Corstorphine and walk back to Tynecastle for a Hearts v Raith Premier game which, predictably, ended 0–0.) The zigzagging bus route took us through the industrial inferno of Grangemouth – a BP company town laid out by architects Escher, Dalí and Bosch and which only mentally-ill executives from the Chemical Division choose to live in – over the Kincardine Bridge into Fife and then back into the Forth Valley. Arriving in Skolville/All-oh-ha – so nicknamed because of the plethora of breweries and Hawaiian climate – a fine smirr of rain was falling, and the dank coldness chilled me to my fine-china bone. In Barnado's I bought a 40p copy of the *Daily Telegraph*'s guide book *Working Abroad* (1988), which I will read cover to cover like a novel.[2]

Recreation Park was shrouded in freezing fog. Six pounds paid at one of the two turnstiles revealed an Aladdin's Cave that had been turned over by violently destructive tomb-robbers. Three sides of the ground were almost flat terracing, with only one long crush-barrier serving as a perimeter surround. The Main Stand cost another quid to enter and once inside this non-cantilevered, corrugated open coffin – erected in 1991 – I found the plastic bucket seating to be a literal pain in the spine. What is the point of seats with no sodding seat-backs? The stand cost £350,000 to build but can only accommodate 426. Surely this wasn't going to be another tiresome re-run of Cowdenbeath, East Stirling or Stenhousemuir? A delicious hot pie, a tasty cup of chicken soup and an excellent glossy programme helped revive my spirits.

The Alberts, who don't even play in the East of Scotland League's *Premier* Division, had travelled up over 100 miles from their base in the Borders. For once the rugby-obsessed market town of Hawick had become a centre of national media attention, what with midweek blizzards leaving thousands of homes without electricity and a local referendum being held on whether 'the fair sex' should be permitted to participate in the Common Riding in June (the latter issue and loaded wording of the questionnaire resulting in family schisms and death threats). Managed by Graham Halfpenny, the Alberts had been unable to train together because of the Arctic weather and more than double the 100 fans they brought with them would have travelled if they hadn't been snow-bound in their unheated houses. (If ScottishPower had been the team's shirt sponsor, the players would probably have turned out bare-chested as a sign of protest.) Five years previously to the day Alloa had hammered Hawick 7–1 at Recreation Park in the same round of the Scottish Cup (when the 'Road to Hampden' hadn't yet been billboarded at every romantic junction by current corporate carpet-baggers Tennents Lager). Although I was expecting a few goals, an amusingly enthralling encounter was the last thing I anticipated seeing.

After a surprisingly skilful, shoot-on-sight start, the Alberts were eventually pinned back. Neil Sinclair, a 32-year-old knitwear-factory worker, then began to do a passable imitation of Lev Yachin, even if some of the unorthodox saves from the black-jerseyed Hawick keeper suggested the nickname 'Blackpool Tower' rather than 'Eiffel'. After a quite breath-taking double save in the 14th minute, his dazed defenders failed to focus properly for the resulting corner. Wasp centre-forward Peter Dwyer headed home unmarked, utilising the powerful neck muscles of a policeman trained to defend himself using the 'Glasgow kiss' manoeuvre. End-to-end football followed, and Callum Graham coolly slotted the ball past Mike Monaghan in the 30th minute to equalise, aided and abetted in beating the Alloa offside trap by 22-year-old Jason Cockburn. (In January 1994 teenage Cockburn had played for Selkirk against Arbroath in a home first-round Scottish Cup-tie, the Border team losing 3–0. I wrote up my *excellent* match report in the back of a photographer's speeding Opel, having left at the full-time whistle to get back to Edinburgh in time to meet a viciously tight deadline. *Scotland on Sunday*'s coverage of this match was the only Scottish paper's not to include the post-match resignation of Red Lichtie manager Danny McGrain. Who the hell resigns immediately after a 3–0 away win? Not one of my finer moments in sports journalism, as the sports editor did not put it.) Before the break Sinclair pulled off a low one-handed diving save to his right, reminiscent of Gordon Banks's stop against Pelé in Mexico or, less hyperbolically, David Seaman's against Gordon Durie at Wembley.

In the one-way-traffic second half, Sinclair again defied the goalkeeping odds. At 1–1 the Wasp forwards were beginning to lose their sting, unbelievably bad finishing (and luck) keeping the Alberts on course for last-minute giant-killing glory. The action was so thick and fast that the *Sportscene* cameraman was crapping himself when taking 15 seconds to change video cartridges. In the 71st minute, however, another simple corner allowed Paul McAneny to head home unchallenged.

The appalling turn-out of home fans – in a total attendance of 452 – was balanced by their infectious good humour. Each miss and/or save was accompanied by pithy but polite protestations, followed by gales of laughter. When Dwyer saw his hooked shot rebound from the crossbar, leaving a totally open goal, he managed to volley over from all of three yards. Having 'Van Vossened' a sitter, the Wasp fans cheerily consoled themselves with the thought that he had only cost £18,000 from East Stirling. 'Arrest yourself, Dwyer – that right foot could put someone's eye oot.' Stewart Mckay shot home with two minutes left to kill the game at 3–1. A fair result and fantastically funny fixture.

A short bus ride to Stirling, with a quick train connection to Edinburgh, had me home in time for the Lottery draw. It may have taken a long time for Game Three between Falkirk and Albion Rovers to be entertainingly eclipsed, but Game 23 had been worth the wait. Who'd have thought that a fixture played in darkest December at the Recs, between two teams nick-named the Wasps and the Alberts, would have turned out to be a couthy and camp Cup classic? Money may buy success but, with the right attitude, bargain-basement teams on a ball-breaking budget can play exciting, attacking and entertaining football as good as anything their more affluent 'betters' can serve up. And to think I was seriously considering leaving at half-time to catch the last direct bus back to the capital at 4.17 p.m. (and then covering up the fact). Virtue definitely has its own rewards. Although the term 'deserving poor' is offensive to all liberal humanists, Alloa are definitely worthy of a charitable visit by any passing neutrals.

FOOTNOTES

1. Less than a week after this victory, Tom Hendrie did sign a player with experience of the Belgian League . . . Not Jean-Marc Bosman but 31-year-old winger Ally Dick (ex-Spurs and *Ajax*). A free agent after having played in Belgium, Australia and South Africa, Dick should make more chances for Dwyer to score and squander. If this signing was a capital-free coup of a deal, Hearts manager Jim Jeffries probably did even better by securing Dundee's Under-21 striker Jim Hamilton for around £200,000. This 'steal' was made possible because Dundee's directors had just called a halt to greyhound racing at Dens Park – the weekly races having cost the cash-strapped club over £800,000! The state-of-the-art kennels are either going to be converted into a 'sin-bin/cooler' for rabid Chic Charnley or refurbished so that Dundee can now try diversifying into the European French Poodle Balloon Football League (a sport that Cadogon's Circus first introduced to Scotland at the Kelvin Hall in the early '70s).

2. Forced to buy nearly all my books second-hand, the late publication of the *Tennent's Lager Scottish Football League Review 1996/97* – in December! – reduced me to near apoplexy when I finally got to hand over £5.95 for it. Having taken over from Younger's Tartan Special as sponsors of the handbook, Tennent's first editorial contribution has seemingly been to dispense with ticket-price information (stupid and incomprehensible bar graphs of each team's ten-year record being substituted in place of prices).

ALMONDVALE STADIUM
Livingston v Ayr United
Second Division, 14.12.96

For the first three months of season 1995–96 I could have watched 'Livingston FC' by cycling along to Edinburgh's Commonwealth stadium (where
the renamed Meadowbank Thistle played on until November, after which
Livingston moved to a purpose-built ground in the New Town of the same
name). I was one of the 473 mourners who attended Thistle's last home
game – a 1–0 win over Stenhousemuir on Friday, 5 May 1995 – and, like the
vast majority of these emotional fans bidding a fond and final farewell, I
never contemplated stepping inside the 16,000-capacity athletics stadium
ever again. Dozens of 'rebel' fans had been locked out of the final home
fixture for orchestrating a vitriolic campaign against chairman Bill Hunter
which included giving him Nazi salutes and chanting 'Blobby, Blobby,
Blobby! Out, Out, Out!' The portly Hunter responded by hiring black-
bomber-jacketed Rock Steady security guards, who ejected the more vocal
protestors.

Like distraught relatives and supporters of innocent execution victims,
the rebels congregated on Marionville Road to watch the demise of their
21-year-old club through gaps in the perimeter fencing. Hunter would have
made a good prison governor in Texas, where inmates being walked to the
electric chair are denied last requests for a cigarette on the grounds that it
would be 'inimical to their long-term health'.

But there was to be no last-minute reprieve from the President (of the
SFA) for the team who had been elected to the League in 1974, albeit in the
form of works team Ferranti Thistle (who immediately moved from their
inadequate ground in Pilton to Meadowbank and changed their unacceptably commercial name accordingly). Crowds may have continued to
average less than 300, after a start which saw Meadowbank Thistle lose
their first 15 matches, but contrary to the negative misinformation
promulgated by Hunter when browbeating opponents against a move,
Thistle were never again a joke club (despite attracting celebrity fans like
John Peel and Rick Wakeman). Promotion to the Premier League in 1988
was only denied by yet another bout of League reconstruction. The
arguments for the 15-mile move to the wilds of West Lothian, to a town of
50,000 inhabitants, may have made social, economic and footballing sense –
all of which have been more than vindicated – but the death of the Thistle
has left a small pocket of real bereavement on the east side of the capital.

Livingston Bus Station resembled a ramshackle aircraft hangar converted
into an assembly-point terminus for WWII refugees (although the double-

deckered charabanc rumbled on as far as Bathgate). Stepping outside into a gale-force wind, the clocktower of the Almondvale Shopping Centre was the first thing I noticed. Designated as the 'town centre', this cathedral to consumer capitalism certainly had no shortage of cash-contributing supplicants. Walking round the massive mall, in a futile attempt to get my hungover bearings, it became clear that I had stumbled on the retailing equivalent of an elephants' graveyard – Safeway supermarket trollies lay abandoned everywhere, upright and on their sides, in huddled family groups and in solitary isolation. Sickly sapling trees had ripped plastic carrier-bags fluttering from their bare branches. The 'five-minute walk' to Almondvale Stadium took almost an hour, as I negotiated death-dealing dual carriageways, a dizzying number of mini-roundabouts and acres of sprawling carparks. Street life was non-existent, the roads and footpaths being mere conduits for ferrying people between home, work and centralised shops. If Los Angeles is the City of Angels, Livingston is the New Town of Right Angles.

Approaching the ground, I was just in time to see hundreds of balloons being released to herald the official opening of the new 1,500-seater North Stand, which brought the total capacity of the three-sided Stickle-Brick stadium up to 6,000. I joined the large travelling army of Ayr fans in the East Stand, their presence at this top-of-the-table clash contributing significantly to a crowd of 3,542 (the season's biggest turn-out up to then in Division Two). Although outnumbered five-to-one, they created all the atmosphere (the Livvy supporters displaying about as much life as fatally wounded Foreign Legionnaires propped up against fort parapets).

Within 60 seconds Livvy's 35-year-old forward Graham Harvey connected with a Mark Duthie corner, heading home unchallenged from two yards. Thereafter Ayr spent 89 frustrating minutes piling forward but, without the stretchered-off Isaac English and the suspended Steve Kerrigan up front, they flattered to deceive. In a frantic finale Darren Henderson almost dislocated his jaw on his own breastbone, mistiming a simple headed chance at the far post. When John Traynor finally got a screaming piledriver on target, goalkeeper Robert Douglas fingertipped the blurring ball onto the underside of the bar. So it was 1–0 to Livvy, then, in their all-black strip, which allowed them to leapfrog all-in-white Ayr to go top (where only Hamilton were managing to stay in touch with the interchanging leaders and favourites for promotion).

The greatest excitement and controversy had been generated by goal-hero Harvey, a part-timer who once turned down John Greig's Rangers and who now gets up at half five in the morning to work as a postman. Shortly after scoring, 'Harvenelli' almost provoked a riot amongst the cheerily aggressive – but non-racist! – Ayr supporters, by making a fist with a protruding thumb. He moved his hand up and down in a vigorous pumping action over his groin area. The Honest Men from Ayrshire exploded in apoplectic outrage. A good few of their concerned citizens insisted on having a police superintendent record the incident in his notebook – during which time Harvey began fondling his tackle. Seconds before the interval, manager Jim Leishman hauled Harvey off, and a post-match radio report stated that Harvenelli had been whisked to hospital because of a groin injury. After his obscene wanking gesture, this smacked of a quite breath-taking (but impressively imaginative) cover-up.

If insisting on a medical examination in order to give his star striker an 'alibi' was an example of Leishman thinking on his flat feet, he's obviously not the tactically challenged and naïvely unsophisticated old-timer that some commentators take him for. (But any manager with a penchant for penning poetry, even if only McGonagallesque doggerel, would be well advised to file it at the bottom of a sock drawer, rather than reciting it to assembled hacks at press conferences.) Dressed 'scruffy casual' in the latest Sue Ryder autumn collection, combined with what looked like canvas deck shoes, the crack-cocaine-extroverted Leishman kicked the ball back into play during the second half – the kicking-foot slip-on shoe travelling higher and further than the ball. Nevertheless 'the Leish Man' has a track-record of success that cashmere-overcoated graduates of SFA coaching courses would be proud to highlight on their laser-printed CVs. Leishman not only led Livvy to the Third Division Championship last season but at Dun-fermline he secured First and Second Division titles (as well as guiding the Pars to the top of the Premier League in early November 1989). In his own non-iambic words, after having decided that the role of *il penseroso* at Montrose was an affectation, he reflected that: 'I had to decide whether I was going to be a tactical genius or just win championships.'

As the second half dragged on, the bitter wind-chill meant I was becoming as cold as I've ever been. The screen ends of all three stands were woeful windbreaks, truncated design embellishments rather than functional additions. The upward-slanting roofs barely projected beyond the front rows, and despite sitting near the press-box at the back my spectacle lenses began to get obscured by the swirling rain. Built by Ayr chairman Bill Barr's construction company, Almondvale looks as if it was bolted together using identacoded self-assembly flat-packs from MFI's Undecorated Shed stadium range.

The match programme had 40 glossy and colourful pages, well designed but written by dyslexic cliché-mongers. In Lee Bailey's 'Star Check' profile, the player who scored Meadowbank Thistle's last-ever goal chose as his favourite player 'Kenny Dalgleish' (who he?), and his preferred culinary concoction was 'Pasta's [*sic*] and all healthy foods'. Highlighting such admittedly minor copy-editing errors may seem like prejudiced nit-picking, but a bizarre style-guide decision had resulted in 'Livi' as the preferred spelling for the club's diminutive. From *The Scotsman* to *The Sun* they are referred to as 'Livvy' whenever abbreviation is required. (This house style was almost as irritating as the otherwise excellent *Total Football*'s use of the term 'footy' – instead of 'footie'.) And even if spelt correctly, the Livvy Lions is not a nickname that will ever be appearing in press match-reports – not unless the 'Lions' ever have to play away in a European second leg at Millwall's new Den.

Not only are the shirt sponsors the giant multinational Mitsubishi, but page ten of the programme listed almost 60 other corporate sponsors who pump money into the club. Most of Almondvale's construction costs were subsidised by the Football Trust, Livingston Development Corporation and West Lothian Council. The final indication that Livvy will be bankrolled to future Premier status within the planned five years came on the back page, where a full-page ad for NEC requested readers to phone up the Personnel Department to see about securing 'superb career opportunities' (even if only soldering microchips onto semi-conductor circuit boards). With semi-skilled job-seekers able to find easy employment as salary slaves on production lines or at the end of customer-service telephone lines, Livingston's expanding workforce means a growing market for season-ticket sales.

This particular New Town expects to double in size by the end of the century, and with 160,000 people living in West Lothian at present, Livingston FC could not ask for a bigger or better potential fan base. The club rent out Savannah five-a-side pitches, offer opulent function suites for hire and visit local schools to give coaching sessions. Livingston are marketing themselves like a successful soap powder, despite being a monopoly supplier of senior football in the area. 'Life is for Livingston' is the naff New Town slogan, and Livingston and Livvy will undoubtedly grow together. If the football club aren't in the Premier League by 2001, I'll celebrate my 40th birthday by eating a remaindered copy of this book.

On Sunday afternoon I watched Inter Milan lose 4–3 to Sampdoria in the San Siro (courtesy of Channel 4). This game and stadium were everything Livingston versus Ayr United at Almondvale were not – and never will be. Even Lucchese against Atalanta in Serie B would have been infinitely more interesting. God, what a contrast – the quaint little Stadia Porta Elisa in Tuscany and anonymous Almondvale in wet West Lothian . . .

I have seen the future of Scottish football – and it's Stepford soccer played in a soulless stadium, located in a counterfeit city of desiccated dreams and stolen supermarket trollies.

FIR PARK
Motherwell v Dunfermline Athletic
Premier Division, 21.12.96

Christmas was coming, along with accumulating entrails from emaciated footballing turkeys which indicated a looming 'Black Wednesday' for some of Scotland's most chronically cash-strapped clubs. (Authorial bankruptcy was a possibility, too, a bulging bank-book at season's start which had contained almost £2,000 now reduced to an anorexic £50.) Motherwell were in such a parlous, penny-pinching predicament that they were unable to afford even free-transfer players, losing released Peterborough striker Lee Power to destitute Dundee. The Dens Park club, however, were rumoured to be up for sale as a 'not-going-anywhere-fast concern' for as little as £200,000 (the figure Hearts had agreed to pay, in still-to-be-started instalments, for the Dark Blues' Jim Hamilton – despite the Tynecastle outfit being in hock to creditors for £6.5 million). On Thursday, 19 December, Falkirk FC had been fined a whacking £25,000 for fielding ineligible trialist John Clark in a 1–0 home victory over St Mirren. Chairman George Fulston and director Neil Binnie, the Scrooge and Marley of Division One, reacted by sacking tyro manager Eammon Bannon, for what was someone else's administrative *faux pas*, and appointing recently axed Kilmarnock boss Alex Totten as their latest stop-gap-sacrificial-lamb-in-waiting (Brockville's boardroom being a barnstorming bampots' bearpit). The Motherwell game attracted a disappointing 4,529 paying punters, with approximately 500 of these travelling south to support Dunfermline (who were over £1 million in the red with three terraced sides of East End Park to be seated before the year 2000). At Ibrox and Parkhead, however, share prices were booming as the first cash projections for pay-per-view TV receipts were published (after Holland's top clubs had just won the right to negotiate their own TV deals independently of the Dutch FA).

With Celtic's game against the parsimonious Pars on the Wednesday night postponed for a third time, I spent the evening reading *A Christmas Carol* instead, shivering in my garret and salivating with light-headed hunger at C.D.'s descriptions of overloaded festive tables (well, not quite, since the central-heating was on full-blast and I was chain-smoking Marlboros, guzzling mini Bounty bars and slurping mouthfuls of hot milky coffee). Bob Cratchit may only have earned 15 shillings a week, but neither he nor Tiny Tim (a Celtic fan?) would have elicited any lachrymose sympathy from Pierre van Hooijdonk who, during acrimonious contract negotiations, told a Dutch magazine that although £7,000 a *week* was 'good for the homeless' it was chickenfeed to 'an international striker'. Cratchit was paid for his Christmas day off work, albeit grudgingly with much Fergus McCann-type grumbling from old Ebeneezer. Would I be? Better bloody had, or my employer would be getting a Ghost-of-Christmas-Present punch on his capitalist coupon.

The train from Glasgow Central trundled across a wasteland of industrial devastation, a scorched-earth landscape where search-and-destroy monetarists had all but obliterated heavy industry and manufacturing capability. Electricity pylons bestrode the bleak urban sprawl, while beneath the carcinogenic electromagnetism of their low-slung cables flickering fires burned in perforated-oil-drum briers on every deserted street corner and lonely patch of demolished rubble. The closure of the Ravenscraig Steel Works in 1991 had failed to incite the predicted workers' revolution. Instead, after the Tory election victory in 1992, PR companies parachuted into North Lanarkshire armed to their Denplan teeth with press releases and state-of-the-art promotional videos. Bespoke-tailored bureaucrats and jumped-up secretarial PAs established beachheads for Local Enterprise Companies in empty office spaces, from where the local unemployed and low-paid populace were bombarded with brainwashing propaganda hyping 'Training and Development' initiatives as the only way forward to achieving 'a post-industrial renaissance and service economy' (where every laid-off steelworker would be retrained as a data-input operative or feng shui fitter). Motherwell itself was absorbed into an Enterprise Zone, with the freight terminal at Mossend and inward investment by BT and Chungwa taking up some of the unemployed slack (albeit mostly in the form of ex-housewives). The town even acquired its own Heritage Centre – while poor Teesside had to make do with the steelmaking business and expensive plant equipment transferred down south – and a new station on its outskirts called 'Airbles' (for those studying at the local college for qualifications in Leisure and Beauty).

The Brandon Shopping Centre was hooching with C1C2 Christmas consumers, the longest queues snaking up and down inside the flagship Scottish superstore of the discount chain '99p Krackers 99p' (which I patronised with my custom, since I'm technically social class DE or F because of being 'hilariously broke'). Motherwell serves as a shopping and entertainment centre for those living in the dormitory towns of Bargeddie, Whifflet, Shotts, Carluke, Bonkle, Bogside, Dykehead, Waterloo, Swinehill, Roadmeetings, Carfin (a Celtic grotto?) and Larkhall. The last-named is a Rangers stronghold where front doors can only be painted red, white or blue (or all three if combined in the form of a Union Jack). It is also known as the 'Scottish Pretoria' by advertisers on Scottish Television – the original 'licence to print money' regional television franchise – whose media buyers constantly seek three-course-liquid-lunch reassurance from their market researchers and product planners that commissioned commercials will 'maximise the client's media spend in true-blue Larkhall'.

Since my last visit to Fir Park in the mid-1980s, Motherwell's ground had changed out of all recognition. The old Main Stand was still there, though, and still gloriously unextended to run the full-length of the pitch – despite the follyesque presence of a protruding, right-angled steel skeleton. A tenner got me inside the East Enclosure, which I had stood in as open terracing. Now covered and seated, its maximum capacity of 3,218 is rarely approached but the most fervent 'Well fans still choose to congregate there – the most captious soccer supporters ever studied through binoculars by anthropologists from Leicester University's Football Research Unit (with the possible exception of Airdrie season-ticket-holders). Both ends had been redeveloped, the two-tier North Stand being reserved for away supporters and the single-tiered Davie Cooper Stand housing home fans and executive-box fat cats.

The overall effect is weird but wonderful and, like Brechin's Glebe Park, Motherwell's stadium could never be mistaken for anywhere else. As a booze-befuddled bridegroom awakening naked and handcuffed in the centre-circle of Fir Park, after a riotous stag night, you'd at least know exactly where you were (although if you were getting married at Fratton Park, Portsmouth, you'd be in serious trouble). Traditional square floodlight configurations top off four corner towers made of cat's-cradled, criss-crossing tubular steel, and although they look strong enough to support crane cabins, jibbed booms and wrecking balls – and must have been horrendously expensive to erect – they are an integral part of the ground's alluring aesthetic. And not only has Fir Park been transformed into a thing of bizarre beauty, but so has its most effective centre-forward. In the 1970s Willie Pettigrew led the Motherwell front line, a prolific but plug-ugly poacher; since 1993 blond bombshell Tommy Coyne has been bulging the onion bag to the orgasmic delight of female Fir Parkers.

The stadium improvements were financed by a 4–3 victory over Dundee United in the Scottish Cup final of 1991 and the subsequent sale of Tom Boyd and China-doll-fragile Phil O'Donnell to Celtic for a combined total of £2.5 million. Tommy McLean had left the Steel Men in fine shape, having finished third in the league in 1994, and his inexperienced and unproven young replacement Alex McLeish appeared to continue the good work by leading 'Well to second place a year later. But by the end of his second season in charge Big Eck had managed a mangled and stress-fractured Motherwell to a dangerously low eighth place (i.e. third bottom), despite having spent over a million pounds on players like John Hendry, Eddie May, Andy Roddie and the brittle-boned Shaun McSkimming. Motherwell were then the first club to feel the ill-wind generated by the Bosman ruling in August '96, losing Paul Lambert to Borussia Dortmund and Rob McKinnon to Twente Enschede for absolutely no marks or guilders.

Going into the Dunfermline game, Motherwell were again lying eighth and chairman John Chapman had put the club up for sale. As far back as mid-October McLeish had been pondering a move, expressed in a plethora of media interviews, to managerless Hibernian, but Chapman had refused to grant the 'sleeping giants of Leith' permission to approach Big Eck officially, since he was contractually tied to Motherwell. Hibs were unwilling, or unable, to pay Chapman compensation or the punitive fines that would have followed for *luring* McLeish to Easter Road. After vacillation worthy of a doomed prince in a Shakespearean tragedy, Big Eck finally and honourably decided not to go through with the hypocritical farce of 'resigning out of the blue', talking terms with a *suddenly* interested Hibs and then signing on the dotted line.

Considering that Chapman was a qualified butcher, my cold and weevil-hosting pie was a disgusting disgrace. I threw it away because it was stomach-churningly inedible, rather than because another Lanarkshire butcher was then at the centre of the world's second worst ever E-coli outbreak (folk in Wishaw keeling over on an almost daily basis, while in the same Wild West town yet another series of doorstep shootings had broken out). When aggressively asked why I was taking photographs of well-wrapped-up 'Well fans, I introduced myself as Jakob Creutzfeldt of *World Soccer*. (Not being 'professional Glaswegians', none of the placated home fans made deliberately unknowing jokes about half-remembering a J. Creutzfeldt who had been an obscure right-back for Partick Thistle in the 1970s.)

Within seconds of kick-off the lumbering and snorting Dunfermline defence appeared to be suffering from mad-cow disease, although in a slaughterhouse of a second half symptoms of bovine spongiform encephalopathy had spread to the Motherwell back four. Motherwell's outfield players looked like ten horseless jockeys or hyperactive jesters in their new strip design of quartered shirts and shorts – in the traditional but normally segregated colours of amber and claret – but they started impressively. Of the 22 players on display, however, only Coyne and team-mate Mitchell van der Gaag had resisted the fashionable blandishments of hairdressers called Nikki for No. 4 on top and No. 2 back-and-sides clipper cuts. Because of similarities of hairstyle, it took a while to identify the Pars defender who sliced wildly past bald Ian Westwater for a 12th minute own-goal – namely Craig Ireland. Three minutes later begloved Marc Miller equalised from the penalty spot.

Despite 'Well continuing to play patient but far from passive football, the home fans were becoming increasingly irascible. Aberdeen 'reject' Andy Roddie gets a torrid barracking from the Fir Park faithful at the best of times, but the frail winger's sensible decision to wear gloves on a sub-zero afternoon incensed the East Enclosurers. His 'wimpy Jessieness' was ridiculed incessantly, resulting in obviously fragile self-confidence shattering horribly. On the half-hour three sides of Fir Park rose to salute sex-and-goal god Coyne, after he slid home Motherwell's second.

The half-time entertainment consisted of Paul Lambert in the centre-circle making the 50-50 draw from a black bin bag. Back home in Scotland because of the Bundesliga's winter break – from early December to February – his entrance onto the park prompted only a mild ripple of resentful applause. As self-appointed spokesman for the 'Dossers fae the Shire', the editor of the scurrilous 'Well fanzine *One Step Beyond* mused mournfully on how Lambert had suddenly become good enough for Scotland after three games for Dortmund but not after three terrific years for the Fir Parkers. Lambert was actually booed off.

In the second period Motherwell started an artillery bombardment of long balls up the park, to the evident relief of the snail's-paced but dinosaur-sized Dunfermline defenders. Pars forward Andy Smith soon found himself clear with only Stevie Woods to beat from five yards, but the big-eared striker took so long to gain control of the ball ricocheting between his ankles that he was closed down by bald Brian Martin (a competent, and sometimes classy, centre-half who nevertheless looks frighteningly similar to the psychopathic Francis 'Red Dragon' Dolarhyde who torments the beautiful blind woman in the final scrotum-tightening scenes of the Michael Mann movie *Manhunter*). With the chance 'gone', Smith simply blootered the ball through a forest of hairy legs for a 55th minute equaliser. When Ivo den Bieman upended a grateful Roddie heading for the corner flag, Coyne confidently stepped up to take the penalty. After Westwater pulled off a fine diving save, all hell broke loose in the East Enclosure. The atmosphere got even more sulphuric with 15 minutes left when Smith's flapping Dumbos allowed him to hang in the air to head home a hopeful, outswinging free-kick.

With time running out for an equaliser, the Motherwell fans began arguing amongst themselves. Quite frankly, I'd never seen or heard anything quite like it as strangers 12 rows apart started screaming blue murder at one another. Demonic dialectics were breaking out right, left and centre, with one particulary heated exchange over Van der Gaag's footballing ability and sexual proclivities.

Final score: 2–3. The Pars danced in the lower tier of their stand and sang 'Cheerio, cheerio' to the stoney-faced Motherwell masochists who had stayed for the final whistle. For a frozen neutral it had been a stonking stramash, played out in a great stadium. Big Eck's last words on his death-bed may be 'Shoulda gone tae Hibs', since his contract is up in the summer, and he may need to inspire another 23 points from Motherwell's final ten games again this season to ensure survival. (A play-off against Airdrie would be a crowd-control nightmare, what with the tendency of both sets of supporters to start rammies amongst themselves.) Assuming Mother-well stay up, however, the good times will surely return.

Any prospective buyer would inherit a debt-free club with a fine finished stadium. With the Old Firm set to dominate well into the 211th century, Motherwell are one of the few 'town' clubs with the potential to snatch a one-off Premier League pennant (or Championship flag, as they did by winning the League in 1932 and breaking a 27-year duopoly held by Celtic and Rangers). On the other hand, they have been relegated from the Premier League twice since its inception in 1975. If the 'Craig' was the heart of the town, Motherwell FC is its soul. Big Eck may not be the Buzz Lightyear of benighted Lanarkshire, but the cliché-quoting redhead might do worse than to repeat the words of the sold-out Christmas toy if a new owner grills him over his future plans for the team. Namely, 'To infinity and beyond!'

Motherwell may not have been generating enough income to pay staff wages, but their loyal fans are their best asset. They may be terrible moaners but at least they normally moan from *inside* Fir Park on match days, kitted out in an impressive range of casualwear from the club shop. In the event, I did get paid for my Christmas Day off (plus an unexpected Christmas bonus!), and this match was error-ridden but passionately exciting Scottish football at its frantic best. Or should that be worst?

BOGHEAD PARK
Dumbarton v Stranraer
Second Division, 26.12.96

Boxing Day at benumbed Boghead, accompanied by Our Kid. It certainly
beat beachcombing in the Bahamas, hand-in-hand with a brunette beauty
like Sandra Bullock or Benazir Bhutto (or even a blue-stocking blonde
bombshell such as Hazel Irvine).[1] After leaving the car in a side-street, a
shifty-eyed steward (and I'm being deliberately vague here)[2] took us aside
and once convinced we weren't 'Sons of the Rock' let us in for half-price,
cash-in-hand. Lynn was advised to say she was his sister, if anyone asked,
and that I was 'her man'. 'What's your name, then?' she asked, not
unreasonably. 'Need-to-know basis only, darlin' . . . Quick, in youse go.' Her
attention-attracting giggling fit only ceased when she saw the inside, her
jaw hitting the underfoot rubble in disbelief. 'God almighty . . .'

I couldn't quite believe it myself — a ground which out-bomb-sited
Cowdenbeath's Central Park.

The Main Stand seated 303 (and cost another £2.50 to enter!), and
beside it a rickety cover housed most of the hungover home support. The
far side was cordoned off, collapsing terracing (*not* a new £750,000 East
Stand as predicted by Inglis). About two dozen sad sacks from Stranraer
stood under the away enclosure, with Dumbarton Rock and Castle rising
through the gloom in the foreshortened distance. We took shelter from the
imminent rain shower under the Overwood Drive end, from where we could
admire the fine filigreed — and leaking — ironwork of the old Turnberry
Station platform roof.

How the mighty have fallen, the Sons having shared the first ever League
title with Rangers in 1891, before winning it outright in 1892. Even as
recently as 1984–85 Dumbarton were playing in the Premier League, but
they haven't won anything since their two-in-a-row triumph of 1892. For
season 1996–97 Dumbarton had been forced by financial necessity —
specifically, a £300,000 overdraft with the Bank of Scotland — to take in
homeless neighbours Clydebank as lodgers for £30,000 a year (and like
most slum landlords had not spent a penny on improving the footballing
equivalent of a rat-infested hovel, except for improved pitch drainage and
two Portaloos for away fans).

In 1994 the Sons followed Greenock Morton's example by extending
their name to 'Murdo MacLeod's Dumbarton', their eponymous boss
achieving promotion to Division One in May 1995 (albeit by collapsing over
the second-spot promotion line way behind the high-flying 'Ton from
across the water). And 1995–96 turned out to be the start of a nightmare

of record-breaking proportions (25 club records tumbling in this season alone). Three days into the Division One campaign, their media-darling manager moved to Firhill to take charge of 'Murdo MacLeod's Magyars of Maryhill', leaving behind a threadbare squad and dissent-ridden board-room. With an opening day League win secured by MacLeod, and two unlucky Cup exits experienced under new manager Jim Fallon, Dumbarton went into their first away fixture. Long-suffering fan David Carson takes up the horror story: 'A visit to Cappielow was . . . a worry, yet thanks to a penalty and a truly sensational [Chic] Charnley strike we found ourselves 2–0 ahead by the interval. And then a curious thing happened during the break. We were relegated. Not statistically, but in spirit. The way in which we hemmed a ten-man Morton team in our own penalty box for the remainder of the game was a grim portent of things to come. Although it finished 2–1 in Sons' favour, the sunburnt tongues of the back four told their own story.'³

Inevitably, Dumbarton were relegated, but before Fallon resigned at the beginning of November '96 the Sons were surpassing, setting or approaching statistical records of such unmitigated awfulness that the club were beginning to attract the sniggering and circling attention of media vultures from London and beyond. These unwanted claims to fame included four seasons without a Cup-tie success (that's 12 first-round exits), 21 defeats in a row (only a 1–1 draw with Stranraer in August helping to avoid equalling Brechin's record of 23 consecutive losses in 1961–62), 34 League games without a win (a 1–0 away win at Clyde in September still not preventing an all-time bad British record), and finally almost 13 months without a home victory.

Old boy Ian Wallace was appointed on 6 November 1996, and immediately told his shell-shocked squad that 'I want to put the fun back into your lives' (having secured eight points from a possible 120 before Wallace's appointment, some players had been phoning in 'sick' on match days). A last-minute equaliser at Boghead secured a draw against Clyde, and a week later I was at Ochilview to see the Sons beat Stenhousemuir 1–0. Thereafter, hapless Berwick became the first team to lose at Boghead in over a year, and pace-setting Ayr United were humbled 4–1 at Somerset Park. Hamilton then came to Dumbarton and ended Wallace's fairy-tale start.

Wallace had been a 20-year-old goal machine when he moved from Dumbarton to Coventry in 1976 for £80,000. Four years later Brian Clough paid £1.25 million for the dumpy little striker with an orange Afro fright-wig. After playing abroad in France and Portugal, Wallace managed Albion Turkugura and Melbourne Croatia in Australia. The latter often attracted crowds in excess of 10,000, but five years ago he returned to Scotland; unable to get a full-time job in football, he bought a newsagent's shop in Glasgow's douce(ish) Knightswood. He still gets up at half five in the morning to open up and Dumbarton must wish that they had appointed him years ago (especially since the board had rejected his application on two previous occasions).

Stranraer hadn't won a match since defeating runaway First Division leaders St Johnstone in the Challenge Cup final in early November, and if they'd lost to revitalised Dumbarton the Sons would have leapfrogged above them to seventh in the basement battle for survival. The visitors took the lead in 14 minutes, however, with press reports on the opener varying wildly in their descriptions of the goal's quality. In the broadsheet-of-record *Herald*, 'Young cracked home a glorious 18-yarder', while in the soaraway sensationalist *Sun*, 'Rob Docherty sliced a shot across the face of the Dumbarton goal to where Gordon Young waited unmarked – and he slotted the easiest goal he will ever score'. Although both PA-stringer pieces were anonymous, *The Sun*'s was spot on.

The new drainage system had been a necessity, since the Boghead sod had been a notoriously muddy mire where substitutes had to be pulled out rather than pulled off, and the pitch remained in reasonable condition during an interesting first half of surprisingly silky soccer from Stranraer (who hit the post).

At half-time my fingers were so cold that I could barely turn the pages of the Holiday Double Issue programme (which cheapskatingly, but understandably, incorporated details of the Ne'er Day fixture against Stenhousemuir). Editor Graeme Robertson had gone on record just prior to Wallace's arrival by saying: 'Everyone tells me things will pick up eventually, but why should they? The fact is we're up shit creek without a paddle.'

Before the restart a passing teenage Son – who was deliberately spilling Bovril down the front of a knitted cardigan Christmas present – informed me that Hibs were losing 1–0. '*Danke schön*,' I replied, re-wrapping my Werder Bremen scarf tighter round my throat.

Stranraer hit the bar at the away end before Lee Sharp (a multi-million-pound transfer from Man U?) equalised in 63 minutes. Wide on the left, he dipped a shoulder, shimmied past his marker and from 22 yards out curled a glorious shot past Gary Matthews into the top far corner. Beyond doubt goal of my season in hell so far (since David McKenzie's strike for Albion Rovers in Game 3 hadn't had the same South American setting-up play). Stranraer went ahead again, deservedly, in the 85th minute, Paul McIntyre heading home from a corner.

The Sons fans then began to drift disconsolately away, and I envied them with real enmity because my feet were blocks of ice (embedded with sharp tacks). Dumbarton continued to pile forward with impressive stamina, due in no small part I'm sure to having a fitness coach who trains the Scottish Navy team at Faslane (a character called Ringo Watts from Liverpool, whose parents presumably worshipped the only Beatle with any real musical talent). Two agonising minutes into injury-time, Toby King's free-kick was met by Sons skipper and stopper Jim Meechan, who glanced his header past a mad-as-hell Matthews: 2–2 and the remaining faithful exploded with exhilaration. With Berwick becalmed at the bottom and Brechin not playing, Dumbarton moved above the latter into eighth place (but only for two days, before losing 2–1 at City's Glebe park on 28 December).

Lynn had another laughing jag on the way back to the car, as I hobbled hunchbacked like a polar explorer in the final stages of fatal frostbite.

Wallace would have been up at 5.30 a.m. on the Friday for the papers, and running a Knightswood newsagent's while managing struggling Dumbarton FC part-time may seem like a disappointing end for Britain's most expensive-ever player (in 1980). What's the attraction of early-morning starts and West of Scotland winters that would freeze your knackers off (especially when compared to being employed by Madeira FC in Portugal or Croatia Melbourne)? God knows, but I wish Wallace well (but not at the expense of Brechin City in the relegation dogfight). Any club that the late Sir Hugh Fraser bought in to has to have something wrong with it. No wonder current MD Neil Rankine wants to sell. And since going-concern newsagent's cost at least £60,000-plus, maybe Wallace could sell up and buy the Sons. At least the 'goodwill' would cost fuck all.

As for the official crowd of 686 – that should of course have been 688.[4]

FOOTNOTES

1. Hazel Irvine is a regular presenter of BBC Scotland's *Sportscene*, when not being whisked away to front the Winter Olympics or Saturday-afternoon *Grandstand* in London. Consummately professional at all times, even when holding Auntie Beeb's high-pressure sports flagship together, one public-school twat of a journalist on an English broadsheet described her presentational style as 'frentic' (which isn't even a proper bloody word). Possessing an honours degree from St Andrews University, Irvine is one of the few women in the sports media whose first love actually is sport (unlike some of the token female columnists and presenters, who either use positive discrimination to secure lucrative writing contracts or trade on their beach-babe bosoms to get in front of cameras). Brian Glanville has (over-)stated the case that 'women sports journalists are an absolute disgrace' but the majority of them do fail catastrophically

149

when attempting the litmus test of football match reporting (where their lack of knowledge and passion for the game cannot be disguised by clunking journalistic generalisations or a provocative flick of blonde tresses). Gender should be irrelevant, of course, and there are many examples of good female writers and presenters such as Julie Welch, Eleanor Oldroyd, Sue Mott and Gabby Yorath, but any female football hackette who whinges about glass ceilings or, worse, concrete roofs is either incapable of understanding the offside rule or has a profile like a crisp packet full of marbles. But I suppose for every Anna Walker there's an equally dire Rob Bonnet . . .

I once met the talented and gorgeous Irvine (if the latter adjective isn't unacceptably 'lookist') at Kilmarnock's Rugby Park, when I got my telephone extension lead stuck in her metal box of microphone equipment. If only I'd been hormonally calm enough to appreciate the undoubted sexual come-on subtext of her extremely short but incredibly polite apology . . . All I could think to blurt out was, 'I'm writing for a broadsheet not a tabloid, you know!' *Jeezuz*. What I should have said was, 'Hey, Haze, want to get your kit off back in my bachelor pad in the West End of the Big G, or what?' I could have been 'Mr Irvine' by now. Talk about *esprit de l'escalier* ('retrospective wit of the press-box staircase'). Hazel is also, allegedly, a Dumbarton fan, but since she comes from Cardross just up the coast on the Helensburgh road I think we can assume that this is not just a convenient 'media team'.

2. I'm being deliberately vague about the steward's identity and specific place of duty, since I wouldn't want to be responsible for his getting disciplined or dismissed. Nevertheless, upon reflection, it was a pretty rum example of individual entrepreneurial initiative considering the dire financial straights Dumbarton were in. When I later accused my sister of sneaking away before kick-off to go out and come back in again, paying for us *both* at the turnstiles, she denied it with the outraged protestations of the beyond-reasonable-doubt guilty. Honestly, I can't take this woman anywhere without her humiliating me by doing the right-on thing . . .

3. 'Going, Going . . . Gone?', *The Absolute Game*, No. 48 (May/June/July 1996), pp. 3–4. This is one of the best-written and funniest articles about a Scottish football club I've ever read. Anthology compilers struggling for pieces about Dumbarton please take note.

4. Clydebank drew Celtic at 'home' in the Scottish Cup third round, but by switching the tie away from Boghead (capacity 5,000) to Firhill they managed to go down 5–0 in front of a Sunday afternoon crowd of 16,102. Dumbarton went out in round two to Cowdenbeath, losing 1–0 at Central Park in front of 294. The draw was made live on *Sportscene* on Saturday, 5 January, with stand-in presenter Alison Walker seriously discussing with Celtic's Peter Grant the non-starting prospect of Clydebank v Celtic being played at Boghead. Grant ended the surreal interview with his 'we fear no one, nowhere' line. Bill Dickie of the SFA and Motherwell presided over the desperately amateurish proceedings, the balls being placed in a clear-glass flower vase (BhS, £15.99). A Tommy Cooperish finale was provided when Dickie stuck his arm in to mix

up the *last two balls* (containing Airdrie and Raith). To be honest, it was the last three, but still . . . No wonder Scottish fans are convinced the draw is fixed to keep Celtic and Rangers apart. The next day the FA Cup draw was also televised live, straight after the Manchester United v Tottenham Hotspur tie. Graham Kelly was as stilted and awkward as his Scottish counterpart, but at least the English version had the razzmatazz and unquestionably fairer innovation of a mini-Lancelot/Guinevere lottery machine for the numbered balls (as opposed to the tedious and time-wasting Scottish tradition of folded pieces of paper inside screwed together ball halves).

STARK'S PARK
Raith Rovers v Dundee United
Premier Division, 28.12.96

The last set of Saturday fixtures in 1996, sandwiched between the depressing dog days of Crimbo and Hogmanay, saw a dozen games postponed because of frozen pitches, in what was beginning to feel like the worst winter since 1947. Running to schedule, however, my train from Edinburgh passed through Aberdour (which, incredibly, once supported an artists' colony of Bohemian beach bums) and Burntisland.

Kirkcaldy was once the linoleum capital of the world, but when the working classes began aspiring to the luxury of fitted carpeting, the underlay fell out of the industry. 'Famous' for its four-mile-long main street and never-ending concreted seafront esplanade, *Kir-cawdy* is a pronunciation nightmare for London-based media persons (a *Grandstand* broadcaster coining the irony-free phrase: 'They'll be dancing in the streets of Raith tonight' as far back as 1967). Economist Adam Smith was born here and at the age of three was abducted by gypsies (who, sadly for today's students of political economy, didn't strangle the garrulous little bastard and future author of *The Wealth of Nations*).

Fifers in general, but 'Lang Touners' in particular, are notoriously fly and 'cawshul', the 50,000 inhabitants of Kirkcaldy exhibiting extreme reticence, undemonstrativeness and aloofness (when sober). I've always quite liked them and although the town is an elongated architectural disaster, I used to drive up there once a year all through the 1980s to see Raith Rovers lose (before being landed with Stark's Park as a regular match-reporting venue). As for Jackie O's niteclub, if you couldn't score here, you couldn't score anywhere. The worst chat-up line I ever heard was slurred in this sexual cattle market. Namely: 'Honest tae fuck, Babycham is a spermicide, ye ken? Drink up, doll, and we'll lubricate yer *lurve* box in the carpark.' Worryingly, this guy pulled. I normally pretended to be engaged, which was okay since most of the white-shoed handbag circlers pretended to be virgins. Jackie O's has gone up-market since then, including a period when they were Raith's shirt sponsors, but I'll never forget those heady nights of super-studs and beautiful 'burdz' being brought horizontally together by lager-fuelled love potions.

During 1996 Raith Rovers had gone through four managers – Jimmy Nicholl (who resigned to take over the insomniac midgets of Millwall), Jimmy Thomson (who lasted 202 days before getting the bullet and the Berwick Rangers electric chair), Jim McNally (as caretaker boss before being banned from the ground for refusing to step in again after manager

No. 4 had departed) and Tommy McLean (who lasted seven days before leaving for Dundee United) – before finally appointing Hamilton's Iain Munro (who had just resigned to take over at St Mirren!). McLean's seven days at Stark's Park in September saw the managerial merry-go-round in Scotland spinning wildly out of control, as if psychopathic chairmen and weak-willed managers meeting on ScotRail services all over the country were reprising the parts played by Robert Walker (Charles Bruno) and Farley Granger (Guy Haines) in Hitchcock's *Strangers on a Train*. United did at least pay £60,000 compensation for Tommy McLean's breaking of his three-year contract at Stark's Park, but feelings of betrayal were exacerbated when McLean invoiced Raith chairman Alex Penman for seven days' wages and expenses. With soccer's usual serendipity, McLean's first game in charge of the Tangerine Terrors was back at Kirkcaldy, where the away dug-out had to be protected by personal security operatives hired from Jackie O's (i.e. bouncers in lounge suits carrying walkie-talkies and electric cattle-prods), brick-proof perspex and head-high sandbags. Raith won 3–2.

Going into this game at the end of December, Raith were struggling to emulate their British League record of 142 goals in 34 games (set in 1937–38), stuck as they were at the foot of the Premier League with a paltry 15 strikes in 18 outings. Memories of winning the Coca-Cola Cup against Celtic in 1994 and going in 1–0 up at half-time to Bayern Munich in the Olympiastadion (in a UEFA Cup run that delighted all of Scotland) were beginning to seem as far-distant in time as old-timers' whisky-induced anecdotes about the great Alex James (whose summer holiday of 1923 included surviving a shipwreck off the coast of Spain before going on to star for Arsenal and Scotland).

Raith may have been sinking back towards their natural level in the hierarchy of the Scottish Football League – '17th or 18th' according to their highest-profile soccerati supporter, Harry Ritchie, a Lang Touner who rose to become literary editor of the *Sunday Times* at the frighteningly young age of 13¾ – but Stark's Park had been transformed since having to shift the home tie against Bayern in 1995 to Easter Road. Passing Raith's rebuilt home on the train, the stadium now looks like a mini-Murrayfield, with blue spidery cantilevered supports on three sides. Two wonderful 3,400-seater stands had been put up at both ends over the summer of '96. Previously the terracing beside the railway line had been replaced by a truncated 939-seat stand. The old wooden stand had been retained, dog-legging round a corner-flag (but in another amazing similarity to Fir Park, terraced houses in Pratt Street mean a gaping 'undevelopable' space that runs half the length of the pitch). Still, it was a vast improvement on three sides of run-down terracing (even if the pitch-level press hutch is still driving match reporters to imaginative flights of fancy when trying to identify and describe players in the build-up to goals).

The physical metamorphosis of Stark's Park may have been a pleasant surprise, but the hiked entrance prices were a liposuctioning blow to my right buttock (where I carry my wallet). To help recoup the £2.3 million investment, fans were being mugged at the turnstiles. Before the new stands went up, eight quid got you into Stark's Park. I had to scramble for loose change in my pockets to meet the £12 entry charge for the Railway Stand, with the programme costing £1.50 – whereas at Motherwell a tenner and a pound had been the respective charges. (An even more damning comparison came at my next game, No. 28, where a tenner got me a seat 'in the gods' at Celtic Park.) And according to 'Outraged of Kirkcaldy' – i.e. Paul Gilfillan, writing in the August '96 issue of *The Absolute Game* – a £220 season-ticket worked out more expensive per game (£12.22) than paying £12 at the gate (if there were no home cup games and friendlies were excluded). Whether paying a large cheque up front or cash at the gate, this pricing policy is definitely the economics of exploitation, especially considering the exit of Raith's best young players for whopping transfer fees in the wake of Nicholl's departure (Hearts buying up Colin Cameron and Millwall taking Jason Dair, Stevie Crawford and Davie Sinclair – although after Millwall had to call in the receivers, Raith lost out on the staggered payments which had been agreed upon originally).

In the Railway Stand I certainly wasn't paying a premium for pampered comfort. Sitting in the back row I regretted for the first time, outside of a bedroom, not being double-jointed. Knee-room was so restricted that passing fans caused havoc, and I had to stand on my bucket seat to let them past. If the crowd had been a capacity 11,877 rather than 5,762, someone could easily have been injured – as they inched along a row like an inexperienced hill-walker negotiating a narrow mountain ledge.

The North Stand was well-nigh full, almost 3,400 chanting and colourful Arabs having travelled down from Tayside; with the identical home equivalent housing less than 2,000. The Raith fans were polite and positive but outshouted and outnumbered – the result of a dire season with little to enthuse over. Trinidad and Tobago star Tony Rougier was unhappy at being the worst-paid player in the Premier League, while in October the signing of a second black player in the form of naturalised Swede Moses Nsebuja had been vetoed at the last minute. Although his agent's 'Best of Nsebuja' promotional video had impressed the board sufficiently to sanction a bid, a second video compilation starring the 23-year-old showed the hung-like-a-stallion striker cavorting in a professionally produced piece of pornography. Although none of his gagging-for-it/gagged female co-stars had any complaints about his performance (stamina or skill-wise), the Raith directors wailed like goosed virgins and blocked any contractual consummation. (Surprisingly, Rangers didn't step in to complete their portfolio of perverted sex maniacs and convicted criminals.)

If the signing of a striker involved in a 'sex scandal' was beyond the moral pale at Stark's Park, one might have thought that a conviction for physical assault in a Leven bar pub-brawl would have been regarded as even more embarrassing to the club (especially if committed by the Raith Rovers captain). But no, hardman stopper Shaun Dennis was back in the team after beating up on one Alan Bence. Signed from local amateurs Lochgelly Albert in 1988, Dennis had already squared up to team-mate Peter Duffield in the tunnel earlier in the season. His poor disciplinary record and criminal conviction didn't prevent new Hibs boss Jim Duffy from recruiting Dennis for £130,000, plus Andy Millen, in early January.

Prior to kick-off, United chairman Jim McLean – manager Tommy's big brother – had slammed the phone down on *Sportsound*'s Richard Gordon, after taking exception to a perceived media witch-hunt against the Merry McLeans. The elder McLean's bad-tempered touchiness was difficult to understand, because the previous day had seen United offloading fringe midfielder David Hannah to Celtic for £650,000 (which, when I heard it on the radio – the astronomical fee, post-Bosman, but not the name – I had assumed to be for Robbie Winters, the Tangerines' best player). Another example of Celtic paying over the odds for the football equivalent of 'prime Florida real estate' in alligator-infested swamp land?

The re-turfed pitch turned out to be the first in my travels that cut up appallingly (in between the rutted ridges). In the second minute United's Swedish striker Kjell Olofsson thwacked a free-kick low, hard and hopeful. Deflecting slightly off Danny Lennon or a frozen divot – a distinction that is not easy to make – the ball hit the back of the net in front of the ecstatic Arabs. Game over. Raith were never going to be able to climb what the normally intelligent Munro called 'a mountain', and United's counter-attacking play went steadily downhill thereafter. I was so bored I read the programme from cover to cover, and although superbly designed and full of readable copy, page 11 drew me up short. The 'Looking Back' feature was almost completely blank, with nothing having happened 10, 50 or 100 years previously. Overleaf on page 12, RGS Design & Print's own ad asked 'Are *you* using us yet?' Am I *blank*, I thought.

At 4.45 p.m. I staggered out with two 'dead legs' and with my teeth chattering because of the cold. Nil-bloody-one, ending the year with a goal average per game of 2.52. Like an old girlfriend who has had a facelift, but who now talks psychobabbling rubbish about 'self-actualisation', I have gone right off Raith Rovers. Wraith Rovers, more like. I hope they stay up but they won't, and Munro is beginning to talk managerial mince. Before this match he said: 'It would be great to be clear of relegation by February or March but we're prepared to battle to the end if required.' If Raith aren't *officially* relegated by February or March they'll be doing well. And like Harry Ritchie, I too wish the Rovers would go back to wearing a white strip with two blue hoops. The current navy blue shirts with white shorts are horrible (although vastly improved when reversed for the 'away' strip).

Bog-awful and *boring*, Raith Rovers are definitely no longer my 'second' team, and like disenchanted San Francisco Giants fan Michael Volpe I think I'll declare myself a 'free-agent fan' (at least in Fife, and for a second team – since Hibs have been ditchwater dull diddies for years, too). Volpe wrote to all the other major-league baseball teams offering his services, whereupon the Giants' arch-rivals, the Los Angeles Dodgers, pulled out all the publicity and PR stops to recruit him. Maybe I'll write to Miss Audrey M. Bastianelli, the Commercial Manager of Dunfermline FC, offering to defect. A candle-lit dinner for three – me, her and match-day mascot Sammy the Tammy – and a season-ticket for East End Park and I'm a Par for life (or until they get relegated).

God, even if the current proposal for a 16-team Premiership in Scotland goes through, Raith's 'natural' level is still one or two places outwith it.

Being in the capital for 'Edinburgh's Hogmanay' (the biggest New Year party in the world), I was dreading the Bell's even more than usual. A crowd of 350,000 piled into Princes Street for the countdown to '97, but I wasn't one of them. Instead I attended a party in the New Town, and although quickly relegated to sexual substitute on a pine bench in the kitchen, I had the satisfaction of reducing a would-be actress to tears, being called 'a smooth-talking son-of-a-bitch' in the process. To be honest she called me something else, which I'm too much of a gentleman (albeit an insecure one) to repeat. Drunk and depressed, I awoke on Ne'er Day in no state to attend a game, even if there had been transport available, and just in time to buy a late edition of the Edinburgh *Evening News*. 'The worst night of my life' blazed the front-page headline – a quote from Keith Little, consultant at the Royal Infirmary's A&E department. In a 24-hour period 579 patients had been treated, all of them drunk, abusive and incontinent. But some were suffering injuries due to being crushed, only luck having prevented Hillsborough-type fatalities.

Red-eyed Falkirk fans caused their Ne'er Day fixture against Airdrie to be postponed, even though a cover had left the pitch perfectly playable. An early-morning radio SOS for help in clearing snow-bound terraces at Brockville only resulted in a handful of Bairns with Hogmanay hangovers turning up to shovel away the snow. The police ruled the terraces too icy for safety. (On Wednesday, 8 January, Falkirk had to replay St Mirren as part of their punishment for fielding the ineligible John Clark in the original fixture, after having had the three points won deducted, and there was almost a riot when the club tried to prevent season-ticket-holders getting in for free; and during the 1–1 draw there were unconfirmed reports of crowd trouble amongst a Bairns support denied adequate catering: namely, outbreaks of attempted cannibalism.) In the few fixtures to beat the Ne'er Day freeze, eyebrow-raising scorelines included Dundee United 4, Aberdeen 0; Hibs 0, Hearts 4; and St Johnstone 7, Dundee 2 (with – shock, horror, probe – Chic Charnley sent off). Partick Thistle beat Clydebank 3–1, but less than 800 paying punters were persuaded to crawl out of their vomit-caked pits to join 1,200 season-ticket-holders. Thistle's bank manager hit the Buckfast before jumping naked into the River Kelvin.

At Livingston's Almondvale Stadium, where Berwick Rangers snatched a last-gasp equaliser in a 2–2 draw – *yes!* – there was tiny-tot trouble in the new North Stand. Chairman Bill Hunter, reverting to his brutal Mr Blobby persona, later went public about the New Town's parents using the stadium as a dumping ground for their problem kids. The club had been giving away a thousand free tickets to local schools but, according to Hunter, the juvenile delinquents had been running amok at home games. 'They don't sit down during the game and they act up. They just don't take a telling.' (*The Sun*, 7.1.97) Maybe a good leathering would have restored public order, although one gets the impression that Hunter would like to sort them out for good with water-cannon and CS gas, riot police and snatch squads.

Two days later my designated driver for the East Fife v St Johnstone game at Methil had his borderline-sober prayers answered when a 9 a.m. pitch inspection resulted in another Saturday postponement (one of many, resulting in a backlog of 44 unplayed fixtures). Contingency plans for seeing St Mirren at Love Street or Whitehill Welfare at Ferguson Park (in the Scottish Cup) also fell foul of the weather. I could have got the train in time – just – to get to Tannadice to see Dundee United play Kilmarnock, but after so many false starts on the first Saturday of 1997, *I just couldn't be arsed.*

So 4 January was my first footie-free Saturday since July.

CELTIC PARK
Celtic v Kilmarnock
Premier League, 8.1.97

Prior to this mid-week match, I hadn't exactly been hot on the trail of that semi-mythical beast, the 6–0 thrashing – so completely losing its track, after a glimpse of the existentially exciting possibility at McDiarmid Park in late October (4–0), that November saw me getting hopelessly bogged down in ever-decreasing circles of dead-end 0–0 draws. I picked up its scent again on 4 January 1997, however, when radio reports from Parkhead confirmed a 5–0 drubbing of Motherwell. In between Christmas and New Year, Dundee had beaten East Fife 6–0 at Dens Park – just two weeks after walloping the frazzled Fifers 7–1 at Bayview – but a Premier six-niller had still to be registered. (For me, a 6–0 home win is a near-perfect scoreline, better than 7–1 say, because consolation goals for the opposition only become non-irritatingly irrelevant when your team hits *double figures*.)

Celtic 6, Kilmarnock 0. And I was there. Along with 45,723 others, but they hadn't been scouring Scotland since 3 August searching for the most sacramental soccer scoreline. To make it even more satisfying, Jorge Cadete hadn't got the cross-hairs of his striker's telescopic sight lined up for the sixth goal until the 90th minute. This fixture had been the first of the season where I had seen my ain folk in the footballing flesh, by which time Celtic's easily won three points still left us 11 points behind Rangers, although with a game in hand. From being top, albeit on goal difference, going into the Old Firm derby of 14 November (which was lost 0–1), Celtic had somehow slipped to being 14 points adrift after losing 3–1 at Ibrox on 2 January. Still, running up six without reply meant our guttering candle of hope was still alight, even if the Ibrox stormtroopers were burning a straight-line, quick-marching path towards nine-in-a-row with a fucking flame-thrower.

Frankly, the Ne'er Day(ish) defeat at Doom Castle was probably the turning point of the two-horse Championship race, marking Celtic's ninth successive failure to beat their arch-rivals. It prompted a £30 million *rise* in Rangers share values, while wiping £6 million from Celtic's listed worth. Plans to go public and float Newcastle United may have pressurised Kevin Keegan into resigning on the morning of the Celtic v Kilmarnock game, but when I caught the middle of a radio report hysterically hyping 'such a high-profile departure', I initially thought Tommy Burns had fallen on his own sword – which in some ways would have been less unexpected than Keegan's decision to cut and run.

Appointed the Pope of Parkhead in July 1994, 37-year-old Burns endured a difficult first season in charge, two years as player-manager at low-profile Killie hardly preparing him for the vicissitudes of being new Chief Executive Fergus McCann's representative on the dug-out touchline at Paradise. Lucky not to be sacked after losing the Coca-Cola Cup final to Raith Rovers in 1994, Burns nevertheless threatened to resign – allegedly – in the wake of winning the 1995 Scottish Cup against the Anabaptists of Airdrie. Even after McCann and Burns were reconciled, the former agreeing to stay out of the dressing-room to concentrate on developing Celtic as a 'corporate global brand name', and the latter accepting banishment from the board-room to focus his nervous energy on restoring Celtic's reputation on the pitch, Burns often looked like buckling under the relentless media attention and inexorable weight of supporting expectation. Neurotic ear-tugging and verbal-tic catchphrase repetition of 'Ehh . . . Sellik Football Club' in trophyless season 1995–96 suggested that the flame-haired left-footer who had delighted Celtic fans as a player between 1973 and 1989 was still out of his inexperienced managerial depth. Pushing eight-in-a-row Rangers to the wire while playing gloriously attractive attacking football endeared him to the support, however, and by the beginning of November '97 Burns had acquired something of a reputation – akin to George Soros in the foreign-exchange markets – for being a canny buyer (if not seller). Brilliant big-money purchases like Pierre van Hooijdonk, Andreas Thom, Jorge Cadete and Paolo di Canio were brought in (the jury still being out on £3.5 million – *gulp!* – stopper Alan Stubbs), along with bargain-basement Bhoy wonders like Tosh McKinlay, Jackie McNamara and Morten Weighorst. Only Phil O'Donnell is an obvious multi-million-pound disappointment.

Nevertheless, this 'nine-in-a-row' season's pressures had obviously been building and Burns had been banished to the stand after overreacting like a member of the Toronto Blessing speaking in blasphemous tongues (although a futile appeal did delay the inevitable punishment). Two nights after this 6–0 win, prior to a nailbiting 2–1 win at Tynecastle, Burns had been asked in a filmed interview shown on *Friday Sportscene* how he coped with the trials and tribulations of being Celtic boss (one of the most stressful jobs in world football, right up there with managing the likes of Barcelona, Juventus, *et al*, and a damn sight more anxiety-inducing than heading up a privatised utility company). After a thoughtful, if ear-tugging silence, Burns replied: 'I speak to God a lot.' I slapped my furrowed forehead in atheistic disbelief. Burns wears his faith on his hair-shirted Hugo Boss sleeve and he went on to describe the solace that bulging mailbags of prayer cards and other inspirational Catholic literature provides him with. Burns hasn't yet exhorted the faithful to pray for dropped Rangers points, and even if God does exist prayers don't influence physical events; at best prayers merely inspire their offerers to display greater moral fortitude, a scientifically explicable psychological side-effect. However, in this novenary season (pertaining as it does to the number nine), if the Celtic manager's devotions result in a League Championship through the intercession of the Holy Virgin, Burns ought to be put on a fast-track development programme to whisk him through the two lobbying stages necessary – beatification and blessedness – before any declaration of sainthood as St Thomas of Parkhead, before the Book of Revelations becomes a shooting script for reality in the new millennium.

The Edinburgh University Celtic Supporters' Club bus left from Bruntsfield at 5.30 p.m. – and neither I nor my ticket-supplier Alan were totally confident about getting a winning result against Killie, whose permanently appointed caretaker boss Bobby Williamson had been getting a few impressive wins for the perennial basement battlers and whose largely similar squad had put a final nail in Celtic's previous, and impressive, title challenge back in April '96 (a 1–1 draw at Celtic Park that I had sat morosely through in the main stand, thanks to a ticket generously provided by a Celtic fan and sometime singer with rock band Complex Brains).

Similarly, when the be-bunnetted Scots-Canadian multi-millionaire McCann had taken over at Celtic in March 1994, saving the club from imminent liquidation brought about by the descendants of the original controlling dynasties, the new MD hardly inspired unreserved optimism that an increasingly dramatic decline could be immediately halted and quickly reversed. But the publicity-shy golfing-holidays tycoon, who muttered away in mid-Atlantic management-speak, hit the shag-piled boardroom floor running, like the BBC2 *Troubleshooter* businessman Sir John Harvey Jones, armed with explosive action plans and strategic five-year timetables. (McCann's initial £9 million investment was a shrewd speculation, rather than an altruistic donation, because his shares were well below their 'asset value' and if he sold up now, rather than in 1999 as promised, he would realise a profit in excess of £40 million.)

Although Parkhead had become a piggery of hotch-potched, patched-up improvements, plans to move to Cambuslang were immediately cancelled. Manager Lou Macari was sacked and Burns 'tapped' away from Kilmarnock, causing acrimonious ill-feeling in subsequent fixtures between the two clubs (although nothing like the long-standing and vicious hatred generated by meetings between Rangers and Aberdeen). Despite losing to Raith in the Coca-Cola Cup final, the much-mocked share issue soon afterwards turned out to be the most successful venture of its kind in British football history (and the current 'ridiculously overvalued' share prices, having risen almost 600 per cent from £65 to £385 in 1996 alone, are largely explained by the fact that only a minuscule quantity of shares are ever publicly traded, sentimental fan shareholders preferring to keep their framed share certificates hanging above fireplaces with dimpled flues all over the East End of Glasgow). The 10,000 fans who initially invested helped raise over £14 million for the club, which helped pay the £500,000 rent for the use of Hampden in season 1994–95, at the start of which three sides of Celtic Park were demolished.

A year previously, the famous Jungle terracing had been converted to a seating area, and for Celtic's last League game in front of the standing Jungle-ites the old board had initiated a fancy-dress competition. The competition for best costume was won by Vincent the Parrot, a put-up job to get a mascot accepted by the support (who would probably have pelted any costumed character 'imposed' on them by the board). At least the new Celtic régime haven't yet introduced match-day mascots in furry suits – e.g. 'Brendan the Bhoy Bedbug'.[1]

The massive new North Stand opened for sell-out business in August 1995, its two tiers capable of accommodating almost 27,000 smiling, Tony Blair-supporting 'stakeholders'. A year later, the 13,000-seater East Stand opened, on what used to be the Rangers End. The Main Stand still houses almost 8,000 fans, and with nearly 3,000 seats erected on temporary scaffolding at the Celtic End the total capacity is now over 50,000. In 1997–98 the planned West Stand should allow 60,000-plus Celtic fans to sit in state-of-the-art comfort.

As the bus driver dropped us off in Dalriada Street, I was so excited that I forgot to buy a programme (and there were none on sale inside). Walking along Janefield Street, with the Eastern Necropolis to the right and *favela*-type tenements to the left, the illuminated Celtic Park loomed overhead like the Mother Ship which appears at the end of *Close Encounters of the Third Kind*. Visible for miles around, 'Paradise Park' is situated in an area of urban deprivation, as if the Toronto Superdome had been taken apart and rebuilt in the centre of New York's Hell's Kitchen. Off-street parking is easy to find but risky to contemplate. (N.B. No area of Glasgow is sectarianly segregated, as in Belfast, but the district of Parkhead has suffered a lack of investment in its housing stock which dates back to the days of the old 'Glasgow Corporation'.)

Once inside the North Stand, the catering facilities were a lot less salubrious than I remembered from my previous visits in season 1995–96 (when I'd been able to luxuriate in one of the 1,600 dark-green padded seats at the back of the lower tier, and whose £25 tickets bought adjustable under-bum heating panels and entry to concourse lounges with licensed bars, buffet tables and colour TV monitors). Although assured that my ordered 'coffee' was not tea, it smelled like tea, tasted like tea and bloody well *was* tea. If I'd been a shareholder I would have written to Fergus McCann personally, adding to the mountains of mail he already receives from mildly disgruntled but proudly pernickety 'investors'.

The panorama laid out below us from our 'Restricted View' seats was stunning; and at a cost of ten quid, being stung for £12 at Stark's Park became even more reprehensible in retrospect. One of 13 pillars in the top level did obscure the right-hand penalty area, but not enough to block out any of the four second-half goals (albeit thanks to some nimble neck contortions). Because the top 11 rows overhang the graveyard, the need for the supporting roof columns could only have been obviated by spending another million pounds on extra concrete foundations.

The match officials were roundly booed on to the pitch, the refereeing conspiracy theory about the men in black being innately hostile to Celtic's cause having been refuelled with liquid nitrogen during the last Old Firm encounter. At 2–1 down, a linesman had chalked off a perfectly good Cadete goal for offside (which Sky satellite replays showed beyond doubt not to have been the case). Unlike in England, none of the match officials involved was allowed to discuss the incident publicly (a tradition of silence that referees themselves had just voted in favour of retaining). The mistake had cost Celtic at least a point, and possibly a Championship, and the con-spiracy controversy then mushroomed with thermo-nuclear intensity when it was alleged that the guilty linesman was a self-declared Rangers fan who regularly drank at a Masonic lodge and who played knockabout games in the Ibrox club's replica kit. So far, so funny. Rogue individual officials may exist, and have certainly done so in the past, but this official's split-second straying into error didn't merit the objurgation that descended on him. To some Celtic supporters' eternal shame, he received vicious death-threats in the mail. As for the Celtic management team, although condemning the written intimidation, they didn't exactly attempt to dampen the flames of supporting speculation about sinister forces combining to keep Celtic in second place.[2] (Like Jock Stein, Burns seems to believe in the conspiracy, but unlike the Big Man doesn't seem to realise that it can be overcome – if it exists – by using it to psychological advantage by putting together a team of 11 individuals so talented and *motivated* that the odd dodgy decision won't be enough to sway final placings over a season.) SFA head Jim Farry suggested that Burns was guilty of using the atmosphere of paranoia and atavistic barricade-manning as 'a heat-shield to cover his own inadequa-cies'. Ouch . . . That was either illegally below the belt or a sucker punch right on the chin . . .

A surprisingly low-key start erupted in seven minutes, when Cadete finished off an excellent three-man move by heading home: 1–0. Cheers of delight turned to howls of derision when Glasgow referee Michael McCurry chalked it off for no apparent reason. All hell broke loose when Main Stand linesman George Clyde flagged Van Hooijdonk incorrectly offside. The language from the supporters which followed is supposed to get fans ejected from the new family-friendly environment of Celtic Park, and I was beginning to succumb to paranoia and mildly industrial language myself before Cadete reopened the scoring in the 18th minute, running in to sidefoot the ball past prostrate Dragoje Lekovic.

Five minutes later a loose ball bounced across the Kilmarnock half. With right-back McNamara running to meet it from 25 yards out I hopefully yelled, 'Boom!' Taking it on the half-volley, the ball screamed into the top of the net. A goal of blootered but balanced brilliance. Di Canio was having his best-ever game for the Hoops, and although the white-booted ex-AC Milan winger only had a flu-hit and makeshift Killie defence to waltz around, he looked like a truly world-class player (Celtic's belated answer to Brian Laudrup?). At one stage he juggled the ball in the air with *seven* increasingly impudent touches. Fans were bowing in 'We're not worthy' supplication whenever he approached a corner flag. Celtic skipper Paul McStay – a Captain Mainwaring of motivational psychology – had to physically restrain the volatile Roman, however, when he was booked for gently sidefooting a dead ball two feet away, but when Steve Hamilton upended Di Canio brutally in the box, inflicting an ankle injury necessitating his withdrawal before the end, McCurry flamboyantly waved away justified appeals for a penalty. At 2–0, half-time was a welcome respite from hoarse vocal cords and a surging adrenaline level. (One thing about 'creative writing' is the total lack of heart-thumping excitement involved in the whole time-consuming process.) Alan's transformation from a softly spoken and bookish young Irishman into a chanting, clapping and combustible Celt just shows how cathartic big-crowd cacophonies can be.

During the break we brought each other up to date with the Celtic Boys Club sex scandal (a club with no *official* connection to Celtic), the decision to stop letting priests in to matches for free, the existence of the Internet Tims (whose on-line contributions such as 'Cloven Hooves – *see* Huns' are a damn sight more entertaining than the official Celtic FC Web site, about which PR officials wax lyrical because of the remarkable interest shown 'from countries like the USA, Brazil, Croatia and Swaziland'), Glen Daly's CD popularity in Dortmund and the existence of the 'Lesbian Lions' wummin's footie team. Using issue 60 of *Not the View* as a basis, I selected my Celtic-supporting celebrity XI: James McMillan; Mickey Rourke, Tom Leonard, Rod Stewart, Michael Caton Jones; Gil Scott Heron, Jim Kerr,

Billy Connolly, Sean Connery; Sharon Stone and Brendan Behan. In a 'Where are they now?' question and answer session, I outlined the sad decline of George Connelly, who played in the 1970 European Cup final but who is now a regular early-morning half-pint-of-lager drinker in Kincardine's CJ's Snooker Club. Alan was as impressed as he should have been by my having shaken hands with Lisbon Lions' Stevie Chalmers and Bobby Murdoch the previous year (and it was quite touching to see the aforementioned Mr Kerr as star-struck when pressing-the-flesh with Lisbon Lions as any of the fans of Simple Minds when requesting his autograph).

In the second half, Cadete made it 3–0 in 65 minutes. In the 79th, Morten Weighorst contemptuously flicked in the fourth with the outside of a boot. But fan fury erupted again when linesman Clyde kept his flag down for a consolation Ally Mitchell goal. 'Christ, Clyde,' shouted a red-faced Tim, 'yer right airm wiz on fuckin automatic pilot in the first half!' The second-loudest cheer of the night greeted ref McCurry's decision to overrule his assistant and chalk it off. With Van Hooijdonk going through the motions for his £4,500 a week, Cadete was exhorting the crowd to keep up the deafening decibel level. (Being part of a 45,000-plus crowd cheering on a team 4–0 up, while convinced that the match officials were determined to help the visitors secure a score draw, was a bizarre but fun experience.) In 87 minutes sub Chris Hay fired in a fifth. With McCurry set to blow one second into the 91st minute, Cadete adjusted his feet and *Spinal Tap* hairstyle before slicing his hat-trick into the bottom far corner – the Portuguese international's 23rd goal in 26 games for Celtic. He celebrated in copyrighted fashion, whirling his right arm with forefinger extended: 6–0 . . .

The bus dropped us off in Edinburgh just after 11 p.m. and Alan and I headed home across the Meadows. At the bottom of the Bridges we bade each other goodnight. As I hit Waterloo Place and Alan the top of Leith Street, we both turned round for a final wave cheerio. Instead, I did a Cadete arm circle and Alan responded in kind. I remained on such a high that I stayed up until half two in the morning watching Channel 4's chaotic new sports discussion programme *Under the Moon*.

Ah, 6–0 . . . The best cure for acute depression/chronic unhappiness that any footie fan can get.

FOOTNOTES

1. The introduction of a match-day mascot at Parkhead is probably only a matter a marketing time, since Pittodrie has Aberdeen Angus, Tynecastle Hearty Harry, and Ibrox Broxy Bear. It must be a terrible job for the man inside, unless he's signing on the dole and gets paid cash-in-hand to moonlight in full view of the local Job Centre

manager. In January '97 Wolverhampton fans complained about being 'grossly intimidated' by Bolton's Lofty the Lion. What did he do – scare them shitless by turning out all the lights in the away section of Burnden Park? In the same month Wolves sacked their mascot – the man in the furry suit, that is, not Warren the Wolf.

2. Bias is notoriously difficult to prove with regard to refereeing decisions – except in the rather obvious case of one referee I could mention, who seems to be convinced that a wine-and-wafer dispensary has been set up in the home dressing-room at Celtic Park – but a Jesuit priest based in Los Angeles has been studying old copies of the *Glasgow Herald* in an attempt to find an objective answer. Like an open-minded scientist, Father Peter Burns expected to find an even distribution of dubious decisions over time, but his tongue-in-cheek researches indicated that Celtic really do suffer from 'Masonic bias' (at least in Old Firm encounters).

Paul Gascoigne's disciplinary record is one that convinces Celtic fans that Scottish referees are scared to send the Fat Bloke off – or are under instructions not to. In over 60 head-banging appearances for Rangers in Scotland, he has never been dismissed. In just ten Champions' League outings, he has been sent for an early bath twice.

3. *Action Replay* is undoubtedly the worst football glossy currently published, but in Issue No. 3, 1996, they gave an interesting update on 'Whatever happened to?' the Lisbon Lions of 1967. In summary: Jock Stein: died of a heart attack in 1985; Sean Fallon: retired; Billy McNeill: media pundit and publican (who underwent successful heart-bypass surgery in early 1997); Ronnie Simpson: member of Pools Panel; Tommy Gemmell: insurance manager and radio commentator; Bobby Murdoch: retired due to ill-health; John Clark: administrator for Strathclyde Fire Department; Jimmy Johnstone: tool company rep; Willie Wallace: sportswear rep in Sydney; Stevie Chalmers: retired/match-day host; Bertie Auld: barman; Bobby Lennox: publican in Saltcoats; Jim Craig: dentist.

If Celtic ever win the European Cup for a second time, the multinational team members will probably all be paper millionaires by the time they retire from the game – or even before they set foot on the pitch hosting any such final.

CAPPIELOW PARK
Greenock Morton v East Fife
First Division, 11.1.97

Although the town-identifying prefix was only added in 1994, this shipbuilding community became a famous literary location in one of Scotland's greatest novels as far back as 1965, when Alan Sharp published *A Green Tree in Gedde* (Michael Joseph). However, like literati Londoners who continually refer to *Trainspotting* – the book and the movie – as being set in Glasgow, pretentious know-nothings occasionally confuse Greenock with the factional 'Graithnock' (see next chapter on Rugby Park). Sharp's 'controversial' novel is dedicated to Greenock, 'to its buildings and chimneys and streets and the glimpses they have afforded me of the river and the hills'. Given a brilliant write-up by the *Financial Times*, their reviewer nevertheless felt compelled to add the rider – because of the half-homosexual character called Harry Gibbon? – that the author was 'in no sense a pornographer'. This probably meant that the book was not a big seller in non-swinging industrial Greenock, although it's the kind of printed praise that any writer would do backflips over. A day after this match the magazine *Gay Scotland* caused outrage in Dumfries with an advert parodying the town's team, headed 'Queens of the North', which Doonhamer fans found even more difficult to swallow than Billy Connolly's joke about renaming their club Queen of the South Nil. A report published on 13 January may have mollified them, however, since Dumfries was rated by Strathclyde University researchers as having the best quality of life in Britain. Greenock's position was not highlighted in the press reports, but presumably it was above Kirkcaldy – the home of Raith Rovers coming 178th out of 189.

Novelist and screenwriter Sharp now lives beneath a warm foreign sun, but he was born in the Wee Dublin area of Greenock, which gave its name to the West End terracing. In his brilliant essay 'A Dream of Perfection',[1] Sharp recounts the thrill of learning the etymology of 'Cappielow' – a Scandinavian word meaning 'a race between mowers'. Sharp himself coined the immortal phrase 'those green savannahs of heart's desiring' and Cappielow's pitch has always been gloriously green because of the almost constant drizzle that refreshes the roots that other round-the-clock rains cannot reach.

Alighting at Cartsdyke Station, the winter weather seemed to have turned (although the games scheduled for Clydebank, Brechin, Albion Rovers, Ross County and Stranraer had all been called off). Instead of stepping out into an air temperature of absolute zero (which Lord Kelvin calculated to be -273.15°C, but which modern scientists have never quite managed to replicate because they've not been doing their experiments at 4.30 p.m. on Saturdays at Scottish football grounds – when the atoms in supporters' fingers and toes really do become totally motionless), I was soaked in raindrops that must have been pleasantly close to my body temperature of 37°C. But by the time I'd walked the 200 yards down to the main Glasgow–Gourock road, the wind-chill factor would have had emperor penguins attacking each other with bloodied beaks (the emperors being the only non-territorial species of penguin, which allows them to nest-huddle together and therefore reduce their metabolic rate – unlike the violently aggressive Airdrie penguins, who play football with their own unincubated eggs).

River-front Greenock is a ghastly combination of dilapidated warehouses and rusting shipyards – Kvaerner being the only yard still operating – and pagoda-roofed post-modern monstrosities built by incoming companies like the Royal Bank of Scotland. Acres of rubble-strewn wasteland separate each example of the two architectural styles (Heavy Industrial and Pseudo Service). I walked almost two miles into the town centre, where some fine Victorian public buildings gave way to a pre-stressed concrete Lafferty's Irish theme pub and yet another bloody hideous modern shopping mall.

I doubled back rather than climb the steep hill to the top of the town, where Greenock rather unexpectedly divides into socially polarised West and East Ends. The former is made up of sandstone villas and 'Brookside Close' developments, while the latter comprises communal tenements without tiled closes and concièrge-less tower blocks (although if facing north residents of either have glorious views of the River Clyde and the rolling hills of lower Loch Lomond and upper Helensburgh, which, if nuked, would effectively wipe out most of the playing and management staff of Rangers FC).

Squelching up Sinclair Street I had become functionally blind, the rivulets of rainwater pouring down my spectacle lenses misting up because of my hot and harried exhalations. Whipping off my smart 'deconstructionist' Italian frames, I squeezed an eyeball with thumb and forefinger to try and get some helpful visual definition. Stand, £1,100! *Au secours!* No, ten quid. I foolishly let a policemen search my backpack, while still wearing it, and my heart was in my mouth because it contained a few spliffs and all the copy and unwritten-up notes for this book (and in retrospect I was far more likely to lose them by carrying the damn things everywhere with me than I would have been by leaving them back at the flat for convicted criminal manuscript burglars).

Once inside I waited for my lenses to clear and then took a bench seat in the 60-year-old Main Stand. Apart from benches having been installed on the steep embankment of the Wee Dublin End in 1978, Cappielow has remained in an architectural time-warp since 1960 (when a roof was put on the terracing opposite the Main Stand). The East Terrace remains open to the elements. The floodlights situated on both roofs surged into high-watt life when activated – unlike the ScottishPower-supplied equivalents at Tynecastle for the visit of Celtic, which remained frustratingly unillumi-nated for half an hour, resulting in a 20-minute delay in getting the game started and a Mexican Wave joke circulating Cappielow to the effect that not only were all linesmen Protestants but so were all electricians (Green-ockers who leave in supporters' buses for the Big G *tend* to be destined for Celtic Park).

Prior to Morton kicking off, the club mascot – a blue-and-white striped dragon! – was getting more and more drookit in his furry costume. Hardly able to put one foam rubber foot in front of another, which would have had Stuart Hall in hysterics if Greenock had been playing their Joker in *It's a Knockout*, a blazered official kicked complimentary *Daily Star* footballs into the crowd instead (where friendships that had survived the Upper Clyde Shipbuilders' sit-in disintegrated over arguments about possession of the freebies).

Morton don't need a moronic match-day mascot, because they have two modern-day local heroes. In the early '60s owner-manager Hal Stewart revived the corpse that Cappielow had become by importing the first wave of Scandinavian players to Scotland. From second bottom of the old Second Division, Stewart led Morton in less than two years to a League Cup final in 1963–64 against Rangers, and although they lost 5–0 they won their Division in the same season, winning 23 games in a row. (My slight huff at my boss for not taking Celtic's title aspirations seriously evaporated when he mentioned in passing that his father had been a first-team regular with Morton in the 1950s, Johnnie 'Flying' Swanson even playing against Celtic and Rangers; despite trying not to be, I was impressed, even if the family footballing talent had obviously skipped a generation.) By 1979–80 Morton actually led the Premier League for a short spell.

Current manager Allan McGraw is the longest-serving manager in Scottish football, and if new identikit stands ever go up at Cappielow one of them will undoubtedly be named after the Hamlet-smoking, craggy-faced guru of attacking football. For the past 20 years he has had knee surgery almost annually and now requires crutches. In 1995 he collapsed with an ulcer problem at East End Park, followed by a near-fatal heart attack a year later. Having pulled through and just missed out on promotion to the Premier Division, this season saw him lose his wife Jean after a short illness. To fill the vacuum of an empty home, he hobbles to a game of some sort six nights of the week. On the subject of managerial pressure he also talks brutal common-sense: 'I don't believe in stress – it's a piece of nonsense! Stress is if you're unemployed and worrying about having no money to pay the bills and feed your family.' McGraw has continued Morton's reputation for being 'the Arnold Clarks of Scottish football, since nothing stays in the shop window for long'. At the end of 1995 Morton sold Derek McInnes to Rangers, and of the current team high-scoring Derek Lilley was likely to move soon.

Morton needed to exterminate East Fife to kick-start their marooned-in-mid-table season, and the expected victory would have meant 13 defeats in a row for the doomed Fifers. After ten years of strip design madness – the nadir of which was an all-red tartan number sponsored by Buchanan's Toffees – Morton had reverted to their classic blue-and-white hoops, with shirt sponsorship by James Watt College.

The ball sponsor, one Billy McIntosh, had been attracted over from Canada by the Ton's site on the Internet, and although ex-Berwick centre-forward Warren Hawke had his kit sponsored by ex-*Scotsport* presenter Arthur Montford, his boots failed to make contact with anything but air molecules in the early stages (and one goal in 41 games led to him being dropped for a game). East Fife were as wobbly as you'd expect from a team who had conceded 62 goals in 21 League games and whose squad featured players recruited from Portadown, Methilhill Strollers, Dundonald Bluebell, Anstruther Colts, Superstar Rangers, Shettleston Juniors, Lochare Welfare, Cupar Hearts, Inverkeithing, Norton House and Colchester United. As the only part-timers in Division One, they had my sympathy; as a part-time writer with a sleep-deprivation-causing day job and a kitchen-table escritoire, I dream of advances and royalties that I can live on, as well as four massive office-furniture desks in a bay-windowed study overlooking Lake Geneva (or even Kames Bay in Millport). Enervated East Fife held out for 15 minutes before succumbing to a cross from Morton's assistant manager and left-back Peter Cormack. Centre-half Colin McFarlane left it and 34-year-old keeper Lindsay Hamilton watched in disbelief as it bounced into the net unaided.

The stoic Morton fans in the stand were getting less philosophical as the missed chances began to defy statistical probability and the known laws of physics (God may not play dice with the Universe but he was playing havoc with Hawke's red-shifted shooting boots). As I flicked through the excellent programme I mused on whether the 'crowd doctor' might have been some kind of group psychotherapist. 'Whose that new fat left-back of oors?' an indulgent Fifer asked. His less than laid-back friend turned to the pre-printed team list. 'Ah dinna really ken . . . Gibb? . . . He's a bloody balloon, whoever he is – wi' aboot as much sense aw direction. Oi, Fat Bloke – naw!'

At half-time a quarter of the patrons in the wooden structure bounded down the Exit stairs to a concrete corridor where smoking was permitted – me among them. The second 45 minutes were even more frustrating for the home fans, as Lindsay Hamilton began to enjoy a game where he wasn't picking the ball out of the net every ten minutes. With all three substitutes on the park for the visitors, they were reduced to ten men when new signing from Alloa Barrie Moffat was carried off with concussion. Macfarlane followed after a second bookable offence. With two minutes left, Morton sub Paddy Flannery broke clear and sidefooted past an apoplectic Hamilton. By full-time most of the 1,800 crowd were on their way home to nice dry living-rooms: 2–0.

Taking shelter from the rain back at the station, I joined about 20 other bedraggled fans huddling together beneath an open-walled shelter about the size of a small car-port. On my Walkman I listened to the live commentary as Celtic defended a precarious 2–1 lead against Hearts (and the sooner the BBC reintroduces a second broadcaster who shouts out numbers corresponding to the numbered squares on a pitch diagram printed in the *Radio Times* the better). Celtic held out – just.

As for Greenock Morton, they'll probably survive but unless the five-year moratorium on League reconstruction is lifted before 1999 – to allow a 16-team Premier Division – the Ton will probably have to accept that the great years of top-flight football from 1977 to 1981 are not going to return before the end of the century. Their one major trophy was the Scottish Cup in 1922, when they beat Rangers 1–0 in the final. If they can avoid the Ibrox superstars along the way, a repeat in the same century just might be possible, which would mean Allan McGraw could die a happy man. God knows he deserves it. As does de-industrialised Greenock, Port Glasgow and possibly end-of-the-line gentrified Gourock. Then again, if they went down like a financial *Titanic* overnight it wouldn't be hard to understand why – they've got a romantic but unacceptably old-fashioned ground that needs millions of pounds invested to bring it up to modern-day standards.

FOOTNOTES
1. 'A Dream of Perfection' by Alan Sharp, pp.209–26, *We'll Support You Evermore* (Souvenir Press, 1976), eds. Ian Archer and Trevor Royle.

RUGBY PARK
Kilmarnock v Dunfermline Athletic
Premier League, 18.1.97

Having read, and bought, every paperback published by William
McIlvanney, my life once imitated art to the extent that I asked a ScotRail
ticket clerk for 'a cheap day return to Graithnock', so irritatingly
intertwined and confusingly connected had the real town of Kilmarnock
become with the Ayrshire novelist's fictional representation of the place in
my sieve-like sewer of a mind. But like match-reporting on the Kilmarnock
teams of 1993–95 (who weren't a Nicotinell patch on the breathtakingly
exciting and successfully sssmokin' League winners of 1965 or the 7–2
conquerors of Antwerp in the Fairs Cup of 1967, or even the brutally
barnstorming promotion chasers from Division Two in 1990), the brick-
and-mortar reality of the town pales in comparison to the rose-and-sepia-
tinted image refracted by the powerful prism of McIlvanney's mind and
memory. Some slightly sexist and sentimental stereotyping is, however,
transformed into high literary art by brilliant turns of phrase, sledge-
hammer storytelling stamina and a screamer of a socialist shot.

A veteran of Ally's Tartan Army and the disastrous expeditionary force
to Argentina, McIlvanney was a great admirer of Jock Stein's Lisbon Lions
rather than a Celtic fan as such. Instead of appointing reserve-team coach
Bobby Williamson as manager after the sacking of Alex Totten, Kilmarnock
FC could have done much worse than to offer the job to McIlvanney. At the
very least his post-match press conferences would have provided some
highly original and entertaining quotes, rather than the cliché-gibbering,
non-sequitur-spouting and self-justifying shibboleth-spraying silliness
inflicted on yawning reporters by successive Killie managers Tommy Burns,
Totten and Williamson. Under McIlvanney's leadership, Rugby Park would
undoubtedly have reverted to being a terraced stage for 'working-class
theatre', instead of the current all-seated auditorium for 'middle-class
cabaret' (and to continue with and extrapolate this analogy, Celtic and
Rangers appear to have Lloyd-Webberish ambitions to promote and develop
'aristocratic rock opera').

Arriving at Kilmarnock Station, I couldn't fail to notice Celtic fans in full
marketing regalia assembling on the platform – part of Scottish football's
strange sociological phenomenon of inverted-pyramid supporting
allegiances, whereby Old Firm fans begin heading for Parkhead or Govan
from every part of Scotland as early as Friday afternoon every weekend.
Indeed, if every Celtic and Rangers supporter were to be electronically
tagged and their green or blue 'radar blips' highlighted on a giant map of

the country, the fortnightly convergence of each colour at three o'clock on Celtic Park or Ibrox Stadium would make for fascinating viewing up to 24 hours prior to kick-off, especially the flashing dots of light representing those unfortunate individuals who never quite make it as far as the Big G to claim their seats – for example, road traffic fatalities, broken-down motorists and alien abductees. Bleeps for the first of these would be largely static, for the second seemingly random-moving as vehicles were abandoned in favour of trains, planes and other automobiles, while for the third the writhings of Saturday-morning sex would be followed by a whooshing light-trail off the screen . . .

I asked two middle-aged Tims to pose by the departures board for a quick photo to illustrate the above point. Having done so with good-natured grace, I hurriedly noted their names in my notebook as the Glasgow-bound train pulled in. 'John Bennie? . . . Spelt with a 'y', aye? . . . No? . . . But that's my name. Bennie. David Bennie!'

'You're not the guy –'

'Yes!? . . .'

'– whose book about Celtic I bought?'

'Yup, that's me.'

After a quick handshake, surname-sharing author and reader departed. The chances of meeting a stranger who'd bought and read my first book must have been minuscule, but for that person to share the same relatively rare spelling of surname, the odds against must have been astronomical (and a couple of weeks later Mainstream forwarded a very nice letter from my equally surprised namesake). It was a weird but wonderful start to my visit to Kilmarnock – even if things began to go almost vertically downhill thereafter.

The drizzle was relentless and I took a zigzagging route down the High Street for intermittent shelter in the cornucopia of charity shops (branches of national 'brand names' being well-lit and warm, while local outlets like the Kilmarnock Colon Cancer Casbah smelled of unwashed incontinence and damp death). Ignoring the 'Bobbie Burns' shopping centre, I nevertheless shopped until I nearly dropped, the cut-price cast-offs for sale in the charity shops giving me the illusion of having real consumer spending power once again. *I'll have that . . . that . . . and . . . Oh, all of those!* Post-Purchase Regret Syndrome wouldn't set in until later, when I attempted to store my purchases in the claustrophobic confines of Rugby Park's concertina-ed rows of cramped seating (and a few days later when trying on a 'Large' Caffrey's T-shirt which, when viewed sideways on in a full-length mirror, made my ironing-board-flat abdominals look like Demi Moore's pregnant belly in her notorious nude *Vanity Fair* cover photo shot).

Taking my seat in the Moffat Stand home end, I immediately regretted not paying an extra two quid for the greater leg-room available in the refurbished Main Stand to my left. With blue-steel cantilevers on top of all three new stands, Rugby Park resembles yet another scaled-down Murrayfield (where Scotland's new £50,000-a-year-minimum professionals were to lose 19–34 to the unemployed but amateur Welsh that afternoon).

The speed with which Rugby Park was transformed from triple-sided terracing (less than a year) and the remarkably low construction costs (less than £4 million) make it seem like an impressive achievement, but only if you're an accountant circling overhead in a helicopter. All three new stands have tip-down plastic seats whose bottoms and fixed backrests meet to form an acute angle. Non-crippling knee-room was obviously not deemed to be a spectating *sine qua non* at the blueprint stage, and the restricted space for sitting can only be justified if the architects were told that Kilmarnock was a town renowned for dwarfism, with the residential area surrounding the ground notorious for its quantity of unexploded anti-personnel land-mines. The fact that only amputated midgets could get comfy in these agony-traps means that the redevelopment of Rugby Park has been a missed opportunity and false economy – made even less comprehensible by the largely unutilised capacity of 18,128. Apart from Old Firm fixtures, those who wish to watch Killie hardly need to be squeezed into the stadium – dragged in kicking and screaming, more like. The total attendance for the visit of Dunfermline was 5,813, of which the Moffat Stand could have housed 4,412. The cramped 'crouching' conditions are so uncomfortable – especially if you have fellow spectators seated to either side – that they would put me off going if I was a swithering local with ten quid and an afternoon to spare (although the powers-that-be who decided that Rugby Park should host the Scotland v Estonia international at the end of March obviously made their decision after stretching out their spindly legs, covered by tartan rugs, in the comfort of the Directors' Box).

As recently as 1994 the 'press box' was a segregated section of dry-rotten benches, with extension leads to old-fashioned phone booths at the back of the Main Stand which invariably got as irretrievably knotted as 18 rats with their tails tied together (with similar frenzied consequences amongst the assembled hacks). The new press row still had wood shavings from last-minute carpentry work all over its surface when it first opened for business, and in some ways was even more irritating because not only did the *faux* brass lamps screwed into the bendy beachwood not light up when switched on but they prevented reporters from spreading out all their paperwork. Yet another example of modern design and up-to-date technology not providing the aesthetic amelioration and functional benefits that they should. (The same could be said of the current Kilmarnock kit, the wonderful blue shirts and shorts, with white facings, from the 1960s having been ditched in favour of jerseys with thin blue-and-white stripes, almost as bad as Cowdenbeath's similarly sick-making colour scheme; and as a match reporter the Killie strip literally gave me a migraine, since the red numbers on the backs of the shirts were not centred on white panels and therefore almost disappeared as recognisable numerals from any distance.)

In the early '60s Kilmarnock were Scotland's leading provincial or town club, finishing runners-up four times before clinching the League title in 1965, but since beating Rangers 1–0 in May 1994 to avoid relegation, Killie have offered Premier League spectators little or nothing in the way of attacking football, flair players or exciting goals.

Despite having drawn 1–1 with visitors Rangers in midweek, Kilmar- nock were still stuck in eighth place as they prepared to do battle with mid- table Dunfermline (who surprisingly had not yet been sucked back into the relegation-haunted basement with Hibernian, Killie, Motherwell and Raith Rovers). The Pars' survival strategy had been to ignore humiliating defeats against the Old Firm while regularly beating those teams beneath them in the table. Kilmarnock's campaign to stay up seemed to be based solely on beating Hibernian three times, as well as sacking Alex Totten without any ready-made replacement in mind. The attempt to recruit Mark Hateley as player-manager backfired embarrassingly when the board offered him a financial deal considerably less generous than the one designed to lure him to Rugby Park as a mere player earlier in the year.

Kilmarnock's determination to do things on the cheap would be understandable if their ex-chairman Jim Moffat – replaced by Ronnie Hamilton in December – wasn't one of Britain's richest businessmen, having made a vast personal fortune in motoring and travel. His exact worth is difficult to estimate, but he could in theory have matched the £40 million investment made in Rangers by Bahamas-based Joe Lewis. Without some kind of cash injection, 'success' for an anaemic Killie side will continue to mean surviving in the Premier League – by boring opponents into a false sense of listless security and then sneaking a couple of fortuitous goals on the break . . .

Nil-nil at half-time summed up the dire proceedings, with any spark of dramatic life being immediately snuffed out by pedantic referee Andrew Waddell (whose 9-to-5 job as a pathologist was the inspiration for the terrible STV series *McCallum*). My pie merited laboratory analysis, because it was made with puff pastry, steak chunks and delicious gravy, the paper carton bearing the legend Scotch Pies from W.W. Wales. Very suspicious, that, edible eats at the footie . . .

By the start of the second period the American-style electronic score-board was beginning to irritate me intensely, with big white hands applauding Killie for getting out of their own half. Dunfermline began to dominate the play but in the 55th minute Killie humped a hopeful ball towards the back post, where Jim McIntyre went down like Jürgen Klinsmann carrying a sack of potatoes. Paul Wright hammered home the penalty. Six minutes later the Pars deservedly equalised, Andy Smith rising above the statuesque home defence to head past Dragoje Lekovic of Montenegro (Killie's only foreign import, signed from Buducnost Podgorica). With just over a minute left, McIntyre whipped over a dangerous cross. Wright bulleted his header in off the underside of the bar, and although Ian Westwater lay on his back holding the ball above his bald head, it had definitely crossed the line: 2–1. With Hibs, Motherwell and Raith all losing, it was a good day for Killie in the end (but not for neutral or knock-kneed spectators).

Mark Reilly, one of Killie's *better* players, is sponsored by Lawnmower and Chainsaw Services, a company who might make more appropriate shirt sponsors than AT Mays (because Kilmarnock are going nowhere – except possibly a guided tour of Division One). Most of the squad are meta-phorical lawnmower pushers, with only Lekovic and Wright charismatic and colourful enough to merit comparison with crowd-pleasing chainsaws. Sadly, however, the cut-off point for constructing a Scottish Super League comes too low to eliminate dreary Kilmarnock from the on-paper, top ten 'élite'.

I got hopelessly lost leaving Rugby Park, a combination of not exiting from the Main Stand and the unexpected presence of a new carpark and training ground, and I wasted 15 minutes walking away from the railway station. The rather smart bourgeois bungalows which surround the stadium form a sandstone maze if you get disorientated, and I had to sprint to catch the 17.28 to Glasgow. Otherwise I would have been stuck in Kilmarnock until nearly seven o'clock, which would have been okay if I'd remembered to bring *The Best of McIlvanney on Football* (given away as a free sampler by *Goal* magazine and written by William's big brother Hugh, the best sportswriter of his generation), and which I could have read in the great wee station buffet. From bitter experience I know that hitting one of Kilmarnock's many pubs wouldn't have meant listening to Tam Dochertys, Dan Scoulers and Charlie Grants performing their latest 'oral novels'.

Still, if ever I have the choice of going to Rugby Park again or staying at home to read, say, McIlvanney's latest award-winning novel *The Kiln*, I know which one I'll plump for. And since it would involve putting my feet up and purring with pleasure, visiting Rugby Park obviously isn't it.

TYNECASTLE PARK
Heart of Midlothian v Cowdenbeath
Scottish Cup, Third Round, 25.1.97

The Jam Tarts versus the Blue Brazil. Fourth-top of the Premier versus fourth-bottom of the Third. City giant Goliaths versus pit village Daveys (even if the former had been 'sleeping' for 35 years and the latter had been without a working mine for even longer). But unlike the English FA Cup, which is only 'sponsored by Littlewoods' and where seismically shocking results are almost guaranteed, in the 'Tennents Scottish Cup' – to give it its fully sold-out commercial name – major upsets are about as few and far between as seed-spillingly sexy scenes in Sir Walter Scott novels (from one of which Heart of Midlothian derive their wonderfully romantic moniker).

Only when meeting Pamela at Haymarket Station did I realise that I'd never actually been to Tynecastle before (not as a Celtic fan, an honorary Hibee, a neutral, or even as a match reporter – roles that had taken me to the Emerald Isle of Easter Road on countless occasions). Although I'd started to semi-support Hibs as a young teenager in Glasgow, kitted out in their gloriously green-and-white cotton jersey of the mid-'70s (life-affirming spiritual armour not yet defaced by a Calor Gas/Carlsberg logo), personal animosity towards the malignant maroon of Hearts only began to grow in 1976, during a school trip to Iona when news of the confirmed 3–0 Rangers victory in that May's Cup final filtered through the transistor radio static as we crossed the short sound of water between Mull and the holy island. Our comprehensive's only Jambo looked homesick (for Gorgie), humiliated and heartbroken. I was laughing so hard that I almost took a header over the starboard side of the small ferry boat.

Hun worship I could understand, even respect; but Jambo love? The 'third force' of Scottish football (potentially, but self-declared) have not actually won anything since the League Cup in 1962, and one of the reasons they're the third-most-disliked club in Scotland (currently, but objectively observed) is their sense of sleeping-giant superiority and penchant for bathetic boasting (as in listing victory in the Tennents Sixes under 'Honours' at the start of the match programme). A League flag has not fluttered over Tynecastle since 1960 – although in 1986 the cult of Chairman Mercer, almost produced a Championship success, Hearts losing the title to Celtic on the last day of the season on goal difference after they went down 2–0 to Dundee at Dens Park – while the last Scottish Cup win was as far back in the mists of time as 1956. Forty years on, the Scottish Cup final was narrowly lost 5–1 to Rangers, while towards the end of 1996 the Coca-Cola Cup final was conceded 4–3 to the same vastly superior opponents. Still, getting humped by the Huns in back-to-back finals was at least an improvement on being shafted by the Diamonds of Airdrie in sado-masochistic semis.

Although the 1996–97 season saw Hearts registering the third-best season-ticket sales in Scotland, their home crowd average of 12,611 was still just behind the 13,000-plus piling into Pittodrie to support an Aberdeen side summarisable as Aitken's Ale House Brawlers. Depending on where the line is drawn, Hearts in the 'modern era' are somewhere between tenth and 15th in terms of achieving silverware success. No wonder 30-something males from the West side of Edinburgh sometimes slide into sozzled self-pity in Rose Street howffs, slurring lamentations about 'Thirty-five years of hurt, ye ken?'. Such a lifetime of supporting misery even included relegation for the first time in 1977 and near bankruptcy.

Never having walked down Gorgie Road before, I was surprised at how similar it was to Leith Walk, both in never-ending length and working-class tenement atmosphere. This area of the capital has always been a closed book to me, and unlike the environs of Easter Road it has not been put on the low-life literary map by the likes of Irvine Welsh (whose lugubrious Leithers and heroin-addicted Hibees must be more fun to read about than to share a close, landing or outside toilet with).

The fact that Pamela had agreed to attend the match was perhaps surprising, since her last experience of Edinburgh football fans had been in Dundee, where Hibee crackhead casuals had attacked her and her then boyfriend because they had been offended by the sight of white and brown skin in close physical proximity (Pamela is Scottish–Sri Lankan). Unsurprisingly, she was rooting for Hearts – with the exception of Gary Mackay, whose alleged racial taunting of Hibernian's Kevin Harper earlier in the season had not gone unreported in the London media.

The crowd eventually totalled a remarkable 11,485, and although £13 seemed a bit steep for entry to the sepulchral Main Stand, the view from Row A of the wooden top level made the financial sacrifice seem less painful. The Wheatfield Stand opposite and the even newer School End Stand to our right were supported by exposed goalframe tubing, rather than yet more cantilevers, and both were serviced by mid-level con-courses or walkways. Strangely, the steel supports were painted pink and somehow managed to appear not unattractive. Beneath our warped wooden floorboards, young boys were able to smoke in their bucket seats (in the concreted Paddock). Only the Gorgie Road end was unfinished, consisting of uncovered seating for away fans. A planned share issue should provide the funds for a new 3,500-seater stand, to be built by Christmas 1997.

'No, you take seat 36,' said Pamela, exchanging ticket-stubs. 'Since that's how old you are next week.'

'Christ, thanks, I'd forgotten about that . . . You know that old Channel 4 series *thirtysomething*? I remember settling down to watch it, cheered up by the fact that I was only 29, with marriage to a Hope-lookalike and a sexy job in advertising to look forward to . . .'

'Talk about six wasted years . . . How's the book going?'

'Don't ask . . . At least seven grounds to go and I feel like a conscripted sailor on board the *Pequod*. Every Saturday morning I've got my own internal Captain Ahab screaming at me to get up out of my nice warm bunk – to climb up yet another God-forsaken stadium's crow's-nest and well-nigh freeze to death . . . Spending this season wading through *Moby Dick* would have made more sense.'

'You love it really, though.'

'I don't – it's literally unreadable . . . Hey, what's up with this coffee? . . . God, it's real. Kenco! . . . Good coffee, good weather, good ground, good crowd – Good God, we'll maybe even get a good game if this goes on.'

Within ten minutes Colin Cameron headed Hearts into the lead, the diminutive forward being yet another bargain brought in by manager Jim Jeffries. Post-Bosman, Jeffries had also snapped up talented Neil McCann and free-scoring Jim Hamilton. Foreign frees had proved equally as effective, a £6.5 million debt not preventing the capture of Pasquale Bruno, Gilles Rousset, Stephane Paille and Stefano Salvatori. He'd also moved on joke Jambos like Neil Berry, David Hagen, Henry Smith, Fraser Wishart, Brian Hamilton, Craig Nelson and Willie Jamieson, getting them off the wage bill if nothing else.

By proving to be a wheeler and dealer of near genius, Jeffries was indirectly responsible for the sackings of Alex Miller and Jocky Scott across the city (at largely debt-free but moribund Hibernian). On the Thursday prior to this game, Hibs drew 2–2 at home to Aberdeen in another third-round Cup-tie. Although ending four straight defeats under new boss Jim Duffy, this score draw was also significant because it meant that Hearts had no longer scored more goals at Easter Road than Hibs. Before Greg Miller and Pat McGinlay's strikes Hearts had scored ten in three games, Hibs nine in 12. And although the local derby rot had been stopped, the Hearts shop was still selling vast quantities of the video *22 in a Row* (featuring highlights of this number of games against Hibernian without defeat).

In the 12th minute David Weir replaced Celtic's Jackie McNamara as the scorer of the most spectacular goal that I'd so far witnessed this season. His 30-yard shot started left, then began slicing towards the top right corner of the net (although seeing it from directly behind the scorer may have made it look even better). 'Pamela, he's a fucking intellectual, too, with a degree in anthropology – well, no, advertising – from America!'

'Well, so's Robbo – he writes that column for *The Scotsman*.'

Hmm . . . Not exactly a clinching criterion that, is it? I mean, does 'Shopping Around With Beryl' make her a member of the shopperati? John Robertson duly made it 3–0 from the penalty spot in the 22nd minute (and although his newspaper column is a good enough read, he is undoubtedly the most entertaining and informative radio interviewee amongst Scottish professionals).

It could have been 6–0 by the break, so abysmal were the Blue Brazil. In 1983 Cowdenbeath earned a replay against Hearts in a League Cup match, before losing on penalties.[1] Centre-half Craig Levein was transferred a few months later for £30,000, but to put the post-Bosman bleating into perspective, this was the last time Cowdenbeath had reared a player good enough to be transferred for big money. Against Hearts, only goalkeeper Neil Russell earned pass marks, and with over 500 people chasing every job vacancy in the Fife town, a Job Centre XI could not have played more ineptly. (Prior to kick-off the Scottish League released figures which confirmed Cowdenbeath as the worst-supported senior club in Britain, with average attendances of 295.)

In the second half Robertson side-footed a Cameron corner home after 63 minutes, after a series of inept corners from the other side of the pitch taken by Steve Fulton. Each time the ex-Celt, christened 'Baggio' by Billy McNeill, prepared to take a corner, kids in the stand wailed, 'Aw naw, it's Four-Ton Fulton!'. An overweight journeyman midfielder with a phizog like a collapsed lung, Fulton never really recovered from McNeill's hyperbolic praise. (As I write, McNeill is at it again, being quoted in the *Daily Mirror*'s 'Mania Plus' magazine: 'He really should be in Hollywood as an actor, probably a leading man.' Ye what? Oi, McNeill – *No!* Even if you are describing Paul McStay – who is becoming increasingly sad-eyed in his declining years – rather than Fulton.) In the 68th minute Neil Pointon made it 5–0. In the dying seconds Robbo's attempt at hat-trick happiness screwed off the foot of the right-hand post, spun along the goal-line, and then went out for a goal-kick beyond the left-hand post. Incredible.

When the final whistle blew, I was convinced that there must have been at least ten minutes left to play, which is a pretty reliable indication of having become immersed in an enjoyable match. The only unpleasant moment had come late in the first half, when 'smoke' from the Gorgie Road end of the timber-dry old stand had begun drifting over half the pitch. Genuinely concerned that a Scottish 'Bradford' may have been about to incinerate another group of innocent fans – with Pamela having to be socked on the jaw to provide me with a limp human shield (as a future best-selling writer, I would have had to consider the happiness-of-the-greatest-number argument) – I was relieved in the extreme to recognise the distinctive smell of fermenting hops, emanating as it did from the nearby distillery. (Don't get me started on the way that death, like a goal, can appear from nowhere out of a clear blue sky.)

Under rotating chairmen Chris Robinson and Leslie Deans, Hearts definitely seem to be stirring from their 35-year-long slumbers, and it's only to be hoped that a debt-to-income ratio that would condemn a Third World country to hyper-inflation and military dictatorship doesn't lead to any further financial crises at Tynecastle. (Two days before the visit of Cowden to Tynecastle, Millwall had to call in the administrators and Bournemouth the receivers.)

Having flirted with Hearts on what was basically a business trip, next season I could see myself being deliberately unfaithful to the harridans and harpies who currently hump the ball down the Easter Road slope. Frankly, I'd prefer to play away from my second footballing home while cheering the blood-red shirts of Torino, but the current maroon of Hearts is a colour I could get used to. And I do prefer Strongbow cider to Carlsberg lager. Hmm . . . I'm definitely on the brink of switching my Edinburgh allegiances – I could divorce Hibernian on the grounds of mental cruelty – and if half the attraction of affairs is sexual novelty, the grass sward at Tynecastle does seem much greener. Like Torino, however, who never recovered from the Superga air crash of 1949 (they're currently in Serie B), I'm not sure Hearts will ever get over Albert Kidd's two late strikes at Dens Park in 1986. Whether crippled by a fear of failure, or made frigid by being scared of success, do I really want to become involved with born losers? Another 35 years of hurt? . . . Ask me again in 2031 – when I'm a sexy and successful 70-year-old and Hearts will surely have won something . . . 'Oh God, no – 69 years of hurt! Let's go and dig up Albert Kidd's corpse and throw stones at it.'

FOOTNOTES
1. Wallace Mercer's final financial link with Hearts was broken soon after the Cowdenbeath game, when he sold his remaining 25 per cent shareholding to Robinson and Deans. As chairman in the 1980s, the cult of Mercerism bedevilled the club. When Hibee sci-fi fans re-read Philip K. Dick's *Do Androids Dream of Electric Sheep?*, it became obvious that the property developer was intent on reinventing himself in the style of 'Wilber Mercer'. As chairman he attempted to sell empathy boxes by mail order, and Hearts fans foolish enough to buy them ended up in trances following 'the upward climb of Wallace Mercer' – which always ended with a virtual-reality stoning, before

returning to consciousness (with genuine bruises!). Manager Alex McDonald had a secret *Swiss Cottage* building society account in the name of 'Buster Friendly' and if the Mercerites were still in control at Tynecastle the whole place might by now have succumbed to total and complete 'kippleisation'.

EAST END PARK
Dunfermline Athletic v Celtic
Premier League, 29.1.97

Although this game was pencilled into my *faux* Filofax for personal
pleasure, I was tempted to give the Wednesday-night visit to the home of
Scotland's very own Crazy Gang a protesting bodyswerve. Just before noon
I had received a telephone call from a credulous acquaintance, who excitedly
insisted Celtic were taking over Wimbledon and joining the English
Premiership. When I expressed sleepy scepticism in my expletive-
punctuated response, he told me to buy a copy of the Glasgow *Evening Times*
(which had splashed the 'story of the decade' over the front and back
covers, as well as pages 2, 3, 4, 44, 45, 46 and 47). Resisting the temptation
of returning to my nice warm bed, I rushed along to Waverley Station to
buy an early edition. Other capital-based Celts joined me on the concourse
and it didn't take much skim-reading to reach the conclusion that the *Times*
was 'flying a fucking kite' (launched into the stratosphere by Ian McGarry,
who had started off in sports journalism as an absolutely brilliant
broadsheet *belles-lettriste*, and who merited every pound and parking-perk
benefit that Glasgow's evening tabloid presumably had to fork out to secure
his writing services).

   The 'exclusive' had no basis in truthful reality, it merely being the result
of footballing politics and newspaper economics. The spin on the story was
designed as a warning to the 15 chairmen of full-time but struggling clubs
who had assembled at Clyde's Broadwood Stadium in Cumbernauld to push
for yet another bout of League reconstruction, with the proposed 16-12-12
set-up not finding favour with Celtic chairman Fergus McCann. By inflat-
ing the story out of all proportion – based on a Machiavellian but hardly
earth-shattering admission by McCann that his board had 'discussed' the
possibility – *The Times* had boosted its sales dramatically. All over Glasgow
new readers must have bought a copy, read the relevant nine pages in head-
shaking but smiling disbelief, and then dumped the paper in the nearest
waste-bin (although I must admit I saved my copy as a memento).

   Having momentarily allowed myself to anticipate Celtic playing the
likes of Manchester United, Newcastle, Liverpool and even Leicester on a
regular basis, the trip to freezing Dunfermline seemed depressingly
unglamorous. But sitting in the Main Stand that night, with three sides of
terracing packed to capacity, Scottish football didn't seem that limited a
stage for the new commercially cavalier Celtic (who with over 40,000
season-ticket-holders were set to smash the million-home-fans-in-a-season
barrier for the first time in their history).

a season in hell

The Pars' mascot Sammy the Tammy made a complete arse of himself by playing air guitar to Sandie Shaw's 'Puppet on a String', but when he persuaded the Dunfermline players to join him in a pre-match huddle – mimicking Celtic's male-bonding exercise – the home supporters applauded appreciatively. Dunfermline were bloody unlucky not to get at least a point, and there's no way their defence could have anticipated the source of Celtic's 36th-minute opener – namely Paul McStay, scoring his first goal in almost 11 months. Just before the interval Jorge Cadete made it seven successive games with his name on the scoresheet. After the turn-around, Celtic's David Hannah managed to miss an open goal from three yards out, and I suggested to Alan that we form a David Hannah Fan Club – which, unlike Cadete's official version, wouldn't cost £14.75 to join and which would only be disbanded early in the 21st century when hapless Hannah broke his scoring duck.

Two-nil: 86 goals in 32 games, taking me that much closer to seeing a century of goals during my season in hell. My goal average remained at a disappointing 2.7 per game (with a little bit of rounding-up).

Celtic in the Carling Premiership? It would be great if they were, but they never will be. In the next few years there is going to be a Scottish Super League and/or the Old Firm playing in midweek European competition. Without Celtic and Rangers, Scottish football would survive, and not just in the sadly semi-professional condition of the Irish game. The cut-throat competition for *trophies* would boost crowds for clubs like Dunfermline, even if total attendances fell dramatically, and without the Glasgow giants Hearts might even live up to their 'third force' tag (behind Aberdeen and Dundee United?). McCann's personal crusade to cull the 40-strong herd of senior Scottish clubs is a sign of the Sky-satellite-subscription times, but rubs against the moral grain if one recalls Celtic's historic powerbase amongst the smaller clubs (in return for considering their long-term futures). But on Planet Football today, I guess it's every corporate multinational and global brand name for itself . . .

Oh, look – there's a blue-and-white-hooped pig floating off to play in the Premiership. Come on, Timbledon, get tore intae them Bournemouth Rangers – they don't like it up 'em! . . .

184

TANNADICE PARK
Dundee United v Hibernian
Premier League, 8.2.97

Dens Park bathed in balmy August sunshine was to be superseded by the unenticing prospect of Tannadice buffeted by February gales. Having been laid low by a dose of virulent Wahun flu – thereby missing Rangers versus Hearts and Celtic against Raith Rovers – I only made it out the door on Saturday morning courtesy of Contact 400 (dry-swallowing four capsules in 60 minutes, rather than the recommended one every four hours). The quadrupled medication stopped my red-raw nose running relentlessly but I felt unpleasantly zonked and uncomfortably dry-mouthed.

Dundee was the same urban disaster, except colder and greyer, with the plans to erect a Hollywood-type sign on Law Hill spelling out 'City of Discovery' in giant white letters inevitably abandoned – the local branch of the Samaritans, who advertise for the 'suicidal and despairing' in United's excellent match programme, fearing the loss of potential clients from the top of the 'T' in cry-for-help jumbee-jumps (with jute clothes-lines either a few feet too long or turned into neck-snapping nooses).

Instead, the city had acquired its very own literary prize, with £5,000 being offered for the best novel set in Dundee (but sadly excluding science-fiction, since this is one of the few genres potentially capable of capturing the essence or soul of jimcracked Juteopolis). Real and would-be writers were prostituting their artistic integrity faster than a professional virgin offered a million dollars for rolling in the hay as part of a two-backed beast. Old and new stories were relocated in the city and even I had retrieved an old file from my PC with the intention of figuring out the commands necessary for automatically replacing every mention of Venice with Dundee. As a working title, *A Venetian Hypothesis about Heaven* became *A Dundonian Idea of Hell*, and with a few extra word-processed changes, the opening paragraph just about stood up under the weight of geographical transposition: 'The 19th-century iron rail bridge' had of course to cross the Tay and not the Lagoon, with the Flying Scotsman replacing the Orient Express. *La Serenissima* became *Ra Citti di Discoveri* and the *Queen of the Adriatic* the *Joker of the North Sea*. The Basilica and St Mark's were replaced by Ninewells Hospital and the Caird Hall, and the Lido by the Fife side of the Tay . . .

I gave up on this futile exercise before losing the plot completely – unlike the lobotomised Livingston fans who, a few days into February, had circled down-town Hamilton in their Messerschmitt bubble-cars looking for demolished Douglas Park. No longer being owner-occupiers, the Accies were of course playing Livvy at Cliftonhill in Coatbridge, but the two New Towners then mistook the floodlights of Fir Park on the horizon for the home of Albion Rovers (whereas Motherwell's ground was hosting a Premier reserve fixture). The dynamic duo eventually got to the game in time to see Accies' final equaliser in a thrilling 3–3 draw. Talk about donkeys led by a Blobby.

With the 'Brothers Grimm' now in totalitarian control at Tannadice – with Big Brother Jim serving as bear-headed chairman and Wee Tam as a curmudgeonly chipmunk of a coach – the McLean Dynasty has been restored to its rightful place at the helm of Dundee's most successful club. Both brothers are gousty gloom-and-doom merchants – a family business once memorably described as 'Misery Incorporated' – but the older McLean won the League for United in 1983, and before that the League Cup twice (as well as masterminding incredible European runs culminating in a UEFA Cup final appearance in 1987).

After eight years without a trophy, McLean senior bumped himself upstairs to make way for Ivan Golac, a charismatic and charming Yugoslav who won the Scottish Cup for the Tangerine Terrors, for the first time in their history, in 1994. (Golac learned English from pop records, whereas his chairman appeared to have gleaned his vocabulary and attitudes from the Old Testament – as in sentences beginning 'Thou shalt not . . .') Within a year of achieving Cup glory, however, Golac was sacked for flirting with relegation. Billy Kirkwood duly led the Arabs into their exiled year in the First Division wilderness, although the promised land of the Premier League was regained after coming straight back up (albeit thanks to last-minute sand-dancing by Partick Thistle's defence in a second-leg play-off match and sun-blindness on the part of referee Les Mottram, who turned down a stonewall penalty for the Jags seconds before United grabbed a late, late lifeline to extra-time and promotion).

One point from a possible 12 at the start of this season sealed Kirkwood's fate, with Tommy McLean being recruited from Raith Rovers before his tea-and-two-slices, slap-down, midnight-to-midnight punishment fasts had time to take effect on the Stark's Park slackers. As well as recruiting a trio of impressive Scandinavians – even if not as wonderfully named as the 1960s trio of Orjan Persson, Finn Dossing and Lennart Wing – McLean junior signed Motherwell's midfield mucker Jamie Dolan. Not normally one to mince his words, Dolan's new manager indulged in an unusual euphemism when he stated: 'Jamie, Dave Bowman [Psycho] and Jim McInally play the game in a way which attracts suspensions, so this signing gives us vital cover.' In other words they're all brutal cloggers.

Since I wasn't heading for the press-box, I didn't break out in a cold sweat about the possibility of my press-pass 'paperwork' not being exactly in order. At Tannadice match reporters have to sign in, but if they slip up like Gordon Jackson boarding the bus in *The Great Escape*, stoney-faced stewards frogmarch representatives of the West Coast 'meedja' mafia to pay-at-the-gate public turnstiles. Before paying my £12 for entry to the top tier of the East Stand, the contents of my backpack were searched as suspiciously as a Palestinian's hand-luggage at Tel Aviv International Departures. The stroppy young constable whose number I noted down with barrack-room-lawyer bravado took some high-decibel convincing that my two remaining Contact 400 capsules weren't 'jellies'. Once inside, signs advised patrons to draw a steward's attention to any pigeon droppings splattered on the plastic seating. After which one of the mean-looking sons-of-bitches would no doubt rub your face in it . . .

The 9,219 crowd were 'entertained' by the Commercial Department's latest PR wheeze – a still-to-be christened lion mascot. I guess it will have to be Larry the Lion, in honour of Lawrence of Arabia (since United fans revel in their nickname 'Arabs').

The Hibee hordes were housed in the L-shaped Main Stand, beneath which collar-and-tied corporate sheiks in executive harems guzzled their way towards heart-attack horizontalism. To the right of the East Stand end, the two-tiered George Fox Stand was an impressive monument to the late chairman. The far end was taken up by the small West Stand. The Fair Play Enclosure will be replaced by a 1,700-seater stand in season 1997–98, giving a total capacity of 14,300. So while Dens Park goes to the structural dogs, down-the-same-street neighbour Tannadice continues to re-invent and up-grade itself architecturally. Budapest's BKV Elore and MTK may play in stadiums that share a load-bearing wall, but they cannot be as depressingly different in regard to spectating facilities. Dens Park was almost cobwebbing over before my eyes – what with its absentee landlord Ron Dixon – and Jim Duffy must have been delighted to escape its crumbling confines for Easter Road (leaving John 'Cowboy' McCormack to take over). If Tannadice is a security-patrolled private housing estate, Dens Park is a gypsy caravan site or a blue-collar trailer park.

On the football side, however, Duffy's first four League games had all ended in defeat, whereas United were going into this match on the crest of run which included eight consecutive League victories. Hibernian's stall was laid out early – constantly playing for offside – and with United's favoured 3-5-2 formation, the windswept centre-circle quickly became a congested vortex of hard-tackling mediocrity. Jim Leighton only had one good save to make before half-time.

Up the East Coast road in Arbroath, the match between 'the Manchester

Uniteds of Angus' and Albion Rovers had to be abandoned after the first 45 minutes because of hurricane-force winds sweeping across exposed Gayfield – with 100ft waves threatening to carry those in the crowd of 367 not lashed to crush-barriers back out to sea.

The presence of defender Erik Pederson, midfielder Lars Zetterlund and forward Kjell Olofsson not only explained the large number of Viking helmets on display (in the stands, not on the pitch) but were the workmanlike base on which United's mini-revival had been built. Good rather than great imports, this Scandinavian threesome had helped to improve United significantly but not spectacularly. Because of the cut-throat nature of the competition in the Premier League, though, any slight improvement in a team's overall standard and consistency of play can result in massive leaps up the table (in United's case to third). When Zetterlund hit the post with a header, when he should have scored, the frustration amongst the Tangerine Terrors began to gather momentum, so to speak.

Having cost a bargain £100,000 from QPR, Dutchman Sieb Dykstra was the busier of the two keepers in the second half, at one heart-stopping point having to scissor-kick away a goal-bound header from Greg Miller (son of old manager Alex, who had ended up coaching at glamorous Coventry). Willie Nesbit Miller was still turning out at right-back for Hibs, with his extra-long sleeves flapping in the wind, and if substitute Robbie Winters had been thrown on earlier he could probably have skinned the distracted defender (who, in retrospect, was obviously dreading the front-page exclusive to be carried in that Monday's Scottish *Sun*, which detailed married Miller's playing away from home with leggy model Leeann Mackay, 22, an infidelity made infinitely more embarrassing by the fact that she was also sharing her favours with Hearts heart-throb Kevin Thomas at the same time and had apparently told a friend that 'Kevin is wonderful in bed – and Willie is just all right'). With ex-Dark Blue destroyer Chic Charnley just one booking away from a five-match ban, and with his Hibernian contract sensibly stipulating pay-per-play payments only, it was left to Pat McGinlay to get sent off. Near the end young Miller blasted woefully wide when straight through on goal.

Nil-bloody-nil, and my nose was running like an open faucet.

With Tommy McLean doling out 'the stupidity pills', Dundee United are unlikely to get relegated again this century. As co-founders of the North-East's New Firm, United's fan base is healthily broad. Angus-based Arabs run supporters' buses out of Brechin, Forfar, Montrose and Carnoustie (for Arbroath), and the team have supporters' clubs in Inverness, Aberdeen, Edinburgh and Glasgow. Bizarrely, the only branch outside Scotland is based in Bermuda (the Tangerine Triangle). I can see the attraction, sort of, but until the mystery of the Tannadice Triangle is solved – home crowds persistently below 10,000 – United are probably doomed never to challenge seriously for another League title. They certainly won't come up against old manager Golac in European competition in season 1997–98, since he was appointed boss of Icelandic champions Akranes soon after the Hibs game. Helping them qualify for the Champions' League should prove to be more fun, if not easier, than running a chocolate factory in Belgrade (where forward-thinking Golac tried to introduce football-themed chocolate bars, although not Charnley Bars sadly, which would require a recipe for a confectionery which exploded in the mouth and took the consumer's head off in a massive taste explosion).

'If living is getting too much to bear,' read the Samaritans' advert in the programme, 'sharing these feelings may help.' After watching Scotland's 0–0 draw with Estonia on Tuesday, 11 February, played in Monaco, I thought I had successfully displaced my disappointment when I found myself willing the World Cup minnows to score with their last-minute sitter. But no, it was another rerun of the emotional wringers suffered against Peru and Iran (plus Costa Rica). Some commentators may mock the idea, but Argentina in 1978 really was Scotland's Vietnam. Unlike America though, our national pride and self-esteem have never really recovered from the psychological mauling (partly because a lack of Scottish internationals coming home in body-bags failed to give us satisfactory 'closure'). Trooping off the pitch, Ian 'Hatchet-Heid' Ferguson shouted at Colin Calderwood, 'Don't clap those fuckers' (the blood-spitting Tartan Army) and pitch-side microphones picked up the comment. All hell then broke loose in the media, but Ferguson apologised and everything was okay again, with Scotland back on course for France in '98. Tssh . . .

Post-modern Stade Louis II in Monaco was stunningly beautiful – even with its Neo-Brutalist concrete obtrusions in the middle – but if located in Tannadice Street it wouldn't have survived the howling North Sea gales for more than a month.

BROADWOOD STADIUM
Clyde v Kilmarnock
Scottish Cup, Fourth Round, 15.2.97

Like Soldier Field, the home of the Chicago Bears, Broadwood Stadium is
built by the shore of a lake (albeit man-made and minuscule). Like the
'Windy City', Broadwood is notorious for its 'gowling hales' (the ground
boasting the highest altitude of any stadium in Scotland). Chicago has
benefited from bustling and colourful immigrant communities, as has the
New Town of Cumbernauld (which started embracing calliper-crippled
Clyde fans overspilling from Rutherglen and the Gorbals 13 miles away in
1956, although the Bully Wee itself only followed in 1994, eight years after
having been evicted from Shawfield in Glasgow's East End, and after
groundsharing in Maryhill and Hamilton). Chicago is famous for its
skyscraper architecture and the soaring Sears Tower; 'Corbu City' for its
glass, concrete and steel boxes and Broadwood for only having two,
touchline, stands (although a new South Stand at one end had recently
upped its capacity to 8,000). Soldier Field boasts a glorious neo-classical
edifice high above the bleachers; the three-sided Tartan Citrus Bowl has
followed the international style of identikit, flat-packed stands. If good
architecture is 'shelter with decoration', Broadwood is an exposed exemplar
of 'expressed structure', a machine for getting buffeted to death in . . .

Although I didn't make the naïve mistake of going to Cumbernauld
Station this time (which requires a 15-minute *taxi* ride to reach Broadwood), alighting instead at Croy (supposedly a 15-minute walk away), I
still thought I'd got off in the wrong place. The station was in the middle
of non-metaphorical nowhere, surrounded by desolate hills and fields.
Feeling like Dr Watson sent down to Dartmoor ahead of his homosexual
and drug-addicted colleague, I half-expected the village idiot who gave me
worryingly vague directions to end his description of my route with a
warning about the Hound of Broadwood (possibly bitter and twisted ex-
boss Alex Smith, whose hang-dog expression and growling self-pity had
been getting steadily worse since September, when he had resigned in
protest at the long-suffering directors' decision to cut back on an enormous
full-time squad and Ajax-inspired soccer academy; into his third year in
charge, Clyde were second-bottom of the Second Division and facing a
third season without promotion, although according to saturnine Smith
another two years would have seen him leading Clyde into the Premier
League).

Up an un-signposted footpath I hauled my mental menagerie of meta-
phorical animals (a chaffing black dog called Depression, a gibbering

190

monkey on my back named Neurosis and a caterwauling meerkat christened Bipolar Maniac). The path eventually emerged at a deserted stretch of dual carriageway, which of course wasn't edged by pavements. At a large roundabout on the north edge of the town – which in 1966 won an architectural award as the world's best-designed community! – I started veering off in the direction of Kilsyth. Then I spotted, through my Swiss Army field-glasses, Broadwood lurking behind a 'landscaped' embankment. No AA or RAC signs? Please . . . Half the fun of being an away infantry fan is the need for Olympic-standard orienteering skills.

Sitting with the home support in the East Stand was a surreal experience. Kilmarnock had brought more fans to Broadwood than Clyde had managed to lure out of the surrounding white-collar-worker housing (despite the New Town having a larger population). A sea of blue and white faced us in the stand opposite – although Killie turned out in pink-and-grey stripes – with the visiting Ayrshire army also having to be billeted in the new South Stand. Clyde normally only have one stand open for business on Saturdays, for crowds of less than a thousand; but although competing up a division, out-of-town tenants Airdrie regularly pull in over two thousand.

Incredibly, there wasn't a breath of wind, which was just as well because at the open end a small advertising blimp was rising high into a clear blue sky (where no doubt its UFO-like presence was interpreted as yet another rip in the fabric of the space-time continuum by the nearby residents of Bonnybridge). At £1.50 the *Clyde View* programme merited its own X-File, comprising as it did 36 glossy and superbly designed colour pages, with copy content almost as good as the professional presentation. It even had a book review page, devoted to contemporary literary fiction! (Well, not quite – the critical analysis was restricted to a puffing of Jack Charlton's autobiography.) Under the editorship of John Taylor, it has won awards for the past five years, including twice as Scottish Programme of the Year (and it won again in 1997).

The not-very-deep subtext of most contributors' prose was that a youthful, enthusiastic and skilful Bully Wee, now managed by Gardner Spiers, were too damn silky and sophisticated for Division Two, with most other teams – specifically Stranraer – guilty of turning the League into a battlefield for Route One trench warfare. Although lying in an out-of-contention fourth place, with a goal difference of only plus four, Clyde had enjoyed a Cup run taking the scalps of Huntly, Ayr United and First Division St Mirren. Three more wins and they would be in a Scottish Cup final for the first time since 1958 (when they were victorious).

The romance of the Scottish Cup? Forget it – the first 45 minutes were

191

like being an unwilling voyeur in a marital bedroom where a flaccid husband and frigid wife were failing to get anywhere near scratching each other's seven-year itches. Even 21-goal hot-shot Eddie Annand – an £80,000 target of Hibernian and a graduate of the Sligo Rovers finishing-school – was struggling to get it up for the wet-and-wailing Mrs Robinsons in the crowd. As for Kilmarnock, I'd never witnessed so much dead meat failing to be flogged into life (although their verbally encouraging supporters were patiently understanding). Having failed to win the £250 half-time draw, I sat attempting to be philosophical about my final descent from panic-stricken genteel poverty (i.e. having a few hundred pounds in capital) to what George Orwell called 'future annihilating' penury (i.e. being reduced to a few jangling coins in threadbare pockets).

In the second period Killie continued to lie back and think of Ayrshire, but Clyde finally showed some signs of girding their chastity-belted loins. Surging down the left like watery semen chased by hot air from a hairdryer, Miller Mathieson picked out widget-sized winger Paul Brownlie with a carefully slide-ruled pass. The ball teed itself up perfectly for clear-through Brownlie, and his ambitious volley from the edge of the box would have made for a spectacular goal if he'd managed to sweetly connect lace with leather. Flailing wildly at thin air, he merely succeeded in falling over (thereby emulating Annand's earlier ass-backwards emergency landing).

At the other end, Killie's Paul Wright blatantly backed into teenage centre-half Jamie Prunty. No one on the pitch or in the stands got overly excited about an indirect free-kick for obstruction at least 94 yards from Dragoje Lekovic's goal-line (although a week later he would be humiliated from similar distances by Dundee United's hat-trick hero Ray McKinnon, who scored direct from dead-ball situations three times). Mike McCurry then made the most bizarre refereeing decision I'd yet seen, in 33 games, awarding the visitors a bad-joke penalty. Wright himself gratefully converted in the 63rd minute (and Killie had always looked like requiring a refereeing hand-job to get off the drooping mark). Kilmarnock profession-ally killed the game, but Clyde's full-time players should have been capable of at least discomforting 'dodgy wop' Lekovic (a frustrated fan's descrip-tion), Maltese left-back Dylan Kerr and pushing-36 centre-half Ray Montgomerie. McCurry was booed up the tunnel by the Bully Wee'ers, who were not happy Broadwood bunnies: 0–1.

Despite the first sign of spring in the form of daylight lasting well past 4.45 p.m., so that the floodlights were not needed, I followed the small band of disappointed Clyde fans back to the station with a heavy heart. Two express trains clattered through Croy without even slowing down, and I wasn't the only man leading a life of quiet desperation beyond the platform's yellow safety line. (Referee McCurry's body would have been unidentifiable if he'd chosen to commute back to Glasgow by train.)

On the Walkman I listened enviously to match summaries of exciting Cup-ties played elsewhere. First Division Falkirk had come from behind to beat the Premier Pars of Dunfermline 2–1, but the barmy Bairns of Brockville's terraces had once again attracted deserved media opprobrium by chanting rudely about their visitors' recently deceased captain Norrie McCathie (Falkirk and Dunfermline fans detest each other with an intensity that is positively Old Firmish).

In the Third Division, at Cowdenbeath's Central Park, home fans had started urging on Queen's Park as the amateur Spiders raced into a 4–0 lead. Despite a consolation goal for the Blue Brazil, greeted in almost complete silence by the crowd of 244, full-time saw shouted demands for manager Tom Steven's resignation. He didn't heed the calls. But five days later he was sacked, one win in 13 games since early November seeing Cowden fall from first to sixth place. Club chairman Gordon McDougall then met secretly with Cowden's stopper Sammy Conn, at the Harthill Service Station on the M8, to offer Conn the post of player-manager. Conn accepted and immediately accused Steven of never having gained the respect of the players (himself included). Splenetic Steven sounded off about how 'these kind of remarks could damage my reputation'. What – more than being sacked by Cowdenbeath?

Maybe Clyde chairman Bill Carmichael could arrange a clandestine meeting at Croy Station to re-recruit Craig Brown to manage the Bully Wee, if the Estonia result in Monaco should cost Scotland a World Cup place in France next year. As Clyde's gaffer at Shawfield, Brown successfully avoided the sack for ten years. Properly managed, Clyde should be struggling to get out of the First Division, not the Second. OKI could be replaced by IKEA as shirt sponsors, and the *gymnastic* academy could diversify into ballet coaching. 'Pas de deux, Pruntly, pas de deux! . . . Now then, now then. Now this is a test, innit, Alex (Miller or Smith) . . . 1–0 down to Stranraer . . . Pirouette, Paul, pirouette! . . . Do I not like, Stranraer, Alex . . .' (Even if this dialogue owes more to Graham Taylor than articulate and intelligent Brown.)

If Soldier Field can host the World Cup opening ceremony for USA 94, there's no reason why Broadwood couldn't accommodate another Challenge Cup final as successfully as the Sunday staging of St Johnstone versus Stranraer on 3 November 1996. A rainswept wind-tunnel is an ideal setting for second-rate Scottish finals, and the organisers wouldn't have to worry about unfair home advantage for the Bully Wee, because they would have lost 1–0 to Stranraer – or possibly Kilmarnock – in a previous round. One can only suspect that Stranraer's winning of the Challenge Cup at Broadwood caused great irritation amongst regular Bully Wee admirers.

Broadwood – a waking bloody nightmare, directed by Le Corbusier.

IBROX STADIUM
Rangers v Dundee United
Premier League, 12.3.97

Failure to get closer than a mile from Pittodrie on 1 March to see Aberdeen play Rangers (see next chapter) necessitated this midweek attempt to infiltrate Schloss Adler/Castle Doom/Fortress Ibrox, thereby ignoring glib advice from acquaintances to 'just make it up' and succumbing to imprecations about 'having to see the Huns' first team, preferably in their Hive'. Feeling like Lieutenant Schaffer (Clint Eastwood) in *Where Eagles Dare*, I resolved to pull it off – since this window of opportunity wouldn't reopen during an increasingly ticket-rationed campaign run-in. If successful, my quest could be over by the end of April; if unable to get a ticket, my travels would almost undoubtedly have ended in 'moral defeat', without having seen in the florid flesh Laudrup, Albertz and Co. (Gazza had been crippled in the pointless but lucrative Ajax Sixes tournament and was recuperating in Soho by going on a marathon bender with Chris Evans and Danny Baker.) Getting a brief for this rearranged fixture (postponed initially because of a combined monsoon-hurricane in February), I had anticipated requiring recourse to a short-wave radio transmitter – 'Broadsword Bennie calling Danny Boy Scalper . . .' – but in the event restricted view seats in the East Enclosure were being advertised in the press for £14 (with briefs on sale to personal callers prior to match-day). And although a crowd of 49,192 turned up, 30-odd seats with sight-lines blocked by the side-wall of the Copland Road Stand remained empty. Broomloan Road stand-dancing Arabs filled all their 700 allocated seats.

Since my visit to Broadwood almost a month earlier, homeless Hamilton Accies had leapfrogged Leggo-land Livingston to take over the second promotion place in Division Two (hooray), Celtic had beaten Rangers 2–0 in the Scottish Cup for their first win over their arch-rivals in ten attempts (hip-hip-hooray), and the following clubs had been officially warned by the SFA about their appalling disciplinary record – Celtic, Hearts, St Mirren, Ayr, Cowdenbeath and East Stirling. The manager of the last-named, Billy Little, was sacked on 7 March, with East Stirling lying 40th out of 40, and he responded by saying: 'Directors think they know all about the game – they know absolutely *nothing*.' The next day two directors took charge of the side for the visit to mid-table Montrose. The Shire's 2–0 win was only their second away victory of the season.

The evening before the Tannadice Terrors ran amok at Ibrox, Celtic had gone down 2–0 to relegation-haunted Kilmarnock at Rugby Park – so that a home win for Rangers would have opened up an eight-point gap before visiting Celtic Park for the second time in ten days for Super Sunday's Match of the Decade Judgement Day in the League on the 16th.

United took the lead after 30 exciting minutes, hitting on the break like a Tayside version of Ajax/Auxerre/Grasshoppers (who had all humiliated Rangers in the Champions' League). Robbie Winters clinically finished a cool build-up featuring Kjell Olofsson wide on the left. From a few rows behind me a home fan bellowed: 'Stop tryin' tae play fuckin' fitba', Rangers – get the bloody ba' up the park.' My friend Gordon, a lapsed Hun who hadn't been to Ibrox since 1975, observed: 'That kind of attitude is why Rangers will never get anywhere in Europe.' Two minutes into the second half, Rangers flooded Sieb Dykstra's penalty area for a corner, and when the ball was contemptuously cleared United took full advantage by one-touch-passing quickly upfield. Olofsson had time to chest down Winters' cross before blasting the ball home. The 700 Arabs reacted as if Ramadhan had been cancelled in favour of a BYOB barbie.

With ten minutes left we dived for the nearest exit – so that I didn't have to risk sitting suspiciously silent for any late consolation goal and in order that Gordon and I could avoid a queue of biblical proportions snaking away from Ibrox Underground Station. The full-time whistle went as we reached the entrance to the Clockwork Orange's lair, with both sides having hit the woodwork in our absence, when the staunch supporters who had stayed to the bitter end made a high-pitched noise similar to that of 40,000 vampires trapped inside St Peter's Square at daybreak – with Pope John Paul II hosing them down with holy water into the bargain. The 2–0 reverse was Rangers' first home defeat in domestic competition this season, and United's 15th unbeaten match in a row. With our return Underground tickets to Buchanan Street, the police waved us through their cordon to the automatic barriers.

On the train back to Waverley, a Ger standing in the aisle actually said: 'We may have lost the battle, but we'll win the war . . . No surrender!' Possibly, but none of the smartly attired, good-humoured and only occasionally foul-mouthed fans around us in the East Enclosure would have come out with this moronic cliché. Maybe David Murray's banning of 'Follow, Follow' as the pre-match song, with Tina Turner's 'Simply the Best' replacing it as the official anthem, has actually put off some of the Battle of the Boyne bigots. Nah . . . The collection of families, females and *foreigners* (Danish) whom we sat amongst must have been a 'small but vocal minority'. Frankly, I knew I would regret infiltrating Castle Doom – even if not for this challenge to my (self-justifying) belief system. Still, I did see the Ibrox idols defeated and played off the park.

PITTODRIE STADIUM
Aberdeen v Dundee United
Premier League, 15.3.97

If the 'long short-cut' to McDiarmid Park in October had been no more
than a bloody annoying detour, my first attempt to bag Pittodrie proved to
be a disastrous dead-end of a 'false economy'. Blanching at £35 for a return
rail ticket to Aberdeen, I downgraded to the 06.55 Citylink coach for a
'bargain' £16. Four hours out of Edinburgh the charabanc shuddered to a
halt in Guild Street Bus Station, after having stopped at every hellhole
hamlet in Fife, Perthshire, Tayside, Angus and Aberdeenshire to pick up
liberated 'lifers', Income Support grannies, CSA-castrated fathers,
multiple-birth mothers, schizophrenic saxophonists, amputated Algerians,
suicidal students from Stonehaven studying sociology and wimple-wearing
Sisters of Mercy. I staggered off with a *memento mori* migraine that I would
have killed to pass on to my best friend in the form of a terminal brain
tumour, only Nietzschean willpower having prevented waves of nausea
turning into crashing sprays of vomit from the Chip Shop Bus Bay at
Inverbervie onwards.

When my sister *finally* showed up in her Micra, she drove straight past
me (later pleading that she had mistaken me for one of the Rangers fans
streaming out of the adjacent railway station – simply because I was
hunched double over a drain in the carpark throwing up *green* bile,
presumably like a crapulous Teddy Bear who had got round the ScotRail
match-day alcohol ban by overindulging in smuggled miniatures of
Chartreuse). Lying in her darkened living-room, dry-retching the lining of
my hernia-imminent stomach into a red basin, she cheerfully sold my ticket
over the phone for the Dons v Huns fixture of Saturday, 1 March, and went
off with the grateful buyer to enjoy the 2–2 draw (during which Andy
'Flying Pig' Goram proved himself half-human by palming an innocuous
cross into his own pigsty net). Her good humour disappeared at full-time,
however, when an unhappy Hun 'gobbed' on her through the security fence.

By 9.50 p.m. I was weakly well enough to watch Celtic's two winning
goals against Hearts on *Sportscene*, propped up on pillows drinking hot sweet
tea. As Lynn took my empty mug, before going out on the razzle, I
projectile-vomited its still warm contents all over her lap with the timing
and accuracy of Regan MacNeil splattering Father Merrin in *The Exorcist*.
She reacted more like bad-tempered Father Karras – wound up by Pazuzo's
taunting of 'Demi, Demi, Demi . . .' – and it's probably just as well she
went into the lush groves of academe rather than the bleak wards of
nursing, since she's got the bedside manner of Beverley Allit with

197

Munchausen Syndrome by Big Brother Proxy. Hell, anyone who can afford a little black number by Nicole Farhi can afford a dry-cleaning bill . . .

Winds originating in the steppes of Siberia continued sweeping across Scotland throughout March, resulting in postponements at gale-buffeted Arbroath and Montrose. Less than two hours after the Highland League encounter between Lossiemouth and Nairn at Grant Park, a floodlight pylon toppled on to the pitch. Relief that the tower had missed the enclosure roof was tempered by the fact that the asbestos panels had lifted off in the direction of Kansas a week previously. Storm-lashed Scotland suffered at least one fatality on a horrendous night for driving, 32-year-old BBC Radio Scotland sports producer Lyndsay Cadden being killed in a two-car smash on the St Andrews–Pitscottie road in Fife. (And as the Irish writer Paul Durcan has observed with real poetic pathos: 'There – but for the clutch of luck – go we all'.)

As producer of *On/Off the Ball*, Cadden was responsible for turning the show round from a disastrous first season, repositioning it from abysmal alternative comedy to full-throttle footie fanzine. Piss-taking presenters Stuart Cosgrove and Tam Cowan have helped convert leaden footsteps into jigs of amusement more than once as I've back-traced my route to railway stations after seeing soul-destroying soccer sacrilege at various grounds during this season in hell – and, as producer, Cadden actually helped add to the gaiety of his benighted nation. Although I never followed up on a kind suggestion by Radio 5 Live journalist Garry Chippington to give Cadden a call, red-lining through his name and phone number in my address book was a melancholy moment. Cadden was good and died young. Unlike, say, the presenter of Radio 5's *606*, David Mellor, who is bloody awful, absolutely ancient and fucking coining it in.

Returning on the Sunday bus, I seriously felt like giving up my ground-hopping odyssey. Instead of four games to go, I now had six – including an extra Ibrox visit – and for the first time I thought I might not make it to a successful conclusion. To paraphrase an old Jewish proverb, if God lived in a glass-fronted split-level ranch house designed by Frank Lloyd Wright, bedsit members of the bourgeoisie like me would pan his windows in with half-bricks and Molotov cocktails . . .

For the 'New Firm' derby against Dundee United I of course learned my lesson and let the train take the strain. When I arrived in Aberdeen the number-one bestseller was still *Work Welfare and the Price of Fish* (Aberdeen City Council, £7.95). A Doric-English dictionary would have been useful to get a handle on the local bastardisation of my own lilting Lowlands language (e.g. '*Fit like, quine, foo ye dain . . . Puckle ae inties . . . Affa weel daen*' translating to 'How are you, mate? . . . Here's some advice . . . Awfully good show'), but John Menzies/*Jone Ming-iz* didn't stock one. Which was *howkin* – i.e. terrible. The Granite City was cold and wet, reflecting a latitude level more northerly than Moscow.

As the main shore-based service port for North Sea oil rigs, Aberdeen has benefited from major oil industry investment (even if young locals have been priced out of the property market). With about 250,000 inhabitants, this wealthy capital for North Sea exploration only has the one senior football club to rally round (or round on?), unlike Scotland's other three divided cities, but the sweetie-wrapper rustling Red Army has a reputation for being about as aggressively hyped-up and voluble as an Italian infantry division under enemy handgun fire. Aberdeen FC's investment in 'star' players has never been allowed to exceed a £1 million ceiling, reminiscent of Switzerland's niggardly refusal to spend money on a standing army for its national defence.

Aberdeen's debt difficulties can be traced back to the follyesque building of the bloody gigantic £4.5 million Richard Donald Stand in 1993, and if a golfer like Gordon Sherry had a head for heights he could drive a dimpled Dunlop from the Beach End roof across the adjacent golf course to the sea 300 yards distant. Hubristically out of proportion, this stand has not only destroyed the harmonious look of Pittodrie Stadium, with its three other low-level stands, but has become a financial albatross around the board's collective neck. A ground capacity of 21,634 is only ever needed for visits by the Glasgow giants, and although New Firm clashes in the 1980s were often all-ticket affairs, the visit of currently high-flying United only attracted 13,645 spectators.

Aberdeen had slipped from second to a feckless fifth, which in January prompted the local *Evening Express* to open a telephone hotline and thereafter print a massive back-page headline stating 'Fans Want Blood' (although the fans' naming of the 'guilty men' was partly offset by an editorial column suggesting it was not *quite* the right time to desert the Dons). Despite this tabloid blood-letting the playing slump *deepened*.

Pittodrie became Britain's first all-seater stadium in 1978, but instead of protesting the undemonstrative Dandies embraced the development wholeheartedly, since it allowed them to sit silently sipping single-grain whiskies wrapped in tartan travelling rugs. And 1978 was probably an even more significant year for Aberdeen than that of their formation in 1903, as it was the year that Alex Ferguson took over from Billy McNeill as manager. For the next eight years the Dons blew apart the Old Firm duopoly at home and cut a red swathe through Europe, culminating in the famous Cup Winners' Cup triumph over Real Madrid in rain-soaked Gothenburg in 1983. But since the mid-'80s Ian Porterfield, Alex Smith, Willie Miller and now Roy Aitken have struggled woefully to emulate Ferguson's glittering record of silverware success.

Celtic legend Aitken took over in 1995 when Aberdeen were sliding towards automatic relegation. A play-off place against First Division Dunfermline was secured and the Fifers were roundly thrashed over two legs. The Coca-Cola Cup was then won 2–0 against surprise finalists Dundee and third place in the League achieved. Season 1996–97 promised further progress but soon turned into a bed-wetting nightmare. In November chairman Ian Donald publicly confessed to being skint – a week before a demoralising 3–0 home defeat to cash-rich Rangers – advising Aitken that the club would have to rely on player sales to finance any transfers in the opposite direction. Manager Aitken was memorably described by journalist Graham Spiers as 'hard-grafting and gabbing', but the latter character trait didn't stop him *gagging* his hedonistically headbanging and clique-ridden squad when allegations of favouritism leaked out to the press – while at the same time calling for referees to be allowed to explain in public their anti-Aitken decisions.

Lynn and I arrived in our seats in the South Stand with a *minute* to spare – just 60 seconds away from me committing siblingcide – where we joined David, Bodil and Anders (supporters of Aberdeen, FC Brann Bergen and Sunderland respectively). Although we had missed club mascot Aberdeen Angus doing his fortnightly *Lord of the Dance* impersonation, Dean Windass was back from suspension looking even more like an overweight Robert de Niro in *Raging Bull* than usual (even with big banana-yellow boots). Deano plays like a heavyweight contender (for the British title belt), unlike his striking partner for the afternoon, butterfly-floating Scott Booth (whose unscarred good looks make Sugar Ray Leonard seem positively bruised and battered by comparison). Windass was imported from Hull City, whereas Booth came through the youth ranks. The latter is a Scotland international with five goals for his country to his name, an Aberdeen fan and local lad who combines intelligence, diligence and skill. But although Windass misses games due to below-the-belt violent conduct, Booth has been unlucky with niggling injuries, leading to comparisons between the mad monomaniac and the *malade imaginaire* hypochondriac. Aitken had just slapped Booth on the transfer list and was willing to let a player rated at £2 million two years ago leave at the end of the season on a free transfer. Colin Todd of Bolton had been set to buy cut-price Booth for £400,000 in February, but after watching him in a 0–0 draw against Hearts prior to settling personal terms, Todd changed his mind. 'Bolton need a lot better' was his damning, and daft, verdict. Is it any wonder Booth's confidence has been torn to shreds?

Aberdeen started smartly enough, which is more than could be said for their hideous strip, the traditional red shirt now having blue trimming and a Living Design sponsorship panel. Indeed the club's cash crisis resulted in the Bridge Street Aberdeen Shop selling replica shirts in the run-up to Christmas with logos for Living Design ironed on over the badge for old sponsors Northsound. Exploited Rudolphs were understandably apoplectic, and club-fan relations were not improved in February when a promise not to change strip designs for two years was reneged on with the announcement that Puma would be taking over from Umbro as kit suppliers come the new season.

After 35 minutes brittle Booth was bumped in the box and Windass blootered the resulting penalty home. I stood up and tried to get a chant going: 'Aiberdeen! . . . Aiberdeen . . . (then, *sotto voce*) Aiberdeeen . . .' Boy, did I feel self-conscious.

At half-time the queue for the Gents was too long to endure and I joined dozens of Dons urinating through a steel fence on a concrete concourse behind the South Stand. To make up for the embarrassment I'd caused Our Kid, I tried to buy a veggieburger for her as recommended by a *Guardian* travel writer, but his weekend in the Granite City obviously hadn't included an actual match-day visit to Pittodrie, because they weren't on the menu (nor 'hot beef sandwiches carved from huge joints').

In the second half United got their unbeaten act together. With woeful Michael Watt ('20-watt Mike') as keeper – in preference to the even less reliable Derek 'Stock Still' Stillie and Nicky 'Shortbread Scion' Walker – and with Toni 'Grand Guignol' Kombouare and Brian 'Dobbin' Irvine in central defence, Aberdeen are always likely to leak goals (the last-named being a practising Christian with multiple sclerosis, whose mildly controversial 'autopathography' *What a Difference a Day Makes* at least shows how a professional sportsman can bravely battle to overcome the prejudices surrounding this potentially pernicious disease). With Watt stranded outside his penalty area, like a whale out of water, Kjell Olofsson was straight through on an open goal but, rather than sidefooting home from 18 yards, the Swede appeared to prefer to walk the ball in – allowing Russell Anderson to race back for a well-nigh miraculous goal-saving sliding tackle. Kombouare set up United's equaliser with 20 minutes left, his mincingly mis-hit clearance bouncing off a relieved Olofsson's shins and trickling over the line.

Final score: 1–1, and United remained unbeaten in 16 games; 1–1, and Aberdeen remained stuck with one win over the same number of fixtures. Sometimes statistics don't lie (unlike five loaves and two fishes feeding 5,000 hungry punters).

Possibly because I'd just been to see Rangers at home in midweek, the idea of Pittodrie as an 'Ibrox of the North' seemed like far-fetched fantasy. Paying £11 to sit in the South Stand and still getting wet when it rained because the truncated roof gives no protection to those sitting even 20 rows back, is surely a sign of a major design flaw. The official entrance in Pittodrie Street resembles a 'tacky excuse for a lavvy entrance' (in the words of a contributor to the A4-sized fanzine *The Red Final* which, at £1, was at least ten times better value than the official obeisance offered by the programme at £1.50).

Director Stewart Milne may be Aberdeen's saviour, having been promoted to 'Executive Vice-Chairman' with a brief to oversee a summer stockmarket flotation designed to compete with Celtic and Rangers. However, as Scotland's 15th richest man with a personal worth estimated at £40 million, investing half of it in the club he has supported since boyhood might be less problematic than letting in unscrupulous City investors. And surely an oil company could be persuaded to advertise on the players' shirts – rather than a double-glazing company, local radio station or an Aberdeen-based financial services company?

Listening, but not dancing to, the Abba Eggsperience at the Lemon Tree Club was a damn sight more entertaining than the football match earlier in the day – and at four quid a damn sight cheaper. Having downed six pints of bitter I awoke in Lynn's house feeling rather tender but ravenously hungry. Breakfast in the Invernecky Italian café on the beautiful beachfront went down a treat, and I would have explored further afield if I hadn't had a train to catch.

Back home in time to see the televised League 'decider' between Celtic and Rangers, it followed the same old Old Firm script of recent years, with some additional scenes of gratuitous violence and hysterical hamming. Celtic 0, Rangers 1. A nine-in-a-row nail in Tommy Burns's managerial coffin (although he deserves a specially minted medal for putting pre-match interviewer Paul Cooney down by advising the overexcited STV mike-man to 'grab a couple of drinks and relax'). Before Aberdeen sacked Alex Smith, he took the Dons to Ibrox on the last day of the 1990–91 season needing only a draw to win the title for the first time since 1985. They pathetically played for one and deservedly lost; had they succeeded, Rangers would now only be heading for six-in-a-row.

Aberdeen FC were appalling, Pittodrie Stadium passable, the Granite City great. The 'sheep-shagging' home fans were pleasant and polite, but maybe they'll get called Dollies from now on (after the recent cloning of a sheep called Dolly by the Roslin Institute). Cloning douce Dons fans might fill Pittodrie but the decibel level wouldn't rise enough to scare the seagulls resting on the guttering of the Richard Donald Stand. Maybe multi-millionaire Milne ought to set up a genetics lab in the city's Marischal College and get Alex Ferguson to donate a test-tube of se . . . sealed spit. Cloning Roy 'the Bear' Aitken would give a lot of disgruntled Dollies a lot of migraines. The Bear and the Sheep may lie down together, but the Sheep won't get a helluva lot of shut-eye (with apologies for paraphrasing to Mr Allen S. Konigsberg of Manhattan).

LOVE STREET
St Mirren v Airdrieonians
First Division, 22.3.97

You've got to admire a club who have resisted the temptation to add a superfluous 'Stadium' or grandiloquent 'Ground' to their residential address or to change their name to incorporate the marketing moniker of their home town.[1] The Paisley Buddies of St Mirren were born in 1877, taking their formal nomenclature from the town's patron saint of thread weaving, and they moved into Love Street when they reached the age of 17 in 1894 (by which time the world-famous 'Paisley pattern' palm-frond design had been nicked from Kashmiri Calvin Kleins, and the ancient Babylonian fertility symbol used to sell everything from shirts to shawls). Situated only a few miles from the green savannah of Ibrox, and therefore prone to losing many of its 100,000 potential supporters to Rangers (and Celtic) in glory-hunting and goal-bagging Teddy Bear safaris up the M8, St Mirren struggle to justify automatic inclusion in any arbitrary Scottish élite.

As previously mentioned, one of my fondest memories is of witnessing Celtic snatch the Championship from the 'Maroon Huns' of Hearts on the last day of the 1985–86 season by thrashing the Saints 5–0 at Love Street. A year later, after having negotiated Paisley's one-way traffic system of white-knuckling complexity, I left my Mini parked in the austerely impressive Victorian town centre. Returning after midnight I found that locals celebrating their first Scottish Cup success since 1959 had been dancing all over the bonnet, a first-stage step to foot-stomping like Michael Flatley all over the roof (the Ferguslie Park Foxtrot?).

The Buddies' boardroom has seen more bloodletting than a bugger-merchants' brothel run by the Borgias, St Mirren's Machiavellian machinations having included the sacking of Alex Ferguson for unacceptably 'industrial language' and the canning of our friend from two of the previous three chapters, Alex Smith – for winning the Cup against Dundee United unacceptably late in extra-time 1–0 ('fan power' having driven sad Smith out of Paisley, Aberdeen *and* Cumbernauld).

Although the current board seemed to have stopped behaving like a Renfrewshire remake of *Logan's Run* – i.e. taking out and sacking any manager approaching three years in the job, never mind 30 years in the game – at the start of this season they reverted to coach-culling type. After four years as manager Jimmy Bone's respected assistant, Kenny McDowell was booted out to 'streamline' salary costs, whereupon Bone made himself voluntarily redundant by resigning in protest. After much dithering, Cup-winning captain Tony Fitzpatrick was appointed, despite a disastrous first spell in charge that eventually led to St Mirren being relegated in 1992 (after 13 uninterrupted years in the Premier League and four forays into Europe).

Fitzpatrick is a popular figure in Paisley, however, and a breath of fresh air in media interviews with his upbeat enthusiasm and unbridled optimism. Resembling Voltaire's Dr Pangloss, he does, however, tend to overegg the Paisley pudding. For example, going into this promotion six-pointer – with Airdrie, Dundee and St Mirren all level on 49 points, but 12 points adrift of St Johnstone with only seven games to go – Fitz was rallying his raw troops with calls for a *Championship* challenge. But weighed down by over a million pounds of debt, St Mirren's promotion push was relying largely on the skinny shoulders of boys barely out of puberty (and as Alan Hansen memorably, but inaccurately, said of Manchester United, 'You don't win anything with kids'). Their man-of-the-match was ex-St Johnstone veteran Tommy Turner, who, at 33, should nevertheless have known better than to noise up the villainous visitors by describing them as 'a pub team'. (Airdrie have a reputation for playing the Beautiful Game like aggressively ugly androids – trained by Czech coach Karel Capek, managed by Robert A. Heinlein and franchise-owned by *Mars Attacks!* director Tim Burton – hitting and hurting rather than hitting and hoping, but kitted out in an attractive away strip of Dutch-orange shirts and white shorts they were to start like a café-bistro XI from Amsterdam patronised by Ajax first-team regulars.)

The rain may not have been ice-cold but it was depressingly unrelenting. Taking shelter in the club shop, I picked up a free copy of *The Saint*, a club newspaper published by the Friends of St Mirren Association (FOSMA – an acronym which could also be applied to non-organised stay-away 'supporters' too, of course: Fucked-Off St Mirren Apathetics). The publication was more readable than the average household freesheet and it had an impressive amount of local trade advertising, as well as a preferential loan scheme offered by the Cooperative Bank. Although not providing *genuinely* generous APR loan rates, just competitive ones, if this developed into a credit union for penurious Paisley Buddies the strengthening of links between club and community would be titanium-like (assuming savers' deposits weren't used to bring any more venal Spanish swan-songers like 'Victor' to St Mirren). But, like Queen of the South, the Saints were obviously making a real effort to combine crucial commercial sponsorship with initiatives to promote authentic community involvement (for example, free tickets for youngsters, an Easter Egg Appeal for local charities and a 'Saintsclub' offering discounts to members).

A damp tenner got me into the Main Stand, where the stewards were friendly and helpful and the supporters fervent but funny. What the fuck was going on? The Enclosure Stand opposite, with its black-and-white striped roof, housed the hard-core atmosphere generators – 'We're black/We're white/We're absolutely shite' – while to the right the open Love Street terrace had no shortage of standers-in-the-rain, whose souvenir Saints umbrellas at £9.99 were proving to be practical instead of gimmicky. At the other end the new Caledonia Stand accommodated approximately 500 diehard Diamonds. And although five-a-side pitches and a gymnasium underneath the stand generate income, it cost £1.5 million to build and its 3,000-odd seats are normally white-elephant empty (or 'unutilised negative space' in SFA-speak). Unlike Aberdeen's Richard Donald equivalent, however, it doesn't dwarf its surroundings.

Scotland's match-of-the-day attracted a crowd of 4,648, barely a third of the ground's total capacity. Within three minutes, Airdrie's aping of Ajax resulted in defender Paul Jack launching an Exocet rocket from all of 35 yards, beating an incredulous Alan Combe high to his right and making Johnny Rep's second goal against Scotland in Mendoza in 1978 look like a mis-hit sclaff. Goal of my season, definitely and for the last time, and scored by an ageing Airdrie defender born in Malaya. For the next 20 minutes, one-dimensional Airdrie performed like holistic Holland on heat – despite having seven geriatric Jambos on their books – and when the increasingly bad-tempered Buddies in the Enclosure started chanting, 'If you hate fucking Airdrie, clap your hands,' the delighted Diamonds in their stand stood up and applauded appreciatively.

Both these sets of supporters have gained notoriety in the past by turning on their own teams the moment performance barometers have nudged towards the inclement – consolation goals conceded, for example, eliciting howls of despair and torrents of abuse.

Paisley prayers were answered after 22 devilishly uncomfortable minutes when their own hirpling Hearts reject Wayne Foster buried an unexpected, and undeserved, chance from just inside the box. Andy Rhodes had no chance of saving it, nor would regular number one John Martin, a legendary character whose failure to appear between the posts must have been due to a medical emergency like a head transplant.

It was 1–1 at the interval, when hundreds of hospitality hangers-on hared off for their half-time 'fayre', no doubt to hobnob with representatives of main sponsors Phoenix Honda. Behind me a down-in-the-mouth Buddy expressed the jaundiced, but probably accurate, view that the extension of turn-around times in recent years to 15 minutes was made to meet the feeding requirements of corporate gannets and other guzzlers of complimentary champagne in wood-panelled surroundings. (And if the Diamonds shirt sponsor is Gillespie Mining, surely the Buddies should be advertising for an AIDS charity like the Terrence Higgins Trust?)

The PA announcements that both Celtic and Rangers were losing went down well with the crowd, especially the former piece of news, but the biggest cheer was reserved for Dundee drawing a 0–0 blank with struggling Clydebank.

Paisley itself is an unemployment black hole, a depressed run-down peripheral suburb of Glasgow – and although historically an independent burgh outwith the Big G's city boundary, it has not been an autonomous town for decades because of local government reorganisation – with all the mill jobs having been lost to the Philippines during Mrs Thatcher's first term. Hillman Imps are no longer made at nearby Linwood, Babcock Engineering has haemorrhaged jobs and Rolls-Royce at Hillington operate with a greatly reduced staff. Glasgow Airport is the major local employer, but not of airline pilots or sexy stewardesses, and as part of Glasgow's *theoretical* bid for the Olympics, Paisley was pencilled in as a possible venue for exhibition baseball – since the residents of Ferguslie Park steal more bats per year than the Boston Red Sox buy.

St Mirren continued to disappoint in the sodden second half, especially 20-year-old Ricky Gillies (whose initials ought to stand for Reynaldo Gento if managerial hype is to be believed; although a few days later a £250,000 offer from Aberdeen was rejected). Canadian-capped centre-half Paul Fenwick may have had his appearance machofied by three nose-breaks since August, but a neutral observer couldn't describe him as 'heading with confidence'. Baby right-back Brain Smith was having such a torrid time, he looked close to blubbering. And, like David Ginola, Junior Mendes was not a winger willing to 'work back' in the post-modern fashion.

An away winner was always on the marked cards, but when it arrived with ten minutes left it was courtesy of a Combe clanger (© Cowdenbeath FC Goalkeeping Academy, from which this sinning Saint graduated magna cum laude in 1993). After murdering the opposing left-back, Jimmy Boyle's hanging cross slipped through Combe's fingers and fell invitingly for Steve Cooper to head home from two feet (away and in height); 2–1 to Airdrie, allowing them to go clear in second place.

When Ajax trained at Love Street prior to humbling Rangers in the Champions' League, Louis van Gaal was apparently so impressed by a crocheted motto pinned up in the home dressing-room that he got a Dutch TV crew to film it. This homily read: 'Hard work beats talent, but only when talent does not work hard.' Having seen the Saints beaten 3–1 by Dunfermline and 4–0 by St Johnstone prior to this poor performance, I'd have to say that St Mirren are neither super-talented nor extremely hard working enough for the Premier League, or even a promotion play-off place. (So that's them up – probably as Champions!) I hope I'm wrong, but attempting to escape the killing fields of the First Division with youngsters given free reign to attack is like trying to win a general election with colourful candidates not forced to be economical with the *actualité* (which is why Tony Fitzpatrick won't be a Premier boss next season and sound-bite-rehearsed Tony Blair will be a Labour Prime Minister after 1 May).

As for Airdrie, they were a pleasure to watch – and by all accounts usually play better away from their temporary home of Broadwood (where they have been groundsharing with Clyde since 1994). Three years ago Broomfield Park was sold to Safeway for £5.5 million, but plans to relocate and rebuild at Raebog on a green-belt site on the outskirts of Airdrie were stymied by a bunch of Nimbys in the nearby village of Glenmavis (where it is a fair bet to say supporters' buses running to Cumbernauld don't stop to pick up many middle-class fans dressed in white replica shirts with big red Vs on the front). A town-centre location at Craigneuk had its development plans for a new stadium called in by Monklands District Council (allegedly after a fax to the Catholic councillors from the Vatican City's cabal of anti-Airdrieonian cardinals. In April 1996 planning permission was refused. A fortnight later, however, with the Council chambers under siege by the normally apathetic Airdrie support – led by a Dutchman called William on a big white horse – the decision was reversed. Orange-flavoured-condom copulating followed in celebration, which almost proved premature when the new Lanarkshire Council based in Motherwell mooted the possibility of a U-turn in November (based on Internet communications received from the Papal Curia's capital gains tax expert claiming that the club owed a fortune to the Inland Revenue, which, happily, they did not).

New Broomfield should be open for business sometime in 1997–98, assuming that the supermarket stash hasn't been reduced to a loose change float after years of rent payments to Clyde not covered by gate-money income for 'home' fixtures. In addition, there have been legal costs, architectural fees and full-time salaries. Players' wages have been more than earned in the past five years, however, under ex-Hearts manager Alex MacDonald – with an incredible cup record that includes reaching ten quarter-finals, five semis and two Scottish Cup finals. Both of the latter may have been lost to the Old Firm – by a single goal on each occasion – but in 1995 Airdrie lifted the B&Q Cup. Not a bad record for a team relegated from the Premier League in 1993, made homeless a year later and forced to train thereafter on public pitches at Strathclyde Country Park. Manager MacDonald may be an unreconstructed Maroon Hun – or 'thrawn wee bugger' as described by his boss at Rangers, Willie Waddell – but as a rough-edged Diamond Geezer you've got to admire his achievements. No wonder his team sometimes get called the Doddies – affectionately (even by Airdrie fans with their hard hearts of stone).

FOOTNOTES

1. *Aaaaaaarrgghh!!!* . . . I'm glad I caught this error before the proofs went to print, but even though Inglis sub-heads his chapter on St Mirren 'Love Street', and newspaper match-reports use the term, the ground's official name is now actually . . . *St Mirren Park* (which I have never heard uttered in my life, nor seen in print until I checked the match-day programme). I guess Love Street Stadium would have been too open to rearranging as the 'Stadium of Love'. Maybe the 'Lullaby of Love Street' ought to be retitled 'St Mirren Park Rap', with its first line updated to take account of modern conditions as well: 'Oh, when the Saints go marchin' *out* [of business] . . .' What next – Paisley Mirren FC playing out of Phoenix Honda Carpark?

CALEDONIAN STADIUM
Inverness Caledonian Thistle v Montrose
Third Division, 5.4.97

In 1960 Inverness Clachnacuddin of the Highland League were almost accepted as members of the Scottish League, but, as happened again in 1974, were eventually turned down because of the long-distance travelling difficulties for visiting teams (the club secretaries of Berwick Rangers, Queen of the South and Stranraer voting against the motion by a show of linked hands from a second-floor windowledge of the League's offices at 188 West Regent Street). Season 1994–95 kicked off with ex-Highland outfits Ross County and 'Caledonian Thistle' having finally been admitted. The latter footballing Frankenstein was the result of enforced Siamese twinning, grafting a 'freeloading' Thistle head on to the armpit of a 'taking over' Caledonian cadaver. As well as merging Caledonian and Inverness Thistle, a further condition of acceptance was the replacement of Caley's Telford Street ground with a brand new stadium by August 1995. The tranquillity of the Highland capital was rudely interrupted, as both sets of fans continued to raise merry hell over the amalgamation. Imagine Rangers and Celtic being forced to combine as 'Glasgow Rantic' in order to gain a place in a European Super League and you'll have some idea of the acrimonious heat generated. Thistle's Kingsmills Park was sold for housing development and Telford Street Park promised to Texas Homecare in return for £750,000.

By the start of this season 'Inverness' had been tacked on in front, which, along with the usual 'Football Club' suffix, gave the club the longest name in the British game, but Inverness Caledonian Thistle were still playing out of Telford Street (with seating for less than 500). In December 1995 the local council – who were insisting on the adoption of the Inverness prefix – had come within one vote of cancelling financial support for a new ground. In May 1996 the club were within hours of going bust, but extrovert club president Dugald McGilvray switched banks and succeeded in raising enough money from local businessmen to underwrite a planned share issue. Without the capital for a new £5.3 million stadium in place, and a new opening date of August 1996 agreed, the club would have been thrown out of the League. A former rally driver from Lochlomondside, McGilvray made his personal fortune from a crawler-crane hire business called, not inappropriately in this footballing context, Weldex.

The final game at Telford Street was played against Arbroath on 5 October 1996, with my missing the 2–0 home win because of industrial action by the RMT union – I could have got into Inverness on the day but not out again – and also because I was labouring under the mistaken belief that before the scheduled first game at the Caledonian Stadium on 9 November, Caley Thistle would be fulfilling a final home fixture as listed in *The Wee Red Book* against Forfar, not realising that the Loons had agreed to switch venues. The bulldozers actually moved in before the Red Lichties team bus had crossed the River Ness, with every destructive swing of a crane's wrecking ball apparently cheered to the doomed rafters by the assembled Thistle fans. Overnight security measures prior to the match had been necessary to prevent tearful Caley fans from walking off with floodlight poles as mementoes for their patios.

When I finally arrived in Inverness to see Caley Thistle, the old Telford Street ground was more than halfway to completion by the Texas sub-contractors. Situated a convenient mile from the station, beside the Caledonian Canal built by Thomas Telford, rain began to pour the moment I tried to photograph the muddy and depressing building site. After a walk of only a few hundred yards, I visited Clach's trim little Grant Street Park, which Caley Thistle now own and use as a *wind-free* training ground, while allowing the Lilywhites to play on in the Highland League for the moment, before selling the site to Wimpey/Pet City/Gala Bingo.

The hike to the Caledonian Stadium was long and boring, ending in a soulless industrial estate; but as one of the fastest growing towns in *Europe*, Inverness actually suffers from appalling urban sprawl, and as a 'Central Belt bigot' I actually felt quite at home outwith the tartan-tatty town centre (where the commercial pressures to exploit the tourist trade only led to Sunday trading as late as July of 1996). At 60,000 the population is now double that of 1960, and with a catchment area of 120,000 the potential is definitely there to support a Premier League team, where McGilvray hopes to be by 2003. (Fifteen miles to the north in the dinky market town of Dingwall, arch-rivals Ross County not only attract comparably large crowds but currently have full-time professional players and a better stadium, and although both clubs cherish dreams of becoming Highland Auxerres, Caledonian Thistle must have historic inevitability on their side because of their stronger economic base.)

As I crossed the busy A9, the Caledonian Stadium beckoned invitingly, but a protective muddy moat and a phalanx of parked JCBs barred my on-foot progress. Doubling back, I prepared to walk an extra half-mile on the just-opened access road, but a teenage fan offered to be my guide through the obstacle course that faced us. Leaping the ditch at its narrowest point, we had to help each other through barbed-wire fences (and as pesky pedestrian patrons, we quite possibly ran the risk of stepping on anti-personnel mines).

211

The cantilevered Main Stand's frontage was only a few yards away from the Moray Firth, and although entry was by pre-purchased ticket only, I managed to get a returned brief for only £7 in the club shop. Sitting in a central section behind the away dug-out, if I turned my head to the right the cantilevered – of course – Kessock Bridge loomed impressively, beneath which the Beauly Firth dolphins put on displays for snap-happy tourists and over which 28,000 vehicles cross daily. This surprisingly heavy traffic also thunders past the small, six-step terrace opposite the stand. Each end terrace is equally Lilliputian in scale, but together they give a total capacity of 5,500. Another truncated stand roof failed to keep the rain off, and for such an exposed location the lack of any plastic panels as sidescreens seemed positively sadistic.

With almost an hour to go before kick-off, I had time to reflect on note-worthy developments elsewhere since the St Mirren game. On April Fools Day ex-Cowdenbeath boss John Brownlie had been appointed manager of wooden-spoon positioned East Stirling (who had been advertising the job with a starting remuneration of £60 per week, which presumably didn't attract an application from Fabrizio Ravanelli of Middlesbrough, since it would have meant a salary cut of £41,940 a week).

On the same day, amateur Queen's Park announced that coach Hugh McCann had resigned, in what turned out to be an inept attempt to 'manage' the news worthy of the Tory Party Central Office. The next day a furious McCann insisted that he had been *sacked*. Rather than get involved in a slanging match, the committee members pulled their black blazers up over their chromium domes and refused to comment.

The day after Scotland beat Estonia 2–0 at Rugby Park on 29 March, Hamilton Accies beat Livingston 2–1 away at Almondvale in a Sunday match beset by controversy. In the week that followed, Hamilton boss Sandy Clark and star winger José Quitongo began to receive poison-pen letters. Clark commented: 'We are now receiving hate mail with Livingston postmarks.' Livid Livvy manager and part-time poet Jim Leishman retorted: 'As far as I know they have only received one letter.'

Apart from Scotland slaughtering Austria 2–0, just an average fortnight really . . . What I really brooded on were my teeth, since my dentist had just described the inside of my mouth as being orthodontically challenged, a cake-hole equivalent of Boghead with one set of upper pre-molars in particular that would have had their safety certificate withdrawn if they had been a Dumbarton football terrace.

At kick-off a crowd of 3,036 had braved the elements to see if Caley Thistle could clinch promotion and the Third Division Championship (a win over mid-table Montrose guaranteeing the former, while any dropped points by second-placed Ross County – 14 points adrift – would have resulted in the title, too). Since I had seen Caley Thistle's 0–0 borefest with East Stirling on 2 November, which had left the Highlanders in fifth place, results had improved dramatically. Their unbeaten run of 19 league games now stretched back to 26 October (a 2–0 defeat at Forfar).

A minute's silence for 'Wee Danny' MacDonald was a moving but eerie experience, because apart from the muted roar of traffic you could have heard a proverbial pin drop (unlike at Ibrox earlier in the year when some Aberdeen fans had booed and chanted during the minute's silence for Scotland and Ibrox legend George Young, or at Pittodrie in 1994 when a *large* minority of the Rangers support did the same thing simply because Sir Matt Busby had been a Catholic; meanwhile, at Stark's Park more than a handful of Celtic fans cheered the news of the Grand National's postponement at Aintree because of an IRA bomb threat, even though these idiots had probably bet heavily on Celtic Abbey).

Caley Thistle stormed forward from the start, but unlike the Highlanders at Culloden they managed to keep their feet (and their heads). Swarming across the widest pitch in Scotland, they had hit the bar within minutes. Big, boney, blond winger Davie Ross set up Iain Stewart inside the box in the 12th minute, and the Inverness side's top scorer calmly slotted the ball past Jim Butter (the lump of lard signed from Queen of the South). After 23 minutes of being besieged by tossed cabers, making-up-the-numbers Montrose got a soft penalty. Colin McGlashan placed rather than lashed the ball past Jim Calder. Three minutes before the break Shaun Smith sidefooted the visitors ahead, and the party atmosphere began to deflate (especially with County winning at Cliftonhill against Albion Rovers).

With an hour gone Ross was replaced by the London-born chief of the De Barros clan, 26-year-old Marco (whose hobbies, according to the match programme, include 'disco dancing, scuba-diving and white-water rafting', and the first two of which he immediately began to practise on the pitch). By ignoring De Barros, Caley Thistle soon got a deserved equaliser, Stewart again finishing clinically after a Brian Thomson free-kick had picked him out. With nine minutes left Stewart bore down on polysaturated Butter and contemptuously lobbed him for an impressive hat-trick, taking Stewart's tally for the season to 28. At 5ft 7in the striker was deemed to be a virtual dwarf by Dundee, but since signing from Lossiemouth in 1995 the 27-year-old Dundonian had scored over 50 goals in less than two seasons. The 3–2 scoreline assured Stewart of a Second Division platform for his undoubted striking talents in the new season, and, with Caley Thistle intent on turning full-time after going up, they'll be hoping to keep him.

At full-time the Caley Thistle players linked hands in the centre-circle and took the applause of their cheering supporters. In season 1997–98 the likes of Queen of the South won't be relishing coming all the way up to the Caledonian Stadium (where, a week later, a 4–1 victory over Albion Rovers secured the Third Division title). Manager Steve Paterson, ex-Manchester United and one-time boss of Huntly, was sufficiently swayed by his team's success to agree to give up his day job as a social worker in favour of a lucrative and long-term contract as full-time coach. Ignoring Central Belt Cassandras, he'd achieved promotion with a squad largely made up of players from the Highland League – or 'dunniewassals' (Highland gentlemen of inferior rank). In the first half, for example, man-mountain right-back Mike Teasdale (born in Elgin) had bellowed at classy ex-Celtic midfielder Charlie Christie (born in Inverness): 'Back tae me, mon!' To which Christie had replied: 'Shut the fuck up the noo, yoo!' Ah, Inverness-English – the most dulcet version of the Western world's numero uno language . . .

If Ross County manage to pip Forfar for the second promotion spot, I'd certainly pay to see an all-ticket Highland derby in Division Two. By next season, a second stand should be in place at the Caledonian Stadium, by which time the plague of rats infesting the stadium will hopefully be totally eradicated. (The rodents hit the headlines in January, an unwelcome consequence of building on an old landfill site.) Whether renamed Inverness City/United or not, Caley Thistle look set for top-flight football in the foreseeable future. Bitter fans of the old Caledonian and Inverness Thistle wouldn't be tempted back even by visits from the Old Firm, but a new generation of Inverness football fans now have an ambitious senior club to grow up supporting.

Frozen cold as well as damply wet, I decided against an overnight stay in one of the many B&B establishments lining Telford Street. On the train back to Edinburgh I flicked listlessly through a copy of *FourFourTwo* (the first of the upmarket glossies devoted to footie). Overdosing on football facts, I wished I'd bought a fiction paperback out of Scotland's largest second-hand bookshop, the wonderful Leakey's.

Missing Telford Street began to prey on my wandering mind, despite not having thought about it since October, but since its omission disqualified me from any possible entry in the *Guinness Book of Records* – for bagging *every* Scottish League ground in season 1996–97 – my technical failure wasn't without at least one plus point. As a Roman amphitheatre-bagger once remarked, arriving late for a Christians versus Lions fixture at a demolished site in Galilee, 'All have sinned and fall short of the glory of *the ground-hopping* God' (who today is probably a glory-hunting Chelsea supporter).

Or in the letter-writing words of John Keats, whose delicate constitution was completely shattered by a walking tour of Scotland in 1818, 'I would rather fail than not be amongst the greatest *groundhoppers*.' (My italicised additions.)

Elsewhere, Raith Rovers were equalising in the last minute for a 1–1 draw against Celtic at Stark's Park. Tommy Burns blamed the disastrous result on the rutted Kirkcaldy pitch. Comparing it to the moon, the under-pressure Celtic boss was quoted as saying: 'Jesus Christ couldn't have put passes together out there.' (Ten days later Rangers won 6–0 at Stark's Park, all but wrapping up nine-in-a-row, and without the Son of God orchestrating things in midfield; Celtic's flame-haired false prophet at least didn't go on record with, 'Infamy! . . . Infamy! . . . They've all got it infirmae!'.)

At Broadwood Clydebank coach Brian Wright quit following a 4–1 mauling from Airdrie. After a 4–0 hammering at Ibrox, Dunfermline boss Bert Paton finally agreed to stop wearing his trademark high-peaked baseball cap (at least not when combined with club blazer and polyester slacks).

Burns may have been suffering from PMT (Pre-Millennial Tension) – and if Celtic don't win the League before then, apocalyptic hell really will break out all around Parkhead – but Caley Thistle could be playing in the Premier League by the turn of the century. I just hope I'm not watching them visit Celtic Park while clacking nervously through a set of false teeth. Dentures by 40? Oh, Christ . . . Like Martin Amis I need a whopping big advance to get my teeth fucking 'fixed'.

BAYVIEW
East Fife v Greenock Morton
First Division, 12.4.97

On the Thursday night before this meaningless match – with East Fife already relegated and Greenock Morton safely stuck in mid-table – I got a phone call offering me a free week's holiday in Gran Canaria. With a sinking feeling in the pit of my stomach, I asked when the charter flight from Glasgow Airport took off. Answer: Saturday morning. Forcing a golf-ball-sized lump of disappointment down constricting vocal cords I managed a croaky 'No', because I had to be in the Fife town of Methil for the above bloody football match. A month earlier, Trinidad and Tobago star Arnold Dwarika had amicably departed the Fifers to sign for the Caribbean side Joe Public FC. 'The one thing I won't miss about this place is the weather!' he had said through chattering white teeth.

At a sun-drenched and humid Kirkcaldy Station I spotted Magsy on the opposite platform and persuaded her to abandon a shopping trip to Edinburgh in favour of guiding me to Bayview (where she was none too happy about having to shell out eight 'ridiculously expensive' quid, which would have been excessive even for her femalely half-hearted favourites Raith Rovers). A shuddering Eastern Scottish double-decker deposited us in Methil's heat-shimmering High Street an hour later. A wonderfully carcinogenic sun continued to beat down as we dined *al fresco* on the pavement outside The Coffee Pot café (whose great-value and delicious menu I give five full-stomach stars to).

Magsy asked if I'd seen the recently released *Fever Pitch* movie (in which the Nick Hornby character is played by Colin 'Mr Darcy' Firth). I hadn't. 'If your Celtic book was filmed, who'd play you?' she oh-so-casually asked.

'Mickey Rourke or Ewan McGregor . . .'

Magsy pondered over her own question and after an ominous silence, and having just seen the re-released *Star Wars*, came up with: 'I know, the actor who played the hero . . . Whatsisname?'

'Hans Solo?' I prompted.

'Nah, Luke Skywalker . . . Mark Hamill!'

'I don't have acne – symmetrical or otherwise.'

Her ego-deflating answer had just enough of a smidgen of justification for it to annoy intensely – as did the complete strangers who circled our table to concur with this ridiculous casting call. Just because we're both boyishly good-looking . . .

'Do you want a *fourth* course or can we go now?' I barked at Magsy.

'Calm down – or have you gone over to the dark side?' she giggled back.

216

Tssh . . . Not only does she know nothing about football, but she's totally ignorant about the critical importance of casting central characters correctly. What you want is 'heightened realism'.

A T-shirted crowd of 440 basked in the unseasonal sunshine, and as the players stood around the centre-circle for a minute's silence dedicated to 'John Boyd of Falkirk' (?), only the seagulls failed to hold their squawking tongues.

Steve Archibald as player-manager had led the Fifers to promotion, behind Stirling Albion, but ensuring survival in the First Division's Darwinian theme-park was always going to be an exhausting struggle in a race against the relegation clock, especially after the board refused to sanction full-time football at Methil. Archibald's slide down the soccer evolutionary scale from Barcelona to Bayview, via Broadwood, must have been a severe shock to his system, but not as massive as being sacked five League games into a new season. Three priceless points had been secured when managing director Julian Danskin, a local lawyer, announced the termination of Archibald's contract due to 'irretrievable differences'. Getting rid of such a high-profile and successful manager, as well as the team's best player, was a boardroom decision of such seemingly inexplicable barminess that it would not be surpassed elsewhere all season.

Replacement boss Jimmy Bone started with a 3–1 home win over Falkirk, but the following week's 6–0 reverse to Partick Thistle at Firhill was to be the first of 15 straight defeats (and East Fife went into the Morton match having failed to notch a second League win and with a miserly haul of ten points). Archibald may not have kept the part-time Fifers up either, but he would surely have avoided mathematically-certain relegation until after March. (The biggest chasm separating the four divisions in Scotland is definitely the yawning one between First and Second.)

The dreary and depressing town of Methil, sandwiched between Buck-haven and Leven as part of an almost seamless coastal conurbation, relies on Kvaerner Oil and Gas as the main local employer. In December, however, the townsfolk found good reason to feel superior to another Fife community decimated by the tenets of Thatcherism – namely landlocked Cowden-beath. For a Christmas edition of the TV programme *They Think It's All Over*, East Fife fans were recorded singing a selection of anti-Blue Brazil ditties, including the coruscating cult classic 'No Soap in Cowden'. The following lyrics were sung to the haunting theme tune of *The Addams Family*: 'They come fae near Lochgelly/They huvnae got a telly/They're dirty and they're smelly/The Cowden Faa-mil-ayyy!'

Predictably, Cowdenbeath's charisma-bypassed councillors were outraged at the slur. When informed about a Hogarthian cartoon-strip running in the

217

East Fife fanzine *Away from the Numbers*, one councillor duly went on record to condemn 'The Cowden Family' for depicting Cowdenbeath as 'full of drug abuse, incest and being allergic to soap'. Editor Michael McColl deserves his own publishing contract, so that he can do for his team what the Revd Ronald Ferguson did for Cowdenbeath in *Black Diamonds and the Blue Brazil*. McColl was memorably quoted as saying: 'Cowdenbeath is the town that time forgot . . . the TV show – it will put the place on the map. Most of them won't see it anyway because very few of them have televisions.' If East Fife draw Cowdenbeath in any of the Cup competitions next season, I'm going to try and make it to the match – if only for my souvenir 'No Soap in Cowden' T-shirt, which I will flaunt with fragrant pride.

Bayview – although it really doesn't have one of Largo Bay unless you climb onto the stand roof with a telescope – is a typically old-fashioned and run-down Scottish ground, with wooden bench-seating in the completely boxed-in and therefore snugly sheltered stand. The other three sides were open terracing, except for a small cover opposite the directors' box. With a capacity of 5,400 (600 seated) Bayview is, however, totally adequate for East Fife's needs in normal circumstances, because even in the First Division they rarely attracted crowds in excess of 1,000. However, New Bayview, a 3,000-seater 'mini-Ibrox', was supposed to be operating by October 1996, but having glimpsed from a distance the largely undeveloped site beside the No.3 dock in what is supposed to be some kind of fashionable marina/converted-warehouse development, I'll believe the new opening date of sometime in season 1997–98 when I sit down in the Second Division's latest identikit stadium.

Because of the National Lottery's negative impact on pools company profits, Football Trust funds have not been as generous as anticipated. Having drawn Rangers at Ibrox in the Scottish Cup in February, though, East Fife shared the gate money (approximately £200,000?) from a crowd of 41,000 who gathered to see the disappointingly respectable 3–0 away defeat, and the necessary funds would now appear to be in place. Apparently, the architects have been instructed to plan for the possibility of an extra 7,000 seats if required – i.e. matching the Premier League Millennium minimum of 10,000 – but New Bayview is doomed to service crowds that will rarely reach four figures for the foreseeable future (and which won't include either David Hasselhoff or Pamela Anderson of *Baywatch* fame – neither of whom have heard of Bayview, never mind their supposed status as East Fife-supporting celebrity fans).

A senior team situated in Methil is now an historical anachronism, and if blueprints for 40 senior sides were being drawn up from scratch today, Methil would be lucky to get on a shortlist of 100.

Although definitely not a top 20 outfit, never mind top 10, in 1938 East Fife became the first club outwith the old First Division to lift the Scottish Cup, and they have also won the League Cup three times (in 1947, 1949 and 1953).

Black-and-gold stripes lining up against blue-and-white hoops reminded me that this was the first 'return' fixture that I had, unintentionally, arranged to see, but unlike at Cappielow in January there were no porridge-coloured clouds scudding overhead. Since Morton's 2–0 win over the Fifers, British Summer Time had arrived and the Greenock club's top scorer, Derek Lilley, had departed for Leeds United in a big-money transfer. Even without him, Morton went ahead within five minutes, Warren Hawke heading home from close range (which I celebrated exuberantly in the home end, lifting up and hugging an embarrassed Magsy as the Ton, appropriately enough, provided me with my century of goals). In the 13th minute Alan Mahood shot through an AWOL Fifers' defence for the visitors' second. Five minutes later Hawke again rose on his Super Hero spring heels to head home number three. Standing behind Lindsay Hamilton's goal I had a great view of all three goals.

A despairing Hamilton's shouts of instruction to his demoralised defence were being totally ignored, whereupon an amused home fan bellowed at the keeper to concentrate on his own game. Hamilton turned round, made a few philosophical comments over the perimeter wall and then push-waved in limp-wristed disgust. The only fans of the 'Bone Idles' to get really riled were a few die-hards in the shade of the terracing cover, who would have got first-class honours if participating in a viva for a degree in Advanced Obscenity.

In the second half Morton's Pride-of-the-Clyde players began showboating like Monaco's Playboys of the Western World and just after the hour mark they paid the (admittedly peppercorn) price. The Fifers' Matt Dyer sclaffed a shot from an acute angle. Morton goalie David Wylie went down in slow-motion and could only get half a glove on the ball, which eventually bobbled over the line. 'Wylie flaps again!' shouted a cheerfully sadistic Methilite, to which Wylie reacted by giving his taunter the universal one-fingered gesture for 'Up yours, mate'. Great hilarity in the home end, where some fans were actually lying flat on their backs with eyelids drowsily half-closed. Morton substitute Marko Rajamaki fired home the final goal with 17 minutes left on the clock.

Final score: 1–4. East Fife against Morton over the season: 1–9. In 32 League matches East Fife had lost 24 times – with 22 goals for and 88 against (so that 1–4 was the Fifers' *average* scoreline). East Fife, then, were not only a statistical embarrassment but a footballing shambles. Personally, however, I'd had a great day out, and although Saturday afternoon in Las Palmas may have got me even more sunburnt, I would have had to forgo the pleasure of seeing five goals, listening to funny terracing crack and standing behind a hot-to-the-touch metal crush-barrier.

Only a late equaliser by Falkirk against Celtic in the Scottish Cup semi-final took the edge off my visit to Bayview. Amazingly, at the bus-stop a Chesterfield-supporting groundhopper raised his blue-and-white scarf in acclamation as the Morton team coach zoomed past (and the next day Division Two Chesterfield were to snatch a thrilling 3–3 draw at Old Trafford against ten-man Middlesbrough in an English FA Cup semi). The bus services out of Methil were gratifyingly frequent and after saying goodbye at Kirkcaldy to my piss-taking Princess Leia lookalike, I set off on the train to cross the Forth Rail Bridge for the last time in my season of cheap-day-returning to Edinburgh. Finally there was light at the end of the tunnel, even if the tunnel did stretch all the way to sodding Stranraer . . .

Kirkcaldy's Raith Rovers had been playing at Motherwell, and after a 5–0 humping, chairman Alex Penman asked manager Iain Munro on the pavement outside Fir Park if he'd 'had enough'. Replying in the negative, Munro was called into Stark's Park on Monday morning and sacked. Jimmy Nicholl honourably refused his old job back (while at Queen's Park Graeme Elder was appointed player-coach). After losing at home to Rangers 6–0 on the Tuesday, relegated Raith hit the back-page headlines once more on the Thursday, after Penman *allegedly* kicked and punched a prostrate photographer outside Stark's Park so severely that the snapper 'had to have his ear stitched back on'.

If East Fife MD Danskin loses to Archibald at the latter's intimated industrial tribunal for unfair dismissal, it's only to be hoped that things don't turn quite so violently ugly on the steps outside the court. (In the event, just two months or so after the visit of Morton, Archibald accepted an out-of-court settlement with the club – less than 24 hours before the case was scheduled to be heard.)

STAIR PARK
Stranraer v Dumbarton
Second Division, 26.4.97

Any part-time player who finds himself being free-transferred to Stranraer's Stair Park must feel like stitched-up Alfred Dreyfus setting sail for his stretch on Devil's Island. The train journey from Glasgow lasts almost as long as the film version of Henri Charrière's autobiographical bestseller *Papillon* — two and a quarter hours to cover approximately a hundred miles. This interminable movie was dismissed by one critic as 'a tournament of brutality unrelieved by any imagination' and the same could be said of the six-year-old League Challenge Cup, in the 1996 final of which, as previously stated, Stranraer overcame St Johnstone 1–0 at meteorologically miasmic Broadwood on a wet and windy November afternoon to win a trophy for the first time in their 126-year history.

Over a thousand supporters of Stranraer FC returned to the town for the celebratory Sunday night shindig, but only goalkeeper Barney Duffy and manager Campbell Money accompanied them back to Stranraer (which geographically and aesthetically merits the metaphorical description of being Scotland's in-grown toenail). The rest of the winning team partied in the niteclubs of Glasgow, since none of them lived in or around the southern ferryport. The only local lad on the books is one Scott McCrindle, who in 1996–97 only managed three first-team appearances as a substitute.

Full-time boss Campbell Money hails from relatively nearby Maybole in southern Ayrshire, and being St Mirren's stalwart steward between the posts for many years is his main claim to fame.

Training sessions take place in either Kilmarnock or Paisley, because Glasgow, where most of the squad is based, is further away from Stranraer than Belfast. But although geographically isolated, no one can accuse the Blues of Stranraer of ever having not lagged behind the times. Formed as long ago as 1870, they didn't attain League status until 1955, and the 12-man committee didn't stop picking the team by a show of liver-spotted hands until as late as 1980. A year later successful experiments with new-fangled electricity led to the introduction of floodlights at Stair Park.

I almost didn't make the 11.23 from Glasgow Central, since I was still suffering from the after-effects of Thursday morning's mother-and-fucking-father of all hangovers. On the Tuesday evening Dundee United had lost their Scottish Cup semi-final replay 1–0 to Kilmarnock at Easter 'Rutted' Road. Yes, the same supermen from Ayrshire who had been shying away from match balls all season as if they had been filled with gaseous Kryptonite. Almost immediately after I had sarcastically slagged them off for struggling woefully to beat Clyde in the Cup in February, Bobby Williamson had them playing like Serie A *stranieri*, in both the Cup and League (including victories over Celtic at Rugby Park and Rangers at Ibrox).

Johnnie Walker whisky is still made in Kilmarnock and after Wednesday night's other semi-final replay at Ibrox, when Falkirk deservedly dumped clueless Celtic out of the competition 1–0, I drank almost a full bottle of the amber anaesthetic (a duty-free present from Gran Canaria). First Division fucking Falkirk!

Watching the highlights 'as live', I became increasingly agitated at the ease with which the battling Bairns were holding out after an early header from Paul McGrillen. The second-half highlights were so elongated that the possibility of extra-time soon became a forlorn hope. I uncapped the bottle and started glugging down the booze when commentator Jock Brown counted down the clock to the point where the hoop-disgracing haddies were 'four minutes into injury-time'. Tommy Burns's gentlemanly decision to allow Falkirk to ditch their epilepsy-inducing blue-checkered shirts in favour of their 'lucky' red away tops had proved to be another tactically naïve disaster. Cup sponsors Tennents must have felt similarly cheated in the wake of both underdogs earning their unexpected day in the May sunshine. Kilmarnock had not lifted the Cup since 1929, nor Falkirk since 1957 (when manager Alex Totten – sacked by Killie in December! – had watched in short trousers as his home-town team triumphed over Kilmarnock).

Bulging Old Firm bankrolls are supposed to insure against such 'tedious' town-twinning showpieces, but this 'People's Final' was a timely reminder of football's inherent unpredictability and a boost to both sets of fans force-fed for at least a generation on an F-Plan diet of junk-food failure. Only the most churlish of Old Firm observers could turn their noses up and reject the 1997 finalists as substandard ingredients for the Cup final cake. And apart from disappointed Arabs and distraught Tims, only jealous Jambos had good reason to curse the provincial finalists (since their scheduled appearance on 24 May had already denied Hearts a UEFA Cup place).

Heading south by south-west, I found myself sitting opposite an attractive blonde power-dresser. A fashion designer called Evelyn Kennedy, rather than an industrial designer named Eve Kendall, I still couldn't resist introducing myself as 'George Kaplan', author of *Confessions of an Unjustified Green Brazilian*. Passing myself off as Roger Thornhill, a Madison Avenue advertising executive, would probably have impressed her more. Telling her about my soon-to-be-concluded adventure, a fat bald bloke waddled past our table mumbling something about literary groundhopping being no more than a 'McGuffin' (a plot device to let me shine as the hero of my own script?). Evelyn did become suddenly attentive when I quoted *The Sun*'s description of how previous manager Alex 'Sanny' McAnespie had been sacked in March 1996 outside Stirling Albion's Forthbank Stadium 'in a notoriously ruthless carpark execution'. In the next block of seats four Dumbarton fans swilled from their cans of Superlager.

Stranraer Station resembled a run-down, end-of-the-line meeting place for Stasi secret agents, situated beside the hydraulic pier extension for Stena Line's catamaran ferry. A sprawling and litter-strewn freight terminal surrounded both pier and station, and the Sons of the Rock looked suitably stunned when told by the ticket clerk that the first train out after the game left at 7.40 p.m., almost three hours after the final whistle.

With the expected lack of signposting for Stair Park, and a fine smirr of cold rain falling, I sought directions from sweet but senile old ladies in the Safeway carpark. Less than a mile away, I soon got my bearings from the floodlight poles. Approaching the ground, one's imminent arrival at Stair Park is heralded by a park bandstand – but being Scotland, or possibly just Stranraer, it was fenced off for safety reasons.

Terracing prices had been reduced to a commendable £4, which I certainly appreciated since I was almost literally running on empty as far as cash fuel for completing my itinerary was concerned (having drawn on my advance, royalties, Public Lending Right earnings – £21.28 – savings and weekly wages to get this far). I stood on the covered Home Town terrace, gazing in disbelief at the opposite end. The Glebe Park hedge paled into evergreen insignificance by comparison, outdone for rural 'charm' by the deciduousness of a wood which almost encroached on to the playing field. To my left a small wooden stand housed 300 fans, most of whom were football-chanting, flag-waving, balloon-releasing Bogheaders. To my right stood the new Main Stand, erected in 1995 for half a million pounds by Barr Construction of Ayr (again!). Cantilevered but sidescreenless in its IKEA identikitness, it seated a maximum of 1,524. With a total capacity of 6,100, over half of Stranraer's 12,000 population could fit inside Stair Park, but the visit of Dumbarton only added 30 onto the average attendance of 600.

Back on Boxing Day, when the famous Dumbarton Rock brass baboons had lost their *cojones* to frostbite, the Sons' and Blues' 2–2 draw had not seemed disastrous for either side, since Brechin City still provided a relegation buffer between them and doomed Berwick Rangers. Since then, however, the City had found some Formula One form (including a win at Stair Park a week earlier to ensure their survival, while at the same time Dumbarton were overcoming Livingston at Almondvale to end the latter's promotion push in a pink blob of embarrassment, since Boxing Day's fixtures had ended with the Livvy Lions roaring five points clear at the top of the table). This game, then, was a relegation six-pointer, Stranraer going into it one point behind the visitors with only three games to go.

Dumbarton's top scorer Hugh Ward had been on the front page of the *Daily Record* earlier in the week, the passionate postman having been on the recorded-delivery end of two black eyes handed out by the cuckolded but estranged husband of a Helensburgh housewife – which explained the Stranraer fan sporting mocking cosmetic keekers of his own. Boghead boss Ian Wallace hadn't hesitated in picking his star striker, however, since Wallace himself had checked out of hospital after *cranial surgery* to watch his team overcome Livingston, sitting in the away dug-out at Almondvale with his head swathed in bandages. 'Postman Panda – you can make first-class deliveries tae ma Missus, onytime' was the wittiest comment I heard from the home support whenever Ward touched the ball (and the largely good-natured barracking may have contributed to his withdrawal after 77 squirming minutes).

Stranraer had the best of a poor first half, but their silently fatalistic fans were easily eclipsed in the enthusiasm stakes by the diehards from Dumbarton. The second half was almost as dire and depressing, but since a defeat for the home side would have seen them, to all intents and purposes relegated, the on-pitch poverty of poetry in motion still held a grim fascination for the assembled witnesses. Both keepers, Barney Duffy and Derek Barnes, just about matched each other in displaying careful competence under psychological pressure.

The usual dip in temperature came about 4.20 p.m., and as I blew into my cold, cupped hands I was becoming reconciled to ending my odyssey in existential gloom with a scoreless draw. With four minutes to go, though, ex-Killie full-back Tom Black floated in a free kick for the Blues. Watching from over 200 yards away, all I saw was a mass of players bunched in front of Barnes trying to get some gravity-defying lift from leaden legs. Signed from Forfar for £10,000 in October, Gary Higgins doubled his season's goal tally by getting his head to the ball first. The Stranraer support suddenly exploded into smiling life. As did I.

With full-time imminent, I got a fan to hold up a promotional Sky postcard featuring Andy Goram with arms raised in exaltation. The copy simply read 'That's a relief' and with the whistling referee in the background I took a picture of it. Whether it came out properly or not, I was just delighted to hear the final whistle being blown by Jim Herald of Newton Mearns. The result meant Stanraer leapfrogged Dumbarton out of second-bottom spot. This relegation battle may have been set to go to the wire on 10 May, but my season in hell was technically over.[1]

Outside in the carpark, with the disappointed Sons streaming towards their transport, I raised a clenched fist and shouted a rehearsed '*Courage – enfer fuyons!*' ('Be brave – let's get the hell out of here!'). I was finally free, after 40 fucking games . . .

After a celebratory half-pint and a brandy, I strolled round Stranraer. As part of the constituency of Galloway and Upper Nithsdale, Tory Trade Secretary Ian Lang looked likely to lose his seat here in five days' time to the SNP – and despite a dire performance by Stranraer-born Colin Calderwood in the heart of the defence as Scotland crashed 2–1 to Sweden in Gothenburg the night before the election, the Nats still snatched the seat to make Scotland a Tory-free zone. (And just as Tony Blair was entering 10 Downing Street as part of a Labour landslide on Friday, 2 May, Tommy Burns of Celtic was being shown the door out of Parkhead because of the team's end-of-season collapse; Tories and Tims across Scotland struggled to take in the enormity of the unfolding disasters, and if such a thing as a Tory Tim exists he must have been in need of heavy sedation and subsequent psychiatric observation; meanwhile, at Links Park, Dave Smith of Montrose was doing a John Major by resigning his leadership.)

Walking westwards along the sludge-coloured seafront, I finally reached the end of a private road. Sitting down and swigging from a can of Sweet Stout, I winced as a burst blister spread stingingly hot liquid over my right sole (making it feel like a foot soldier's bloodied stump). The Seacat ferry picked up speed as it headed for the small gap at the head of Loch Ryan (a sea-loch). I considered disrobing and 'disappearing' into the water *à la* Reginald Perrin or John Stonehouse, but I was too cold, or committing suicide by holding my breath until my brain exploded, but I wasn't drunk enough to overcome in-built survival reflexes. Instead, I limped back to the station and watched in awe as the Stena Line plane-cum-ferry, the *Hoek van Holland*, used its four jet engines to reverse into docking position (Stena Line are Stranraer's shirt sponsors). As the train pulled out, I stuck a tape into my Walkman. 'Let's Go Round Again' by the Average White Band had me shaking my head in you-must-be-joking disagreement. Never again, I thought.

At Paisley I introduced myself to a match reporter who had been covering the game (because although I have quite a *high* boredom threshold, Michael Crichton's *Disclosure* had exceeded it many miles back down the line). In Central Station, *Scotland on Sunday*'s Raymond Travers and I headed for the nearest concourse bar. As amusing in pint-sinking person as in journalistically barbed print, I had to cut short what could have developed into an all-night session.

Sprinting to catch the last train from Queen Street to Waverley, I just made it in breathless time by ignoring a tightening chest and shooting pains down my left arm. As long as I didn't go into cardiac arrest before Linlithgow, I was looking forward to my *surprise* 'Happy 40th Game' party. But my heavily dropped hints had been in vain, since the apparently deserted flat was in fact totally empty, without 40 friends hiding in the dark waiting to leap out (which would have been a real shock since I'm not even on first-name terms with 40 people). Even four close friends assembled to celebrate my admittedly anorakish achievement would have been appreciated, and, feeling slightly sorry for myself, I wrote up my notes, brought my statistics up-to-date and chain-smoked with the lights out until the overdose of nicotine made me feel nauseous. Exhausted – it had been a long day and a long nine months – I crawled into bed.

Still, I'd made it with two League Saturdays to go and with £26 left in the budgetary biscuit tin (even if most of it rattled to the sound of copper against sheet metal when shaken). As for Stranraer's chances of staying up – I was well past the point of caring one way or another. Having successfully seen Stair Park, it could have sunk into the Irish Sea as far as I was concerned.

FOOTNOTES

1. Come 10 May, live issues remained to be settled in every division except for the First (see Conclusion for final League placings). In Division Three, East Stirling avoided the wooden spoon by beating Arbroath 3–0 (thereby inflicting 40th place on the Manchester Uniteds of Angus – whose manager Tommy Campbell almost immediately jumped ship to Montrose). Forfar and Ross County both won at home, but the Loons from Angus – whom Campbell had left for Arbroath earlier in the season – scraped promotion on goal difference. In Division Two, Stranraer survived by the skin of their Stair Park dentures for a second season in a row, two late goals against Stenhousemuir securing a 2–1 victory and condemning Dumbarton to a second successive plummet down a Division. Ayr won out over Hamilton for the Second Division title by beating Berwick away.

At the foot of the Premier League, Kilmarnock, Motherwell and Hibernian were all in the play-off position at one point during a dramatic afternoon of rollercoaster radio listening, but three draws ensured that they all finished in the same positions they were in when play kicked off at 3 p.m. (a late start at Fir Park notwithstanding); 73rd-minute equalisers for Kilmarnock and Motherwell, against Aberdeen and Dunfermline, ensured that Hibs' 1–1 draw against Raith condemned the Leith laggers to play-off purgatory. On Saturday, 17 May, they beat Airdrie 1–0 at Easter Road in a brutal first-leg. Five days later at Broadwood, Hibs won 4–2 in another headbanging encounter to make sure of their survival.

In the Scottish Cup final, at Ibrox on 24 May, Kilmarnock beat Falkirk 1–0.

On 8 June, Scotland beat Belarus 1–0 in Minsk to almost guarantee World Cup qualification for France. The second-half penalty was converted by Gary McAllister, whose bravery in stepping forward to take it cannot be underplayed, since Macca's matchwinner took place almost a year to the day after his spot-kick miss against England during Euro 96.

What are the facts? Not those in Homer [or Hornby], Shakespeare [or Simon Inglis], or even the Bible [or even The Wee Red Book]. *The facts for most of us are a dark street, crowds, hurry, commonplaces, loneliness and, worst of all, terrible doubt which can hardly be named as to the meaning and purpose of the world [or the SFA].*

 —William Hale White, aka Mark Rutherford, writing in the year of his death, 1913

Having watched over 60 hours of football, I'm now in the extra-time phase of attempting to draw a few conclusions. Summing up the sad statistics first, I visited 37 separate stadiums, attended 40 matches and witnessed 105 goals (an average of 2.6 per game) – all of which cost almost a thousand quid. Every club with a ground of its own I saw in first-team action, and Scotland's three 'homeless' teams I watched playing once apiece in away fixtures. I also took in one Premier reserve game and one international match (both at Ibrox, adding up to three different visits). Dunfermline's East End Park I inspected twice. Albion Rovers I saw most often, five times in total (beating Dundee United because one of their five was a reserve fixture). One-nil was the most frequent scoreline (six times). The managerial casualty rate was pretty horrendous, with 50 per cent of clubs changing their manager – at least once – during the season. (Oops, there goes the 21st club out of 40 to dispense with the managerial services of an incumbent boss – Partick Thistle sacking Murdo MacLeod on 23 May.)

Only missing Inverness Caledonian Thistle turning out at Telford Street, before they decamped to the Caledonian Stadium, prevented me from 'bagging' a game at every Scottish League ground in operation during season 1996–97 (an achievement that has been done many times before, apparently), but I still finished my groundhopping odyssey with no stadiums left unhopped. In other words, as I write I've seen a competitive first-team game at every ground currently hosting senior League football in Scotland.

Am I glad I decided to take on, and to all intents and purposes succeeded in rising to, the challenge? Hmm . . . Well, I'm absolutely delighted I've done it, and fucking ecstatic that I won't ever have to do it again (at least not in a single season and on a backpacker's budget). At times it was an almost vertically uphill struggle but I had anticipated, to a degree, what I was letting myself in for. Compare and contrast my differing reactions to negotiating and agreeing contractual terms over the telephone for my first book *Not Playing For Celtic* and then for this one, my second contribution to the growing canon of football literature (and which, technically and pompously, now constitutes an authorial *oeuvre*). Back in 1994 I put the handset back on its cradle and then danced around in whooping and air-punching celebration, as if I had just scored the last-minute winner in a cup final. In 1996 I replaced the receiver and proceeded to slide down an adjacent door-jamb in stunned silence, appalled at the prospect of 'researching' *A Season in Hell*, and resembling a distraught defender who had just sliced an attempted goal-line clearance into his own net for an injury-time decider in a relegation play-off.

Hence, in all honesty, I approached my off-the-cuff itinerary of Scottish stadiums to be sought out and slagged off with more than a modicum of resentful cynicism, because in addition to being haphazard in planning and eventual execution it was hardly a journey of epic proportions or inherent literary potential (and my initial lack of enthusiasm explained the lazy and ludicrous decision not to venture further afield than Hampden or Easter Road for my first two games, when I should have been taking advantage of the fine weather to tick footballing frontier towns like Dingwall or Inverness off my list).

In the weird and wonderful world of publishing, *weltschmerz-y* (or world-weary) would-be writers have signed on the contractual dotted line to undertake every arbitrary A to Z route imaginable – whether it be island-hopping or Munro-bagging in Scotland, climbing the seven highest peaks in all seven continents, Greyhound-bussing and hitchhiking across America via every hick town called 'Glas-gow', circumnavigating the globe single-handed in a dhow without the aid of radio, radar or attached retinas, or going around the world in 80 days accompanied by the same number of bacon-sarnie swallowing BBC technicians – but any genuine glory to be gained is not achieved by simply completing such futile exercises, no matter how exotic the locations encountered, but through the memory-filtered and wordsmith-processed attention to detail on the written page. Boghead on Boxing Day, therefore, is as potentially rich a source of material as the Bernabeu during a Basque bombing blitz.

For this book I have had to punch so hard above my first-draft weight, to give it whatever powderpuff quality it may possess, that I've been pushing the edge-of-the-*brown*-envelope both mentally and physically (and with the exception of Jeffrey Archer, all good writing is re-writing).

For the ten months August 1996 to May 1997, my life as a typically underachieving but uniquely neurotic 35-/36-year-old has revolved almost exclusively around reading newspapers (my dreary day job), visiting football stadiums most Saturdays, and sitting alone with only a throbbing writing-bump for company trying to convert chaotic notes and undated clippings into reasonably lucid value-added prose. Three quotes from three fine writers largely sum up my day-to-day existence during this period:

> '. . . the sickening virus of envy, spite and affronted despair which comes from reading too many newspapers'
> – Michael Bywater, *Independent on Sunday*, 12 January 1997

> 'Of the 40-odd matches regular observers must take in, usually 30 of these will be stomach-churning, and the remainder vaguely accomplished . . .'
> – Graham Spiers, *Scotland on Sunday*, 2 February 1997

> 'I want to cut my throat when I think I shall never write the way I want, or set down a quarter of what I dream'
> – Gustave Flaubert, editor of Rouen FC's fanzine *N'importe*

Yep, aye and *oui* without question. But occasionally a newspaper will print something quite brilliant inspired by an artistic muse rather than the 'Blue Bugloss' deadlines of hack journalism, to be clipped and filed under 'Miscellaneous' (and lost forever!). The direst football match can explode into unexpected life with a great goal, and out of the 40 fixtures that I notched up, nine were a real pleasure to watch – at Brockville (2–3), Forthbank (1–3), McDiarmid Park (4–0), Recreation Park (3–1), Fir Park (2–3), Celtic Park (6–0), Tynecastle (5–0), Caledonian Stadium (3–2) and Bayview (1–4). However, all four 0–0 draws – at Station Park, Firs Park, Glebe Park and Tannadice – were as excruciatingly dull and depressing as the Ur-scoreline of Scottish football would suggest (and at 10 per cent of my total, it was the joint-second most frequent result, along with 2–1). And as for writing, once in a while the usual pig's-ear prose turns into a silk-purse paragraph, which when re-read later provides a mild glow of pride as having originated in such a normally undiamantiferous mind.

BELL'S SCOTTISH LEAGUE

PREMIER LEAGUE

	P	W	D	L	F	A	Pt
Rangers	36	25	5	6	85	33	80
Celtic	36	23	6	7	78	32	75
Dundee Utd	36	17	9	10	46	33	60
Hearts	36	14	10	12	46	43	52
Dunfermline	36	12	9	15	52	65	45
Aberdeen	36	10	14	12	45	54	44
Kilmarnock	36	11	6	19	41	61	39
Motherwell	36	9	11	16	44	55	38
Hibernian	36	9	11	16	38	55	38*
Raith Rovers	36	6	7	23	29	73	25

FIRST DIVISION

	P	W	D	L	F	A	Pt
St Johnstone	36	24	8	4	74	23	80
Airdrie	36	15	15	6	56	34	60*
Dundee	36	15	13	8	47	33	58
St Mirren	36	17	7	12	48	41	58
Falkirk	36	15	9	12	42	39	54
Partick Thistle	36	12	12	12	49	48	48
Stirling Albion	36	12	10	14	54	61	46
Morton	36	12	9	15	42	41	45
Clydebank	36	7	7	22	31	59	28
East Fife	36	2	8	26	28	92	14

SECOND DIVISION

	P	W	D	L	F	A	Pt
Ayr Utd	36	23	8	5	61	33	77
Hamilton	36	22	8	6	75	28	74
Livingston	36	18	10	8	56	38	64
Clyde	36	14	10	12	42	39	52
QOS	36	13	8	15	55	57	47
Stenhsmuir	36	11	11	14	49	43	44
Brechin	36	10	11	15	36	49	41
Stranraer	36	9	9	18	29	51	36
Dumbarton	36	9	8	19	44	66	35
Berwick	36	4	11	21	32	75	23

THIRD DIVISION

	P	W	D	L	F	A	Pt
Inverness CT	36	23	7	6	70	37	76
Forfar	36	19	10	7	74	45	67
Ross County	36	20	7	9	58	41	67
Alloa	36	16	7	13	50	47	55
Albion Rov	36	13	10	13	50	47	49
Montrose	36	12	7	17	46	62	43
Cowdenbeath	36	10	9	17	38	51	39
Queen's Park	36	9	9	18	46	59	36
East Stirling	36	8	9	19	36	58	33
Arbroath	36	6	13	17	31	52	31

*In a two-legged pay-off, Hibernian overcame Airdrie 5–2 on aggregate
Tennents Scottish Cup Winners: Kilmarnock; Coca-Cola Cup Winners: Rangers; League Challenge Cup Winners: Stranraer

If groundhopping around Scottish League grounds, with all the vicissitudes involved, can be interpreted as a metaphor for an individual's lonely journey through life, what can this season's final League placings be made to represent? Try putting yourself in the position of one of the above teams with regard to: (a) current financial status; (b) degree of personal happiness; and (c) career development level.

Getting my own friends and acquaintances to try this, I've been taken aback by the hubristic height (hypocritical?) of their self-assessments. (Some of these individuals only need to sink six pints on a Saturday night in order to start cursing their lives of quiet despair with heartfelt intensity.) Although no one opted for Rangers or Celtic in any category, most varied with their selections from mid-table in the Premier League to the top half of the First Division.

My newly acquired 'second teams' of Queen of the South, Brechin City and Albion Rovers – in that order and replacing decades of soft-spot, and sad-sack, supporting of Hibernian and Raith Rovers – are actually pretty damn close to what my objective choices would have been anyway, so I'll just stick with them for the sake of this exercise.

Financially, my spluttering sources of income are akin to the well-nigh ruinous revenues raised by the Wee Rovers, with literally less money in the bank than the club treasurer must deposit in a Coatbridge night-safe after deducting cash expenses from the gate-money generated by Cowdenbeath visiting Cliftonhill on a wet and windy Wednesday evening (when a crowd of less than 200 would not be unprecedented). Psychologically, I'm the City, because the angst-ridden Angus outfit are almost permanently fighting to avoid relegation to the dark tunnel of Division Three. (Arguably an even better analogy for my normal mental state would be with the Junior sides of Hurlford United and Luncarty, from Ayrshire and Perthshire respectively, who regularly compete with each other in trying to run up the longest record of consecutive defeats in Scottish football.) Careerwise, I like to think of myself as the Doonhamers of Dumfries, playing in a lower division than I deserve to be in but with the potential in 1997–98 to move up a league (where in the First, Queen of the South wouldn't lose money by running a full-time set-up, and I could possibly set myself up as a full-time and self-supporting writer in a garden shed somewhere, like Roald Dahl, but without the mansion at the top of the garden; and it's no coincidence that Division Two's five full-time sides filled the top five places). The Doonhamers for the European Cup? No, of course not. Me being awarded the Nobel Prize for Literature? Equally ridiculous. The Queens winning the Premier League? Imaginatively conceivable but realistically impossible. Bennie for the Booker? The same (although after Keri Hume picked up a massive win bonus for finishing top of this particular literary league with *The Bone People*, anything is possible). Dumfries as a southerly outpost of Premier League football? Why the hell not? Me getting my name above a book title? Ditto. Christ, some of the teams and writers lauding it above the Queens and me are so full of shit that whites of their eyes have turned a scatological shade of brown . . .

During season 1997–98 I shall revisit the homes of my new trio of alternative XIs – Palmerston Park, Glebe Park and Cliftonhill Stadium – at least once. If and when Airdrieonians and East Fife open 'New Broomfield' and 'New Bayview', I shall make my whining way to Airdire and Methil (and Falkirk, too, if 'New Brockville' appears on the Grangemouth horizon), if only to fulfil the full membership requirements of 'The Scottish "38" Club' (which is not a holiday company dedicated to providing sun, sand and erectile-dysfunctional sex for middle-aged heuchter-teuchter hedonists approaching the Big Four-O).

It exists to encourage fans 'to watch a game on every Scottish League ground' and even Associate Members receive the brilliantly produced bi-monthly newsletters (which I wish I had been receiving during the past nine months). Although 500 people are estimated to have visited every ground, the club's current membership consists of 83 Full Members and 79 Associates (i.e. those still on their groundhopping travels), with 70 per cent of the total based in England and Wales, 24 per cent in Scotland and 6 per cent abroad (but no breakdown of the presumed preponderance of Stenhouse-muir-supporting Scandinavians in the make-up of the overseas membership was available at the time of writing). I'm not normally a great 'joiner' – but 'The Scottish "38" Club' certainly deserves the oxygen of some publicity and greater support from north of the border. With my heart set on full membership – like the iconic Inglis and the other 82 members of the élite 'who have visited all the current home grounds of the Scottish League clubs' – and with my hankering after the commemorative goodies on offer like club tie, badge and certificate, I was slightly concerned about the 'technicality' of having missed Telford Street. I need not have worried, needless to say, since full membership was not possible for another, unforeseen and unimagined reason – namely my failure to visit Cliftonhill, Boghead and Broadwood *twice* (to see the groundsharing tenants of Hamilton, Clydebank and Airdrie playing at 'home'!). The explanatory literature, which a journalist acquaintance passed on to me, mentioning associate membership available for those in the process of making the full 1-to-37 tour was therefore a bit misleading. So bear in mind that 40 visits are required in *total* (unless you have spectated at the old grounds of the above 'homeless' trio and can remember or trace the exact dates and attendance figures as proof of visitation).

Stuck in tantalising and frustrating limbo, so-near-and-yet-so-far like a handful of others apparently, I will attempt to make up the necessary numbers next season, but if new stadiums open in the interim for other clubs like East Fife and see me slipping *backwards*, I will have to accept defeat and apply for anticlimactic associate membership. (Details of the club are available from Mark Byatt, Founder and Organiser, The Scottish '38' Club, 6 Greenfields Close, Loughton, Essex IG10 3HG.)

Having completed the grand tour, the classified results on TV and radio will never be the same. What were just names on fixture lists and pools coupons have become triggers for recollections of actual teams and real places. On Sunday mornings, I'll no doubt ponder over each division's results in my newspaper with hungover intensity, punctuated by gurgles of pleasure and groans of despair. During this season I've visited places that I'd otherwise have died without seeing, however fleetingly – Forfar, for example – and with them all marked 1 to 40 on a map in my study, I can stand lost for minutes at a time in retrospective admiration at my personal achievement. More evocative still is my football Year Planner – no more than a glossy piece of cardboard divided into columnar months – with Saturdays highlighted in red. I've filled in all my stadiums, fixtures and scorelines with loving care, and I can now sit in my favourite armchair with a cup of coffee and a pack of Marlboros just staring, for up to an hour, at this thing balanced on my thighs. Like Proust dipping madeleine cake into a cup of tea, and being overwhelmed by the remembrance of things past, my Year Planner brings poignant and pissed-off memories flooding back (of goals, people, weather conditions, smells, places and various states of emotional being).

Although theoretically in favour before I began this odyssey, I'm now a fundamentalist believer in and hard-line proselytiser for the one change that could improve Scottish football (both playing in and spectating at) out of all current recognition – namely, the introduction of SUMMER FOOTBALL! It's got to come eventually, even if an extended winter break is a necessary first step. In the words of St Johnstone's hard-man Austrian midfielder Attila Sekerlioglu: 'The Scottish weather is incredible.' As in incredibly bad, Attila, ya? Playing twice a week April-through-October would gain far more fair-weather fans than those lost to fortnightly holidays on the various Costas. As for all-seated stadiums, outwith packed Parkhead and impregnable Ibrox they're atmosphere killers, and as a fan there is nothing to beat resting your elbows on a crush-barrier.

Before starting this book I was against all suggestions being made to increase the size of goalmouths – especially from American TV executives prior to the World Cup in 1994 – but I now believe the dimensions definitely ought to be increased to compensate for today's larger and taller goalkeepers (some of whom, as recently as 1978, still played bare-handed without sticky-palmed gloves imported from the Continent). No rule change would be required but it would lead to a directly proportional increase in the number of goals scored. And if a meaningless football match has any philosophical point to its 90 minutes of 'sound and fury signifying nothing', it has to be the orgasmic joy of goal-scoring. A game without a goal is *not* like a fish without bicycle. Nil-nil draws, although not out-lawable, out to be punished with 0.999 repeater points for each side involved in one. Nil-nil is existential monotony and alienation writ large on a football field — even more frustrating than tantric sex, and giving fans refunds for having to endure each manifestation of goal-scoring impotence might motivate home sides to get their goalkeepers up into the opposition's penalty box for last-minute corners.

With regard to the perennial debate over league reconstruction — which isn't even the most important question, never mind answer to Scottish football's undoubted problems — I'd go for . . . oh, 16-12-12. Also, as in England in the past, the team finishing bottom of the senior heap — Arbroath this season — ought at least to have its top-flight survival subject to a process of re-election. Arguably, automatic relegation for the team finishing 40th ought to be introduced, with their replacement decided by round-robin play-offs between the Highland League champions and those winning the Ayrshire, Central and Eastern Junior Leagues. If Edinburgh United triumphed under this system, Meadowbank Stadium would be restored to its rightful place as a Scottish League ground (and having seen all the rest, there is no way that the old home of defunct Meadowbank Thistle can be dismissed as having the worst atmosphere of any senior Scottish ground).

As for the next Third Lanark, I'm not at all sure there will be one by the end of the century, but if one team is likely to go belly-up financially it must be Clydebank (for whom everything connected with the club is turning increasingly pear-shaped). Having left all-seated Kilbowie to the elements and vandals, they now face a second season groundsharing with Dumbarton. Substituting the 'green' in Noam Chomsky's famous test-phrase (which has perfect syntax but no semantic worth), Clydebank's epitaph could be: 'Colourless red ideas sleep furiously.' Or if retaining the original green, the title of Tommy Burns's autobiography.

For anyone considering following in my blistered and chilblained foot-steps (which in just five years or so could conceivably be part of an organised heritage tour for soccerati aficionados of this book, with my decapitated head in a glass-fronted tank of formaldehyde providing the commentary via tracing needles hooked up to an EEG machine), I'd advise doing about 75 per cent of the grounds by train and the remaining quarter on four wheels. Ideally, I'd have preferred having a yellow 250 SEL Mercedes at my disposal, like the one featured in *Betty Blue*, plus a female map-reading companion like that movie's Beatrice Dalle. In Dante's *Divine Comedy*, the hero was led through heaven by his beloved Beatrice, with his guide for hell and purgatory being pedantic Virgil – and even an anoraked and vestal Wayne from Walthamstow would have been welcome company for me on my travels. Although I actually enjoy my own company – too much for my own good, I sometimes suspect – doing 40 matches in a season would have been more fun with a Merc-load of moneyed and unmarried mates.

In 1873 Arthur Rimbaud published his own *Une Saison en enfer*, which was critically slaughtered and led to the author retiring from writing at the tender age of 19. He eventually died aged 37 in Marseille, after having an infected leg amputated (but his interesting employment CV included a spell as a cashier for a travelling circus and a period as a camel-train driver – not positions you see advertised in British Job Centres nowadays). At 36 my dodgy knee is currently killing me and if this book doesn't earn back its advance I may well meet a similar fate on holiday in Millport in the summer of 1998. Alternatively, I may do a poor heterosexual's 'Bruce Chatwin' and embark on a tour of Spanish League grounds carrying only a calfskin haversack (although in my case it would contain no more than a Pentel Ultra Fine, John Menzies reporter's notebooks, a paperback copy of *The Football Grounds of Europe* and a half-bottle of Bell's). After all, fashionable publishing hybrids which combine travel memoirs and confessional male autobiography, marketed as supposedly cutting-edge cultural critiques, are apparently what appeal to modern bookbuyers.

Although supporters are constantly lauded by members of the footballing establishment as being the most important people in the game, anyone who follows a particular team knows that in reality their blind loyalty is constantly taken advantage of. Every office-bearer in the Scottish Football Association and Scottish League, as well as every ego-tripping club chairman, ought to be working at their leather-topped executive desks with plaques bearing the following inscription bang in front of them: 'It's the fans, stupid!' But because fans are motivated by an obsessive love for the game, they almost invariably get shafted from behind (and by an iron fist not hidden within a velvet glove).

I guess the acid-test question for anyone professing to have an in-depth, groundhopping knowledge of Scottish football would have to be: 'Where the hell is Stenhousemuir?' Most people I ask, albeit out of the blue, respond as I did before having visited the unhappy hunting ground of the Warriors – placing them almost anywhere between southern Ayrshire and North Angus – but all I can say is that once groundhopped, Stenny are never forgotten.

Personally, a more pertinent question now is, 'Where the devil in Spain are Celta Viga located?' As a Glasgow Celtic supporter, ten-in-a-row neurosis has already started manifesting itself and for at least some part of season 1997–98 I hope to be in Celtic Park cheering on the harassed Hoops. The hype has already begun. But for season 1998–99 following Celta Viga as a 'socio' would at least be a 'Season in the Sunshine' . . . I really ought to look them up in a reference book before investing any more supporting emotion in them, because knowing my luck – and despite their mid-table position in the First Division – Celta Viga are probably just some Spanish-type equivalent of Stenhousemuir, stranded inland and just north of Manzanares on the inhospitable and malarial Castilla la Mancha plain . . .

Anyway, if having read this tour of Scottish grounds you've enjoyed the armchair experience, then great. If it inspires you to take in a few games at stadiums away from your home patch, all the better (even if you cussedly ignore authorial advice and head off for Almondvale Stadium on foot and in darkest winter). If, as Heidegger suggested modern technology is the art of arranging the material world so that most people don't have to experience it directly, you Dear Reader, have no excuse if you're still flirting with the idea of bagging a competitive game at every Scottish League ground in a single season – because I've already done it for you (with the 4F feet to prove it). Be warned, be very warned – if boredom hasn't turned you rigid by January, the cold will certainly have done so (as well as blue). Two seasons is the minimum practicable time-scale if you want to retain your sanity and your savings.

As I write, only a couple of months remain before three out of four of Scotland's representatives in Europe kick-off a new season in preliminary-round ties in July (Scotland having fallen below a seeded ranking of 16 to an acutely embarrassing 19th). Domestically, the new season officially kicks off again on 2 August 1997, with Premier and First Division clubs starting their League campaigns and the rest clashing in Coca-Cola Cup ties – which is where I came in all those months ago, beginning this personal odyssey on 3 August 1996 with Queen's Park versus Ross County. As I can easily recall, it ended 3–1, after extra-time, and although I haven't started to forget any of my 40 memorised scorelines, specific goals and scorers are already beginning to drift out of sharp focus and beyond conscious recollection.

Hmm . . . Setting out from base camp at Hampden Park in early August and arriving at the broad sunlit uplands of Stranraer's Stair Park in late April doesn't have much of a sense of symmetry, does it? Or symbolism. Or logic. But even without any rhyme or reason to my route, I got there in the end. As does every Scottish football club at the end of every season. Stone-tablet statistics and results may suggest that most teams finish as failures, but come each new season the slate is wiped clean and eternal hope once again triumphs over bitter experience. The twists and turns of footballing fate, both on and off the pitch, are so unpredictable that no super-computer, like the Gary Kasparov-humbling Deep Blue, will ever be able to extrapolate forward in order to list final League placings or to complete cup runs with any degree of accuracy whatsoever.

During 1996–97 the standard of play may have been absolutely hellish, with a few honourable exceptions, but the angels with dirty faces (and mouths and minds) on the terraces and in the stands just about made the on-pitch torture bearable. And if you have to endure watching utter shite almost every alternate Saturday, your sense of humour is obviously going to be skewed towards the scatological. (I *may* never become a professional writer, one whose team selections and formations from a basic squad of 26 alphabetical letters are successful enough to attract lucratively large crowds, but having seen part-time and full-time players running around like headless and knee-capped broiler chickens, I have no doubt I could have hacked it as a professional footballer.)

Having had my bookish sensibilities forged to the strength of Ravens-craig steel in various footballing furnaces up and down this Godforsaken land, however, I think that the football authorities really ought to see about erecting a tomb in honour of the 'Unknown Supporter'. Whoever is commissioned to compose the inscription on any monument, it should definitely not be the person who wrote the following copy, and which appeared in an 'advertorial' notice for the Rangers v Celtic BP Scottish Youth Cup final at Broadwood on 14 May 1997:

> THIS MATCH IS NOT CASH ENTRY BUT BY TICKET
> ONLY, TO BE PURCHASED AT THE TURNSTILES . . .
> PLEASE HAVE THE CORRECT MONEY READY TO AVOID
> DELAYS AT THE TURNSTILES.

Ah, exact-fare footie-following at last, with the first-ever ticket-only-pay-at-the-gate fixture . . . This example of 'diverging parallelism' just about sums up Scottish football and how it is organised, from top to bottom. Farcical yes, but funny too – even if the laughter in the gale-force gloom has a slightly hysterical edge. And to supporters of the much-maligned 'wee diddy teams', I have only one more thing to say: having stood in your midst, I salute you.

So, as I prepare to blow the full-time whistle on my Season in Hell, I can but look forward to my next one. Paradise Park — that Graveyard of Dreams — here I come . . .

David Bennie
Edinburgh
25 May 1997